CHARLES GILPIN AS "EMPEROR JONES"

PLAYS OF
NEGRO LIFE

A SOURCE-BOOK OF
NATIVE AMERICAN DRAMA

Selected and Edited by

ALAIN LOCKE

Formerly Professor of Philosophy, Howard University
Editor of THE NEW NEGRO

and

MONTGOMERY GREGORY

Formerly Professor of Dramatics, Howard University
Director of The Howard Players

Decorations *and* Illustrations *by*

AARON DOUGLAS

HARPER & BROTHERS, *Publishers*
NEW YORK *and* LONDON, MCMXXVII

PLAYS OF NEGRO LIFE

ACKNOWLEDGMENTS

For permission to print or reprint certain of the plays in this book the editors wish to thank the following authors:—Eugene O'Neill, Ridgley Torrence, Ernest H. Culbertson, Paul Green, Willis Richardson, Frank H. Wilson, John Matheus, Eulalie Spence, John W. Rogers, Jr., Lucy White, Jean Toomer, Georgia Douglas Johnson, Thelma Duncan, and Richard Bruce, and also the following publishers and authors' representatives:—*The American Play Company, The Macmillan Company, Henry Holt and Company,* the *Robert McBride Company, Opportunity, a Journal of Negro Life,* for a series of prize plays from the *Opportunity Contests* of 1925-26-27, *Samuel French, Inc., The Howard Players* for three plays from their repertoire, *The Crisis, The Carolina Magazine,* and *Theatre Arts Monthly.*

For permission for the use of photographic and illustrative material, thanks and acknowledgment are made to Maurice Goldberg, Francis Bruguiere, Rabinovitch, *Theatre Arts Monthly,* and to the collaborating artist, Aaron Douglas.

Special personal thanks for valuable suggestions and cooperation are due to Mrs. Edith J. R. Isaacs, Editor of *Theatre Arts,* Miss Mary Hoyt Wiborg, Ridgley Torrence, Paul Green, Barrett H. Clark, Professor Frederick Koch of the *Carolina Playmakers,* Dr. W. E. B. Du Bois of the *Krigwa Little Negro Theatre,* and Charles S. Johnson, Editor of *Opportunity.*

A. L.
M. G.

TABLE OF CONTENTS

INTRODUCTION: The Drama of Negro Life, *Alain Locke*   xiii

TWENTY PLAYS OF THE CONTEMPORARY NEGRO THEATRE

THE DREAMY KID, *Eugene O'Neill*   1
THE RIDER OF DREAMS, *Ridgley Torrence*   25
RACKEY, *Ernest H. Culbertson*   51
THE NO 'COUNT BOY, *Paul Green*   69
THE FLIGHT OF THE NATIVES, *Willis Richardson*   97
WHITE DRESSES, *Paul Green*   117
IN ABRAHAM'S BOSOM, *Paul Green*   139
SUGAR CANE, *Frank H. Wilson*   165
'CRUITER, *John Matheus*   187
THE STARTER, *Eulalie Spence*   205
JUDGE LYNCH, *John W. Rogers, Jr.*   215
GRANNY MAUMEE, *Ridgley Torrence*   235
THE BIRD CHILD, *Lucy White*   253
BALO, *Jean Toomer*   269
PLUMES, *Georgia Douglas Johnson*   287
THE BROKEN BANJO, *Willis Richardson*   301
THE DEATH DANCE, *Thelma Duncan*   321
THE EMPEROR JONES, *Eugene O'Neill*   333
THE DANSE CALINDA, *Ridgley Torrence*   373
SAHDJI, AN AFRICAN BALLET, *Richard Bruce*   387
AUTHORS AND PLAYS   401
A CHRONOLOGY OF THE NEGRO THEATRE, *Montgomery Gregory*   409
BIBLIOGRAPHY OF NEGRO DRAMA   424

LIST OF ILLUSTRATIONS

CHARLES GILPIN AS "EMPEROR JONES"   *Frontispiece*
THE HAPGOOD PLAYERS IN "THE RIDER OF DREAMS"   *facing p.*   30
"THE RIDER OF DREAMS"   "   42
THE DALLAS LITTLE THEATRE PLAYERS IN "NO
    'COUNT BOY"   "   70
"THE FLIGHT OF THE NATIVES"   "   100
THE WOOD SCENE FROM "IN ABRAHAM'S BOSOM"   "   142
JULIUS BLEDSOE IN THE CROSSROADS SCENE FROM
    "IN ABRAHAM'S BOSOM"   "   152
THE SCHOOLROOM SCENE FROM "IN ABRAHAM'S
    BOSOM"   "   160
'CRUITER   "   194
PAUL ROBESON AS "EMPEROR JONES"   "   220
THE AUCTION BLOCK SCENE FROM "THE EMPEROR
    JONES"   "   270
"THE BROKEN BANJO"   "   310
THE EMPEROR   "   340
THE FUGITIVE   "   350
FOREST FEAR   "   360
SURRENDER   "   370

INTRODUCTION: THE DRAMA
OF NEGRO LIFE

INTRODUCTION

THE DRAMA OF NEGRO LIFE

The drama of negro life is developing primarily because a native American drama is in process of evolution. Thus, although it heralds the awakening of the dormant dramatic gifts of the Negro folk temperament and has meant the phenomenal rise within a decade's span of a Negro drama and a possible Negro Theatre, the significance is if anything more national than racial. For pioneering genius in the development of the native American drama, such as Eugene O'Neill, Ridgley Torrence and Paul Green, now sees and recognizes the dramatically undeveloped potentialities of Negro life and folkways as a promising province of native idioms and source materials in which a developing national drama can find distinctive new themes, characteristic and typical situations, authentic atmosphere. The growing number of successful and representative plays of this type form a valuable and significant contribution to the theatre of today and open intriguing and fascinating possibilities for the theatre of tomorrow.

This anthology garners the yield of this experimental and ground-breaking decade as far as the one-act play is concerned, and in that form, which has been the bulk of the recent development, presents the worthwhile repertory of the Negro Theatre to date. [Here really is a new province in our national literature. From opposite approaches, there has been a notable collaboration between the Negro playwright attempting, on the one side, to advance Negro drama as such and to provide the talent of the Negro actor with a fit vehicle and a native medium and, on the other side, the quest of modern American realism for new material and a deeper, firmer grip upon the actualities of American life. Half the plays in this volume represent one wing of this advance, and half, the other. Together, although the field is obviously in its first stage of development,—indeed for that very reason, they show how promising this new field really is. [For if the first decade of intensive effort can have given us several of the most noteworthy and representative American plays that have ever been written, and can have suddenly raised the general level of plays of this subject matter from vaudeville and farce to significant folk comedy and tragedy, there is every reason to expect that another decade will fully realize Eugene O'Neill's forecast that "The possibilities are limitless and to a dramatist open up new and intriguing opportunities: the gifts the Negro can and will bring to our native drama are invaluable ones"] And likewise fully confirm Ridgley Torrence's fine hope when he said, "I have sometimes imagined that the Negro, other things being equal, might produce the greatest, the most direct, the most powerful drama in the world."

The Negro experience has been inherently dramatic: surely the substance of great drama is there. No group experience in America has plumbed greater emotional depths, or passed so dramatically through more levels of life or caught up into itself more of those elements of social conflict and complication in which the modern dramatist must find the only tragedy that our realistic, scientific philosophy of life allows us. Indeed the essential, elemental forces of great drama in all time,—epic turns of experience, tragic intensity of life, discipline and refinement of the emotions, have been accumulating, like underground well-springs, for generations in Negro life, and now are beginning to seek artistic vent and find free-flowing expression.

Certainly the vitalizing spirit of drama is there also. Generations of enforced buffoonery and caricature have not completely stifled the dramatic endowment of the Negro; his temperament still moves natively and spontaneously in the world of make-believe with the primitive power of imaginative abandon and emotional conviction. It is agreed that, as actor and as audience, the Negro temperament promises to bring back to a jaded, sceptical stage some of the renewing, elemental moods and powers of the early drama. If to these unpurchasable things are added, as seems likely now, a worthwhile medium of serious dramatic expression and a seasoned, intelligent contact with the arts of the theatre, the future appears most promising both for the Negro drama and for the Negro actor. With such a background, sporadic Negro geniuses like Ira Aldridge in the past, and Paul Robeson, Charles Gilpin, Frank Wilson in the present, will take shape in the company of talents they focus around them as fixed constellations of the American stage, and eventually there is destined to rise a national Negro Theatre where the black playwright and the black actor will interpret the soul of their people in a way to win the attention and admiration of the world.

Vital as the Negro actor and dramatist are to this development, theirs is and can be no monopoly of the field. White actors have been very successful in some Negro parts; Negro actors have a similar range of interpretative scope not yet fully realized or opened up. There are plays with Negro

characters that are to all intents and purposes not racially
distinctive enough to be classified as Negro plays; and a play
like *Judge Lynch,* included in this collection, with entirely
white characters, may yet be so much a play of the peculiar
situations of race, as to be indisputably a drama of Negro
theme and motive. If the expectations of Negro drama as a
fruitful phase of American drama are to be fully realized,
the field even when it finds its peculiar ingredients in the
problems and issues of racial conflicts and partisanships or
takes its cues from particular folkways, must be a freeman's
estate, with that reciprocity and universality of spirit which
truly great art requires and itself helps to establish.

[However the drama of Negro life is not yet fully free;
though lately very conscious and valiant efforts have been
made to free it from its immediate handicaps. For the present the problem play of this subject has yielded far too much
of that sordid realism without purgation of terror or universality of pity which great tragedy still demands. If this
has been the handicap from the point of view of the white
dramatist, there has been the corresponding blight of propaganda and the taint of sentimentality with the average Negro
dramatist. But in a short space of time, we must remember,
a new seriousness has had to be injected into the whole subject matter and a bramble of false and superficial stereotypes
cut down and plowed under.] Similarly the Negro playwright
has had to abandon his puppets of protest and propaganda
and take to flesh and blood characters and situations. Eventually, without doubt, the Negro playwright will claim his
natural advantage of greater intimacy of knowledge and feeling, but even then, this can result in partial monopoly only.
Indeed for the present, the white dramatist is his advantaged
rival, by virtue of his more natural objectivity toward this
special material of the race life and his more intimate school-

ing in the theatre. [But if the mastery which is within sight, but not yet achieved, is to come at all, it must arise not from objective study merely, but from deep spiritual penetration into the heart and spirit of Negro life.]

Though the problem play seems to dominate the situation for the time being, the folk play, it would seem, is really the more promising path for the sound development of Negro drama. When the problems of group adjustment are nearer resolution, there will perhaps come from both sides a perspective and elevation which will make out of the life tragedies of one generation the great problem and history plays of a generation that can afford to view them with pity and terror instead of chagrin and hate. Meanwhile, every attempt, even in make-believe, to distance the situation is, I believe, helpful. But it is not the primary function of drama to reform us. The drama that will refine and entertain, that may even captivate us before long, is likely to be the uncurdled, almost naïve reflection of the poetry and folk feeling of a people who have after all a different soul and temperament from that of the smug, unimaginative industrialist and the self-righteous and inhibited Puritan. That the folk-play is so rare as yet is, however, not to be marveled at, if one recalls how recent the free play of spirit is in Negro life. But the growth in the last five years of Negro Little Theatre groups in nearly a dozen centers furnishes for the first time opportunity to establish a drama nourished intimately by its own audience, unhampered by commercial dictation, and free of the worse features of conventionalized exhibitionism. [But to this body freedom of the Negro drama must also come inner freedom which only the Negro dramatist and the enlightened audience of the future can bring. Just as much as the Negro's situation in the past has forced him to a counter-attitude in life and a spectator's attitude toward himself, it has cut at the roots of fine drama in him. Forced to laugh outwardly and weep inwardly, the Negro has until lately only been in the position of successful clowning. But with greater spiritual freedom and self-control, we may now confidently await the great actor, the moving interpreter, just as with better emotional compensation there will come the power to smile satirically and reflect with ironic composure. And with that spirit, the Negro drama will be less moved but more moving, less controversial but more challenging, and more universal even in sounding its most racial notes. With all due allowance for a possible mirage of special hope and interest on our part, it is to be hoped that the reader will see in reality at the horizon the great American tragedy and comedy at which we must in time arrive.

ALAIN LOCKE.

New York City,
  May 18, 1927.

THE DREAMY KID

A PLAY IN ONE ACT

By

EUGENE O'NEILL

*Reprinted by special permission of the author
and the American Play Company New York City*

CHARACTERS

MAMMY SAUNDERS
ABE, her grandson—"The Dreamy Kid"
CEELY ANN
IRENE

Scene: Contemporary New York: a Negro settlement
district.
Time: An early winter evening.

First performance at the Provincetown Playhouse,
October 31, 1919

THE DREAMY KID

SCENE: MAMMY SAUNDERS' *bedroom in a house just off Carmine Street, New York City. The left of the room, forward, is taken up by a heavy, old-fashioned wooden bedstead with a feather mattress. A gaudy red-and-yellow quilt covers the other bedclothes. In back of the bed, a chest of drawers placed against the left wall. On top of the chest, a small lamp. A rocking-chair stands beside the head of the bed on the right. In the rear wall, toward the right, a low window with ragged white curtains. In the right corner, a washstand with bowl and pitcher. Bottles of medicine, a spoon, a glass, etc., are also on the stand. Farther forward, a door opening on the hall and stairway.*

It is soon after nightfall of a day in early winter. The room is in shadowy half darkness, the only light being a pale glow that seeps through the window from the arc lamp on the near-by corner, and by which the objects in the room can be dimly discerned. The vague outlines of MAMMY SAUNDERS' *figure lying on the bed can be seen, and her black face stands out in sharp contrast from the pillows that support her head.*

MAMMY SAUNDERS. (*Weakly*) Ceely Ann! (*With a faint querulousness*) Light de lamp, will you? Hits mighty dark in yere. (*After a slight pause*) Ain't you dar, Ceely Ann? (*Receiving no reply, she sighs deeply and*

3

her limbs move uneasily under the bedclothes. The door is opened and shut and the stooping form of another colored woman appears in the semi-darkness. She goes to the foot of the bed sobbing softly, and stands there, evidently making an effort to control her emotion.)

MAMMY SAUNDERS. Dat you, Ceely Ann?

CEELY. (*Huskily*) Hit ain't no yuther, Mammy.

MAMMY. Light de lamp, den. I can't see nowhars.

CEELY. Des one second till I finds a match. (*She wipes her eyes with her handkerchief, then goes to the chest of drawers and feels around on the top of it, pretending to grumble*) Hit beat all how dem pesky little sticks done hide umse'fs. Shoo! Yere dey is. (*She fumbles with the lamp.*)

MAMMY. (*Suspiciously*) You ain't been cryin', is you?

CEELY. (*With feigned astonishment*) Cryin'? I clar' ter goodness you does git the mos' fool notions lyin' dar.

MAMMY. (*In a tone of relief*) I mos' thought I yeard you.

CEELY. (*Lighting the lamp*) 'Deed you ain't. (*The two women are revealed by the light. MAMMY SAUNDERS is an old, white-haired negress about ninety with a weazened face furrowed by wrinkles and withered by old age and sickness. CEELY is a stout woman of fifty or so with gray hair and a round fat face. She wears a loose-fitting gingham dress and a shawl thrown over her head.*)

CEELY. (*With attempted cheeriness*) Bless yo' soul, I ain't got nothin' to cry 'bout. Yere. Lemme fix you so you'll rest mo' easy. (*She lifts the old woman gently and fixes the pillows*) Dere. Now ain't you feelin' better?

MAMMY. (*Dully*) My strenk don' all went. I can't lift a hand.

CEELY. (*Hurriedly*) Dat'll all come back ter you de doctor tole me des now when I goes down to de door wid him. (*Glibly*) He say you is de mos' strongest 'oman fo' yo' years ever he sees in de worl'; and he tell me you gwine ter be up and walkin' agin fo' de week's out. (*As she finds the old woman's eyes fixed on her she turns away confusedly, and abruptly changes the subject*) Hit ain't too wa'm in dis room, dat's a fac'.

MAMMY. (*Shaking her head, in a half whisper*) No, Ceely Ann. Hit ain't no use'n you tellin' me nothin' but de trufe. I feels mighty poo'ly. En I knows hit's on'y wid de blessin' er God I kin las' de night out.

CEELY. (*Distractedly*) Ain't no sich a thing! Hush yo' noise, Mammy!

MAMMY. (*As if she hadn't heard, in a crooning singsong*) I'se gwine soon fum dis wicked yearth—and may de Lawd have mercy on dis po' ole sinner. (*After a pause —anxiously*) All I'se prayin' fer is dat God don' take me befo' I sees Dreamy agin. Whar's Dreamy, Ceely Ann? Why ain't he come yere? Ain't you done sent him word I'se sick like I tole you?

CEELY. *I tole dem* boys ter tell him speshul, and dey swar dey would soon's dey find him. I s'pose dey ain't kotch him yit. Don' you pester yo'se'f worryin'. Dreamy 'ull come fo' ve'y long.

MAMMY. (*After a pause, weakly*) Dere's a feelin' in my haid like I was a-floatin' yander whar I can't see nothin', or 'member nothin', or know de sight er any pusson I knows; en I wants ter see Dreamy agin befo' ——

CEELY. (*Quickly*) Don' waste yo' strenk talkin'. You git a wink er sleep en I wake you when he comes, you heah me?

MAMMY. (*Faintly*) I does feel mighty drowsy. (*She*

closes her eyes. CEELY *goes over to the window and, pulling the curtains aside, stands looking down into the street as if she were watching for some one coming. A moment later there is a noise of footfalls from the stairs in the hall, followed by a sharp rap on the door.*)

CEELY. (*Turning quickly from the window*) Sssshh! Sssshh! (*She hurries to the door, glancing anxiously towards* MAMMY. *The old woman appears to have fallen asleep.* CEELY *cautiously opens the door a bare inch or so and peeks out. When she sees who it is she immediately tries to slam it shut again, but a vigorous shove from the outside forces her back and* IRENE *pushes her way defiantly into the room. She is a young, good-looking negress, highly rouged and powdered, dressed in gaudy, cheap finery.*)

IRENE. (*In a harsh voice, evidently worked up to a great state of nervous excitement*) No, you don't, Ceely Ann! I said I was comin' here and it'll take mo'n you to stop me!

CEELY. (*Almost speechless with horrified indignation, breathing heavily*) Yo' bad 'oman! Git back ter yo' bad-house whar yo' b'longs!

IRENE. (*Raising her clenched hand, furiously*) Stop dat talkin' to me, nigger, or I'll split yo' fool head! (*As* CEELY *shrinks away* IRENE *lowers her hand and glances quickly around the room*) Whar's Dreamy?

CEELY. (*Scornfully*) Yo' axe me dat! Whar's Dreamy? Axe yo'se'f. Yo's de one ought ter know whar he is.

IRENE. Den he ain't come here?

CEELY. I ain't tellin' de likes er you wedder he is or not.

IRENE. (*Pleadingly*) Tell me, Ceely Ann, ain't he been here? He'd be sure to come here 'count of Mammy dyin', dey said.

CEELY. (*Pointing to* MAMMY—*apprehensively*) Ssshh! (*Then lowering her voice to a whisper, suspiciously*) Dey said? Who said?

IRENE. (*Equally suspicious*) None o' your business who said. (*Then pleading again*) Ceely Ann, I jest got ter see him dis minute, dis secon'! He's in bad, Dreamy is, and I knows somep'n I gotter tell him, somep'n I jest heard ——

CEELY. (*Uncomprehendingly*) In bad? What you jest heah?

IRENE. I ain't tellin' no one but him. (*Desperately*) For Gawd's sake, tell me whar he is, Ceely!

CEELY. I don' know no mo'n yo'.

IRENE. (*Fiercely*) You's lyin', Ceely! You's lyin' ter me jest 'cause I'se bad.

CEELY. De good Lawd bar witness I'se tellin' you de trufe!

IRENE. (*Hopelessly*) Den I gotter go find him, high and low, somewheres. (*Proudly*) You ain't got de right not ter trust me, Ceely, where de Dreamy's mixed in it. I'd go ter hell for Dreamy!

CEELY. (*Indignantly*) Hush yo' wicked cussin'! (*Then anxiously*) Is Dreamy in trouble?

IRENE. (*With a scornful laugh*) Trouble? Good Lawd, it's worser'n dat! (*Then in surprise*) Ain't you heerd what de Dreamy done last night, Ceely?

CEELY. (*Apprehensively*) What de Dreamy do? Tell me, gal. Somep'n bad?

IRENE. (*With the same scornful laugh*) Bad? Worser'n bad, what he done.

CEELY. (*Lamenting querulously*) O good Lawd, I knowed it! I knowed wid all his carryin's-on wid dat passel er tough young niggers—him so uppity 'cause he's boss er de gang—sleepin' all day—an' Lawd knows what he

does in de nights—fightin' wid white folks, an' totin' a
pistol in his pocket—(*with a glance of angry resent-
ment at* IRENE—an' as fo' de udder company he's
been keepin'——

IRENE. (*Fiercely*) Shut your mouth, Ceely! Dat ain't your
business.

CEELY. Oh, I knowed Dreamy'd be gittin' in trouble fo'
long! De lowflung young trash! An' here's his ole
Mammy don' know no dif'frunt but he's de mos' inner-
cent young lamb in de worl'. (*In a strained whisper*)
What he do? Is he been stealin' somep'n?

IRENE. (*Angrily*) You go ter hell, Ceely Ann! You ain't
no fren' of de Dreamy's, you talk dat way, and I ain't
got no time ter waste argyin' wid your fool notions.
(*She goes to the door*) Dreamy'll go ter his death sho's
yo' born, if I don't find him an' tell him quick!

CEELY. (*Terrified*) O Lawd!

IRENE. (*Anxiously*) He'll sho'ly try ter come here and see
his ole Mammy befo' she dies, don't you think, Ceely?

CEELY. Fo' Gawd I hopes so! She's been a-prayin' all de
day——

IRENE. (*Opening the door*) You hopes so, you fool nigger!
I tell you it's good-by to de Dreamy, he come here! I
knows! I gotter find an' stop him. If he come here,
Ceely, you tell him git out quick and hide, he don't
wanter git pinched. You hear? You tell him dat,
Ceely, for Gawd's sake! I'se got ter go—find him—
high an' 'low—(*She goes out leaving* CEELY *staring
at her in speechless indignation.*)

CEELY. (*Drawing a deep breath*) Yo' street gal! I don'
b'lieve one word you says—stuffin' me wid yo' bad lies
so's you kin keep de Dreamy frum leavin' you!
(MAMMY SAUNDERS *awakes and groans faintly.* CEELY

hurries over to her bedside) Is de pain hurtin' agin, Mammy?

MAMMY. (*Vaguely*) Dat you, Dreamy?

CEELY. No, Mammy, dis is Ceely. Dreamy's comin' soon. Is you restin' easy?

MAMMY. (*As if she hadn't heard*) Dat you, Dreamy?

CEELY. (*Sitting down in the rocker by the bed and taking one of the old woman's hands in hers*) No. Dreamy's comin'.

MAMMY. (*After a pause—suddenly*) Does you 'member yo' dead Mammy, chile?

CEELY. (*Mystified*) My dead Mammy?

MAMMY. Didn' I heah yo' talkin' jest now, Dreamy?

CEELY. (*Very worried*) I clar ter goodness, she don' know me ary bit. Dis is Ceely Ann talkin' ter yo', Mammy.

MAMMY. Who was yo' talkin' wid, Dreamy?

CEELY. (*Shaking her head—in a trembling voice*) Hit can't be long befo' de en'. (*In a louder tone*) Hit was me talkin' wid a pusson fum ovah de way. She say tell you Dreamy comin' heah ter see yo' right away. You heah dat, Mammy? (*The old woman sighs but does not answer. There is a pause.*)

MAMMY. (*Suddenly*) Does yo' 'member yo' dead Mammy, chile? (*Then with a burst of religious exaltation*) De Lawd have mercy!

CEELY. (*Like an echo*) Bless de Lawd! (*Then in a frightened half-whisper to herself*) Po' thing! Her min's done leavin' her jest like de doctor said. (*She looks down at the old woman helplessly. The door on the right is opened stealthily and the* DREAMY KID *slinks in on tiptoe.*)

CEELY. (*Hearing a board creak, turns quickly toward the door and gives a frightened start*) Dreamy!

DREAMY. (*Puts his fingers to his lips—commandingly*) Ssshh!

(*He bends down to a crouching position and holding the door about an inch open, peers out into the hallway in an attitude of tense waiting, one hand evidently clutching some weapon in the side pocket of his coat. After a moment he is satisfied of not being followed, and after closing the door carefully and locking it, he stands up and walks to the center of the room casting a look of awed curiosity at the figure in the bed. He is a well-built, good looking young negro, light in color. His eyes are shifty and hard, their expression one of tough, scornful defiance. His mouth is cruel and perpetually drawn back at the corner into a snarl. He is dressed in well-fitting clothes of a flashy pattern. A light cap is pulled down on the side of his head.*)

CEELY. (*Coming from the bed to meet him*) Bless de Lawd; here you is at las'!

DREAMY. (*With a warning gesture*) Nix on de loud talk! Talk low, can't yuh! (*He glances back at the door furtively then continues with a sneer*) Yuh're a fine nut, Ceely Ann! What for you sendin' out all ober de town for me like you was crazy! D'yuh want ter git me in de cooler? Don' you know dey're after me for what I done last night?

CEELY. (*Fearfully*) I heerd somep'n—but—what you done, Dreamy?

DREAMY. (*With an attempt at a careless bravado*) I croaked a guy, dat's what! A white man.

CEELY. (*In a frightened whisper*) What you mean—croaked?

DREAMY. (*Boastfully*) I shot him dead, dat's what! (*As CEELY shrinks away from him in horror—resentfully*)

Aw say, don' gimme none o' dem looks o' yourn.
'Twarn't my doin' nohow. He was de one lookin' for
trouble. I wasn't seekin' for no mess wid him dat
I could help. But he tole folks he was gwine ter git
me for a fac', and dat fo'ced my hand. I had ter git him
ter pertect my own life. (*With cruel satisfaction*) And
I got him right, you b'lieve me!

CEELY. (*Putting her hands over her face with a low moan
of terror*) May de good Lawd pardon yo' wickedness!
O Lawd! What yo' po' ole Mammy gwine say if she
hear tell—an' she never known' how bad you's got.

DREAMY. (*Fiercely*) Hell! You ain't tole her, is you?

CEELY. Think I want ter kill her on de instant? An' I didn'
know myse'f—what you done—till you tells me.
(*Frightened*) Oh, Dreamy, what you gwine do now?
How you gwine git away? (*Almost wailing*) Good
Lawd, de perlice don' kotch you suah!

DREAMY. (*Savagely*) Shut yo' loud mouth, damn yo'!
(*He stands tensely listening for some sound from the
hall. After a moment he points to the bed*) Is Mammy
sleepin'?

CEELY. (*Tiptoes to the bed*) Seems like she is. (*She comes
back to him*) Dat's de way wid her—sleep fo' few minutes, den she wake, den sleep agin.

DREAMY. (*Scornfully*) Aw, dere ain't nothing wrong wid
her 'ceptin' she's ole. What youh wanter send de word
tellin' me she's croakin', and git me comin' here at de
risk o' my life, and den find her sleepin'? (*Clenching
his fist threateningly*) I gotter mind ter smash yo' face
for playin' de damn fool and makin' me de goat. (*He
turns toward the door*) Ain't no use'n me stayin' here
when dey'll likely come lookin' for me. I'm gwine out
where I gotta chance ter make my git-away. De boys is

all fixin' it up for me. (*His hand on the door knob*) When Mammy wakes, you tell her I couldn't wait, you hear?

CEELY. (*Hurrying to him and grabbing his arm—pleadingly*) Don' yo' go now, Dreamy—not jest yit. Fo' de good Lawd's sake, doin' yo' go befo' you speaks wid her! If yo' knew how she's been a-callin' an' a-prayin' for yo' all de day ——

DREAMY. (*Scornfully but a bit uncertainly*) Aw, she's don' need none o' me. What good kin I do watchin' her do a kip! It'd be dif'frunt if she was croakin' on de level.

CEELY. (*In an anguished whisper*) She's gwine wake up in a secon' an' den she call: "Dreamy. Whar's Dreamy?" —an' what I gwine tell her den? An' yo' Mammy is dyin', Dreamy, sho's fate! Her min' been wanderin' an' she don' even recernize me no mo', an' de doctor say when dat come it ain't but a sho't time befo' de en'. Yo' gotter stay wid yo' Mammy long 'nuff ter speak wid her, Dreamy. Yo' jest gotter stay wid her in her las' secon's on dis yearth when she's callin' ter yo'. (*With conviction as he hesitates*) Listen heah, yo' Dreamy! Yo' don' never git no bit er luck in dis worril ary agin, yo' leaves her now. De perlice gon' kotch yo' suah.

DREAMY. (*With superstitious fear*) Ssshh! Can dat bull, Ceely. (*Then boastfully*) I wasn't pinin' to beat it up here, git me? De boys was all persuadin' me not ter take de chance. It's takin' my life in my hands, dat's what. But when I heerd it was ole Mammy croakin' and axin' ter see me, I says ter myse'f: "Dreamy, you gotter make good wid ole Mammy no matter what come —or you don' never git a bit of luck in yo' life no more." And I was game and come, wasn't I? Nary body in dis worril kin say de Dreamy ain't game ter de core, n' matter what. (*With sudden decision walks to the foot of the bed and stands looking down at* MAMMY. *A note of fear creeps into his voice*) Gawd, she's quiet 'nuff. Maybe she done passed away 'n her sleep like de ole ones does. You go see, Ceely; an' if she's on'y sleepin', you wake her up. I wanter speak wid her quick—an' den I'll make a break outa here. You make it fast, Ceely Ann, I tells yo'.

CEELY. (*Bends down beside the bed*) Mammy! Mammy! Here's de Dreamy.

MAMMY. (*Opens her eyes—drowsily and vaguely, in a weak voice*) Dreamy?

DREAMY. (*Shuffling his feet and moving around the bed*) Here I is, Mammy.

MAMMY. (*Fastening her eyes on him with fascinated joy*) Dreamy! Hit's yo'! (*Then uncertainly*) I ain't dreamin' nor seein' ha'nts, is I?

DREAMY. (*Coming forward and taking her hand*) 'Deed I ain't no ghost. Here I is, sho' 'nuff.

MAMMY. (*Clutching his hand tight and pulling it down on her breast—in an ecstasy of happiness*) Didn' I know you'd come! Didn' I say: "Dreamy ain't gwine let his ole Mammy die all lone by he'se'f an' him not dere wid her." I knows yo'd come. (*She starts to laugh joyously, but coughs and sinks back weakly.*)

DREAMY. (*Shudders in spite of himself as he realizes for the first time how far gone the old woman is—forcing a tone of joking reassurance*) What's dat foolishness I hears you talkin', Mammy? Wha' d' yuh mean pullin' dat bull 'bout croakin' on me? Shoo! Tryin' ter kid me, ain't yo'? Shoo! You live ter plant de flowers on my grave, see if you don'.

MAMMY. (*Sadly and very weakly*) I knows! I knows! Hit

ain't long now. (*Bursting into a sudden weak hysteria*) Yo' stay heah, Dreamy. Yo' stay heah by me, yo' stay heah—till de good Lawd take me home. Yo' promise me dat! Yo' do dat fo' po' ole Mammy, won't yo'?

DREAMY. (*Uneasily*) 'Deed I will, Mammy, 'deed I will.

MAMMY. (*Closing her eyes with a sigh of relief—calmly*) Bless de Lawd for dat. Den I ain't skeered no mo'. (*She settles herself comfortably in the bed as if preparing for sleep.*)

CEELY. (*In a low voice*) I gotter go home fo' a minute, Dreamy. I ain't been dere all de day and Lawd knows what happen. I'll be back yere befo' ve'y long.

DREAMY. (*His eyes fixed on* MAMMY) Aw right, beat it if you wanter. (*Turning to her—in a fierce whisper*) On'y don' be long. I can't stay here an' take dis risk, you hear?

CEELY. (*Frightenedly*) I knows, chile. I come back, I swar'. (*She goes out quietly.* DREAMY *goes quickly to the window and cautiously searches the street below with his eyes.*)

MAMMY. (*Uneasily*) Dreamy. (*He hurries back and takes her hand again*) I got de mos' 'culiar feelin' in my head. Seems like de years done all roll away an' I'm back down home in de ole place whar yo' was bo'n. (*After a short pause*) Does yo' 'member yo' own mammy, chile?

DREAMY. No.

MAMMY. Yo' was too young, I s'pec'. Yo' was on'y a baby w'en she tuck 'n die. My Sal was a mighty fine 'oman, if I does say hit myse'f.

DREAMY. (*Fidgeting nervously*) Don' you talk, Mammy. Better you'd close yo' eyes an' rest.

MAMMY. (*With a trembling smile—weakly*) Shoo! W'at

is I done come ter wid my own gran'chile bossin' me
'bout. I wants ter talk. You knows you ain't give me
much chance ter talk wid yo' dese las' years.

DREAMY. (*Sullenly*) I ain't had de time, Mammy; but you
knows I was always game ter give you anything I got.
(*A note of appeal in his voice*) You knows dat, don'
you, Mammy?

MAMMY. Sho'ly I does. Yo' been a good boy, Dreamy; an'
if dere's one thing more'n 'nother makes me feel like I
mighter done good in de sight er de Lawd, hits dat I
raised yo' f'um a baby.

DREAMY. (*Clearing his throat gruffly*) Don' you talk so
much, Mammy.

MAMMY. (*Querulously*) I gotter talk, chile. Come times—
w'en I git thinkin' yere in de bed—w'at's gwine ter come
ter me a'mos' b'fore I knows hit—like de thief in de
night—en den I gits skeered. But w'en I talks wid yo'
I ain't skeered a bit.

DREAMY. (*Defiantly*) You ain't got nothin' to be skeered of
—not when de Dreamy's here.

MAMMY. (*After a slight pause, faintly*) Dere's a singin' in
my ears all de time. (*Seized by a sudden religious
ecstasy*) Maybe hit's de singin' hymns o' de blessed
angels I done heah fum above. (*Wildly*) Bless Gawd!
Pity dis po' ole sinner!

DREAMY. (*With an uneasy glance at the door*) Ssshh,
Mammy! Don' shout so loud.

MAMMY. De pictures keep a whizzin' b'fo' my eyes like de
thread in a sewing machine. Seems 's if all my life done
fly back ter me all ter once. (*With a flickering smile—
weakly*) Does you know how yo' come by dat nickname
dey all calls yo'—de Dreamy? Is I ever tole yo' dat?

DREAMY. (*Evidently lying*) No, Mammy.

MAMMY. Hit was one mawnin' b'fo' we come No'th. Me an'
yo' Mammy—yo' was des a baby in arms den ——

DREAMY. (*Hears a noise from the hall*) Ssshh, Mammy!
For God's sake, don't speak for a minute. I hears
somep'n. (*He stares at the door, his face hardening
savagely, and listens intently.*)

MAMMY. (*In a frightened tone*) W'at's de matter, chile?

DREAMY. Ssshh! Somebody comin'. (*A noise of footsteps
comes from the hall stairway.* DREAMY *springs to
his feet*) Leggo my hand, Mammy—jes' for a secon'. I
come right back to you. (*He pulls his hand from the
old woman's grip. She falls back on the pillows moaning. Dreamy pulls a large automatic revolver from his
coat pocket and tiptoes quickly to the door. As he does
so there is a sharp rap. He stands listening at the
crack for a moment, then noiselessly turns the key, unlocking the door. Then he crouches low down by the
wall so that the door, when opened, will hide him from
the sight of anyone entering. There is another and
louder rap on the door.*)

MAMMY. (*Groaning*) W'at's dat, Dreamy? Whar is yo'?

DREAMY. Ssshh. (*Then muffling his voice he calls:*) Come
in. (*He raises the revolver in his hand. The door is
pushed open, and Irene enters, her eyes peering wildly
about the room. Her bosom is heaving as if she had
been running and she is trembling all over with terrified
excitement.*)

IRENE. (*Not seeing him calls out questioningly*) Dreamy!

DREAMY. (*Lowering his revolver and rising to his feet
roughly*) Close dat door!

IRENE. (*Whirling about with a startled cry*) Dreamy!

DREAMY. (*Shutting the door and locking it—aggressively*)

Shut yo' big mouth, gal, or I'll bang it shut for you!
You wanter let the whole block know where I is?

IRENE. (*Hysterical with joy—trying to put her arms around
him*) Bless God, I foun' you at last!

DREAMY. (*Pushing her away roughly*) Leggo o' me! Why
you come here follerin' me? Ain't yo' got 'nuff sense in
yo' fool head ter know de bulls is liable ter shadow you
when dey knows you's my gal? Is you pinin' ter get me
kotched an' sent to de chair?

IRENE. (*Terrified*) No, no!

DREAMY. (*Savagely*) I gotter mind ter hand you one you
won't ferget! (*He draws back his fist.*)

IRENE. (*Shrinking away*) Don' you hit me, Dreamy! Don'
you beat me up now! Jest lemme 'xplain, dat's all.

MAMMY. (*In a frightened whimper*) Dreamy! Come yere
to me. Whar is yo'? I'se skeered!

DREAMY. (*In a fierce whisper to* IRENE) Can dat bull or
I'll fix you. (*He hurries to the old woman and pats
her hand*) Here I is, Mammy.

MAMMY. Who dat yo's a-talkin' wid?

DREAMY. On'y a fren' o' Ceely Ann's, Mammy, askin' where
she is. I gotter talk wid her some mo' yit. You sleep,
Mammy? (*He goes to* IRENE.)

MAMMY. (*Feebly*) Don' you leave me, Dreamy.

DREAMY. I'se right here wid you. (*Fiercely to* IRENE)
You git the hell outa here, you Reeny, you heah—
quick! Dis ain't no place for de likes o' you wid ole
Mammy dyin'.

IRENE. (*With a horrified glance at the bed*) Is she dyin'—
honest?

DREAMY. Ssshh! She's croakin', I tells yo'—an' I gotter
stay wid her fo' a while—an' I ain't got no time ter be

pesterin' wid you. Beat it, now! Beat it outa here befo' I knocks yo' cold, git me?

IRENE. Jest wait a secon' for de love o' Gawd. I got somep'n ter tell you ——

DREAMY. I don' wanter hear yo' fool talk. (*He gives her a push toward the door*) Git outa dis, you hear me?

IRENE. I'll go. I'm going soon—soon's ever I've had my say. Lissen Dreamy! It's about de coppers I come ter tell you.

DREAMY. (*Quickly*) Why don' you say dat befo'? What you know, gal?

IRENE. Just befo' I come here to find you de first time, de Madam sends me out ter Murphy's ter git her a bottle o' gin. I goes in de side door but I ain't rung de bell yet. I hear yo' name spoken an' I stops ter lissen. Dey was three or four men in de back room. Dey don't hear me open de outside door, an' dey can't see me, 'course. It was Big Sullivan from de Central Office talkin'. He was talkin' 'bout de killin' you done las' night and he tells dem odders he's heerd 'bout the ole woman gittin' so sick, and dat if dey don't fin' you none of de udder places dey's lookin', dey's goin' wait for you here. Dey s'pecs you come here say good-bye to Mammy befo' you make yo' git-away.

DREAMY. It's aw right den. Dey ain't come yit. Twister Smith done tole me de coast was clear befo' I come here.

IRENE. Dat was den. It ain't now.

DREAMY. (*Excitedly*) What you mean, gal?

IRENE. I was comin' by de front way when I sees some pusson hidin' in de doorway 'cross de street. I gits a good peek at him and when I does—it's a copper, Dreamy, suah's yo' born, in his plain clo'se, and he's watchin' de door o' dis house like a cat.

DREAMY. (*Goes to the window and stealthily crouching by the dark side peeks out. One glance is enough. He comes quickly back to Irene*) You got de right dope, gal. It's dat Mickey. I knows him even in de dark. Dey're waitin'—so dey ain't wise I'm here yit, dat's suah.

IRENE. But dey'll git wise befo' long.

DREAMY. He don't pipe you comin' in here?

IRENE. I skulked roun' and sneaked in by de back way froo de yard. Dey ain't none of dem dere yit. (*Raising her voice—excitedly*) But dere will be soon. Dey're boun' to git wise to dat back door. You ain't got no time to lose, Dreamy. Come on wid me now. Git back where yo' safe. It's de cooler for you certain if you stays here. Dey'll git you like a rat in de trap. (*As Dreamy hesitates*) For de love of Gawd, Dreamy, wake up to youse'f!

DREAMY. (*Uncertainly*) I can't beat it—wid Mammy here alone. My luck done turn bad all my life, if I does.

IRENE. (*Fiercely*) What's good you gittin' pinched and sent to de chair gwine do her? Is you crazy mad? Come away wid me, I tells you!

DREAMY. (*Half-persuaded—hesitatingly*) I gotter speak wid her. You wait a secon'.

IRENE. (*Wringing her hands*) Dis ain't no time now for fussin' wid her.

DREAMY. (*Gruffly*) Shut up! (*He makes a motion for her to remain where she is and goes over to the bed—in a low voice*) Mammy.

MAMMY. (*Hazily*) Dat you, Dreamy? (*She tries to reach out her hand and touch him.*)

DREAMY. I'm gwine leave you—jest for a moment, Mammy. I'll send de word for Ceely Ann ——

MAMMY. (*Wide awake in an instant—with intense alarm*) Don' yo' do dat! Don't yo' move one step out er yere or yo'll be sorry, Dreamy.

DREAMY. (*Apprehensively*) I gotter go, I tells you. I'll come back.

MAMMY. (*With wild grief*) O good Lawd! W'en I's drawin' de las' bre'fs in dis po' ole body—(*Frenziedly*) De Lawd have mercy! Good Lawd have mercy!

DREAMY. (*Fearfully*) Stop dat racket, Mammy! You bring all o' dem down on my head! (*He rushes over and crouches by the window again to peer out—in relieved tones*) He ain't heerd nothin'. He's dar yit.

IRENE. (*Imploringly*) Come on, Dreamy! (*Mammy groans with pain.*)

DREAMY. (*Hurrying to the bed*) What's de matter, Mammy?

IRENE. (*Stamping her foot*) Dreamy! Fo' Gawd's sake!

MAMMY. Lawd have mercy! (*She groans*) Gimme yo' han', chile. Yo' ain't gwine to leave me now, Dreamy? Yo' ain't, is yo'? Yo' ole Mammy won' bodder yo' long. Yo' know what yo' promise me, Dreamy! Yo' promise yo' sacred word yo' stay wid me till de en'. (*With an air of sombre prophecy—slowly*) If yo' leave me now, you ain't gwine git no bit er luck s'long's yo' lives, I tells yo' dat!

DREAMY. (*Frightened—pleadingly*) Don' you say dat, Mammy!

IRENE. Come on, Dreamy!

DREAMY. (*Slowly*) I can't. (*In awed tones*) Don' you hear de curse she puts on me if I does?

MAMMY. (*Her voice trembling with weak tears*) Don' go, chile!

DREAMY. (*Hastily*) I won't leave dis room, I swar ter you!

(*Relieved by the finality in his tones, the old woman sighs and closes her eyes.* DREAMY *frees his hand from hers and goes to* IRENE. *He speaks with a strange calm*) De game's up, gal. You better beat it while de goin's good.

IRENE. (*Aghast*) You gwine stay?

DREAMY. I gotter, gal. I ain't gwine agin her dyin' curse. No, suh!

IRENE. (*Pitifully*) But dey'll git you suah!

DREAMY. (*Slapping the gun in his pocket significantly*) Dey'll 'have some gittin'. I git some o' dem fust. (*With gloomy determination*) Dey don' git dis chicken alive! Lawd Jesus, no suh. Not de Dreamy!

IRENE. (*Helplessly*) Oh, Lawdy, Lawdy! (*She goes to the window—with a short cry*) He's talkin' wid someone. Dere's two o' dem. (*Dreamy hurries to her side.*)

DREAMY. I knows him—de udder. It's Big Sullivan. (*Pulling her away roughly*) Come out o' dat! Dey'll see you. (*He pushes her toward the door*) Dey won't wait down der much longer. Dey'll be comin' up here soon. (*Prayerfully, with a glance at the bed*) I hope she's croaked by den, fo' Christ I does!

IRENE. (*As if she couldn't believe it*) Den you ain't gwine save youse'f while dere's time? (*Pleadingly*) Oh, Dreamy, you can make it yet!

DREAMY. De game's up. I tole you. (*With gloomy fatalism*) I s'pect it hatter be. Yes, suh. Dey'd git me in de long run anyway—and wid her curse de luck'd be agin me. (*With sudden anger*) Git outa here, you Reeny! You ain't aimin' ter git shot up too, is you? Ain't no sense in dat.

IRENE. (*Fiercely*) I'se stayin' too, here wid you!

DREAMY. No you isn't! None o' dat bull! You ain't got no mix in dis jamb.

IRENE. Yes, I is! Ain't you my man?

DREAMY. Don' make no dif. I don' wanter git you in Dutch more'n you is. It's bad 'nuff fo' me. (*He pushes her toward the door*) Blow while you kin, I tells you!

IRENE. (*Resisting him*) No, Dreamy! What I care if dey kills me? I'se gwine stick wid you.

DREAMY. (*Gives her another push*) No, you isn't, gal. (*Unlocking the door—relentlessly*) Out wid you!

IRENE. (*Hysterically*) You can't gimme no bum's rush. I'm gwine stay.

DREAMY. (*Gloomily*) On'y one thing fo' me ter do den. (*He hits her on the side of the face with all his might knocking her back against the wall where she sways as if about to fall. Then he opens the door and grabs her two arms from behind*) Out wid you, gal!

IRENE. (*Moaning*) Dreamy! Dreamy! Lemme stay wid you! (*He pushes her into the hallway and holds her there at arm's length*) Fo' Gawd's sake, Dreamy!

MAMMY. (*Whimperingly*) Dreamy! I'se skeered!

IRENE. (*From the hall*) I'se gwine stay right here at de door. You might's well lemme in.

DREAMY. (*Frowning*) Don' do dat, Reeny. (*Then with a sudden idea*) You run roun' and tell de gang what's up. Maybe dey git me outa dis, you hear?

IRENE. (*With eager hope*) You think dey kin?

DREAMY. Never kin tell. You hurry—through de back yard, 'member—an' don' git pinched, now.

IRENE. (*Eagerly*) I'm gwine! I'll bring dem back!

DREAMY. (*Stands listening to her retreating footsteps—then shuts and locks the door—gloomily to himself*)

Ain't no good. Dey dassen't do nothin'—but I hatter git her outa dis somehow.

MAMMY. (*Groaning*) Dreamy!

DREAMY. Here I is. Jest a secon'. (*He goes to the window.*)

MAMMY. (*Weakly*) I feels—like—like de en's comin'. Oh Lawd! Lawd!

DREAMY. (*Absent-mindedly*) Yes, Mammy. (*Aloud to himself*) Dey're sneakin' cross de street. Dere's anudder of 'em. Dat's tree. (*He glances around the room quickly—then hurries over and takes hold of the chest of drawers. As he does so, the old woman commences to croon shrilly to herself.*)

DREAMY. Stop dat noise, Mammy! Stop dat noise!

MAMMY. (*Wanderingly*) Dat's how come yo' got dat—dat nickname—Dreamy.

DREAMY. Yes, Mammy. (*He puts the lamp on the floor to the rear of the door, turning it down low. Then he carries the chest of drawers over and places it against the door as a barricade.*)

MAMMY. (*Rambling as he does this—very feebly*) Does yo' know—I gives you dat name—w'en yo' des a baby—lyin' in my arms ——

DREAMY. Yes, Mammy.

MAMMY. Down by de crik—under de ole willow—whar I uster take yo'—wid yo' big eyes a-chasin'—de sun flitterin' froo de grass—an' out on de water ——

DREAMY. (*Takes the revolver from his pocket and puts it on the top of the chest of drawers*) Dey don't get de Dreamy alive—not for de chair! Lawd Jesus, no suh!

MAMMY. An' yo' was always a-lookin'—an' a-thinkin' ter yo'se'f—an' yo' big eyes jest a-dreamin' an' a-dreamin'

—an' dat's w'en I gives yo' dat nickname—Dreamy—
Dreamy ——

DREAMY. Yes, Mammy. (*He listens at the crack of the door—in a tense whisper*) I don' hear dem—but dey're comin' sneakin' up de stairs, I knows it.

MAMMY. (*Faintly*) Whar is yo', Dreamy? I can't—ha'dly —breathe—no mo'. Oh Lawd have mercy!

DREAMY. (*Goes over to the bed*) Here I is, Mammy.

MAMMY. (*Speaking with difficulty*) Yo'—kneel down—chile —say a pray'r—Oh Lawd!

DREAMY. Jest a secon', Mammy. (*He goes over and gets his revolver and comes back.*)

MAMMY. Gimme—yo' hand—chile. (*Dreamy gives her his left hand. The revolver is in his right. He stares nervously at the door*) An' yo' kneel down—pray fo' me. (*Dreamy gets on one knee beside the bed. There is a sound from the hallway as if someone had made a misstep on the stairs—then silence. Dreamy starts and half aims his gun in the direction of the door. Mammy groans weakly*) I'm dyin', chile. Hit's de en'. You pray for me—out loud—so's I can heah. Oh Lawd! (*She gasps to catch her breath.*)

DREAMY. (*Abstractedly, not having heard a word she has said*) Yes, Mammy. (*Aloud to himself with an air of grim determination, as if he were making a pledge*) Dey don't git de Dreamy! Not while he's 'live! Lawd Jesus, no suh!

MAMMY. (*Falteringly*) Dat's right—yo' pray—Lawd Jesus, Lawd Jesus. (*There is another slight sound of movement from the hallway.*)

THE CURTAIN FALLS

THE RIDER OF DREAMS

A ONE ACT PLAY
FOR THE NEGRO THEATRE

By

RIDGLEY TORRENCE

Reprinted by special permission of the author and The Macmillan Company, from "Granny Maumee, The Rider of Dreams, Simon the Cyrenian"; Copyright, 1917, by The Macmillan Company

CHARACTERS

Lucy Sparrow, a washerwoman
Madison Sparrow, her husband
Booker Sparrow, her young son
Uncle Williams, a more prosperous neighbor

Scene: A one-room cottage interior, in a small town in the
   South
Time: An early October evening

First performance by the Hapgood Players, the Garden
Theatre, New York City, April 14, 1917

THE RIDER OF DREAMS

SCENE: NIGHT IN A ROOM *used for kitchen, dining room, and laundry by a colored family. A lamp is set upon a central table laid with a spotless tablecloth. Baskets of clothes stand on several chairs. At the back is a cookstove and to the left of this a door. There are also doorways to the right and left of the room.* LUCY SPARROW, *a worn, sweet-faced woman of forty, is sprinkling clothes at an ironing board at left with her back turned to the table beside which, on a high stool, is perched a small boy,* BOOKER SPARROW. *Both the boy and the woman, as well as the room, show a painstaking neatness despite the disorder necessary in the process of a professional "wash".*

LUCY. Who make you?

BOOKER. God. Ain't the mush done now?

LUCY. It's done but I ain't done wif you. You got to learn good befo' you can eat good. Who redeem you?

BOOKER. Christ. I'll stop being hungry for it if I don't get it now.

LUCY. Bettah lose youah wishes an' youah ahms an' laigs an' everything youah body's fix wif an' keep youah immortal soul. Who sanctify you?

BOOKER. The Holy Ghost. I don't want nothing but mush.

LUCY. Well, you ain' goin' to git hit twell you luhns de questions. What de chief en' of man?

27

BOOKER. Chief end of man is to glorify God and enjoy himself forever.

LUCY. (*Coming swiftly forward and confronting him with a threatening look*) Enjoy *hisself!* I ain' neveh teach you dat. You know betteh'n dat. Man got no right to enjoy hisself. He got to enjoy Gawd. You knows dat as well as you knows eatin'. An' you got to say it an' what's mo' you got to live it. Now what de chief en' of man?

BOOKER. Enjoy God forever.

LUCY. Dat's mo' like it. (*She turns her back and going to the ironing board resumes her labors, still talking*) I'm raisin' you fo' de Kingdom an' you'ah goin' in de Kingdom ef pushin' 'll land you dere. Because dis time anutheh yeah you may be in some lonesome graveyard. (*Singing*)

In some lonesome graveyard,
Oh, Lawd, no time to pray.

(*As she sings* BOOKER *stealthily slips off his stool and going around to the opposite side of the table takes a spoon with which he approaches a dish set upon a warming shelf fixed to the stove. He furtively dips his spoon in the dish and begins to eat.* LUCY *continuing her singing*)

Play on youah harp, little David,
Little Davy, how ole are you?
"I'm only twelve yeahs ole."

(*She turns and discovers* BOOKER) What! You stealin'! I'll show you! (*She gives him a cuff and a shake, depositing him again upon his stool*) You shorely is on de way to de fieh but I'm goin' to pluck you out ef it skins you alive. Steal, will you? What de sevenf commandment?

BOOKER. (*Sniveling*) Thou shalt not steal.

LUCY. See dat.   You knows it but you des won't live hit. Well, I'm goin' live it into you.   I'm goin' slap sin out of you.   (*She gives him another shake*) An' de grace into you.   Now you say dat commandment sevumty times seven.   Begin.   Say hit.

BOOKER. Thou shalt not steal.   Thou shalt not steal——

(*The door at back opens and* MADISON SPARROW *stands in the doorway looking on the scene within the room.   He is a tall, loose-jointed, lazy-looking man.   In one hand he carries a long green bag.*)

MADISON. (*After a survey of the situation*) What de boy do?

LUCY. He steal, dat what he do.

MADISON. Um.   What he steal?

LUCY. Mush.   I tole him not to tech it.

MADISON. Well, he was hongry, weren't he?

LUCY. Dat ain' de p'int.   'Tweren't his till I give it to him.

MADISON. (*Places the bag carefully by the doorway, throws his hat upon it, then seats himself at the table*) Bring on dat mush. I'm tia'hd of dese fool doin's. Dey ain't no git ahead wif um.   If de boy wants mush let him git mush.

LUCY. (*Placing food before him on the table*) Yes, but not rob it.

MADISON. Who talkin' 'bout robbin'?

LUCY. Madison, dat's de wrong kin' of trash fo' dis baby to heah.   Go lay down, honey.   Tek de bowl wif you. (BOOKER *whines but takes a dish and goes to doorway at left.*)

MADISON. No, hit's de right kin' of preachin'.   I'm tia'hd of all dat ol' fashion way of doin'.   Ef I wuz to wuk my ahms off dat ol' fashion way I couldn't git no furder.

LUCY. What you bin wukin' at dis yeah, Madison?

MADISON. Dat's it. You know dat I'm bin lookin' fo' it and couldn't find hit.

LUCY. What you wuk at last yeah?

MADISON. You knows I wuk in de strippin' factory.

LUCY. Jes' two weeks.

MADISON. You knows I wuk till I strain my back. But neveh min' about all dat. I done tuhn oveh a new leaf. I goin' to be a business man. I goin' to let de otheh man wuk.

LUCY. 'Sposin' everybody was to do dat away.

MADISON. Let 'em do it. I don' ask nothin' of nobody. I goin' to have every toof in my haid covehed wif gol'. I'll get youah'n an' Book's fix dat way too. I goin' to have plenty society grub in me all de time. I ain't goin' to let my fam'ly suffeh. I got too sweet disposishun fo' dat. I'll git 'em whateveh I want.

BOOKER. (*Lingering in the doorway*) When you get rich will you get you the guitar, Daddy?

(LUCY *waves* BOOKER *through doorway. He vanishes.*)

MADISON. I'll git it an' I got it. Watch me now. (*He goes over to the bag by the door and reaching in it produces a handsome guitar*) Dat's de beginnin' er good times, boy.

LUCY. (*With sickening apprehension*) Madison, where you get dat insterment?

MADISON. Dat's de Lawd's insterment, Lucy. He done pervide it.

LUCY. Oh, Madison, dat ain't youah'n.

MADISON. 'Tis now, honey.

LUCY. No, youah las' dime you spent Sunday an' I ain' give

Photo by Maurice Goldberg

THE HAPGOOD PLAYERS IN "THE RIDER OF DREAMS"

you no money since. You got it wifout payin' for it.
You charged it.

MADISON. Yassah, I got it wifout payin' for it an' I goin' to
keep on a-gittin' it wifout payin' for hit as long as de
gittin's good.

LUCY. How you like to be treat dat way?

MADISON. What way?

LUCY. If you was keepin' a store, to have folks charge things
when dey didn' know how dey could pay.

MADISON. I'm willin' fo' to be treat dat way ef dey can do
hit. Let 'em come an' git my things if dey finds any.

LUCY. (*Breaking down*) Oh, I cain' stan' hit. Youah sinkin' fas' down to de fiery lake an' you's pullin' my baby
down too.

MADISON. No, I's raisin' him up an' I goin' lan' us all in a
sof' place on dat Easy Street I heah 'em singin' 'bout so
long wifout seein'.

LUCY. (*Suddenly examining the guitar*) Wheah you git dis
guitar?

MADISON. What guitar?

LUCY. Dis. Oh, Madison, dis is 'Zek'l Williams' own guitar
dat he wouldn't sell. Dis is de guitar dat nobody couldn'
buy. How you come by it?

MADISON. Look heah, woman. You act like I *stole* de
guitar. You don't think I'm a thief, do you?

LUCY. How you come by hit?

MADISON. I got it off Wilson Byrd.

LUCY. Dat sneakin' w'ite man. How'd he git it?

MADISON. I didn' ask him.

LUCY. What you give him fo' hit?

MADISON. Oh, dat's anotheh story. Him an' me's goin' in
business togetheh.

LUCY. Oh, Madison, dat w'ite man stole dis guitar. Oh,

take it back dis minute an' snatch youah soul from de bu'nin'.

MADISON. Who, me? What you take me fo', gal? Take back a guitar to de rich man what own de very house we live in!

LUCY. Well, we soon will buy hit.

MADISON. Dat's right. We will. But dat ain' de question. I didn' git dis guitar fo' to return it, I git it fo' to play it. I boun' to play it cause I'm goin' to be er rich man soon an' I got to have a-plenty music in me.

LUCY. You goin' to git rich playin' guitar?

MADISON. (*Laughing comfortably*) Eh, yah, yah. Whoopee! No indeedy. I flies higher dan music flies. I'm one er dese heah kine er 'lectioneerin' mens which make der money work fo'um. Dey sen's one dollah out in de heat an' sweats her twell she rolls home wif anutheh.

LUCY. How you goin' to put money out, Madison, lessen you wuks an' gits de money?

MADISON. (*Cunningly*) Oh, don' yo' botheh youah haid long er dat. I bin down low and folks trample me des same as a wu'm, but now I'm goin' spread my wings an' sting 'em like a king bee. Whaffo' I lay dere an' let'm trample me? 'Twere because I lack conference. I puts my 'pen'ance on dis promis', I puts my 'pen'ance on dat, an' dey all fails me.

LUCY. You ain't neveh put youah trus' in Gawd.

MADISON. Yassuh, I did, an' Gawd He up an' gimme de go-by too. What He bin doin' fo' me? Nuthin'. Now I goin' spit on my han's an' whu'l in an' trus' myse'f. An' I feels lots betteh. I can feel conference wukin' all oveh me. I casts 'em all off. I'm lookin' out fo' myse'f. M-m-m—It took me long time to git heah but now I'm heah let 'em look out for me. (*His voice rises to a chant*) M-m-m—Midnight on de sea. All de lights out. I'm carryin' hod on Jacob's laddeh to build me a new house an' I'm buildin' it high, man. Don' tech me. I'm a flame of fieh an' I'll singe you sho'. If dey asks fo' me tell 'em say, "I saw somethin' sailin' up but he was headin' fo' a high hill on de sun an' my eyes failed me." Tell 'em say, "He had de fo' win's runnin' like stallions to fetch up wif him but dey carried 'em out, and buried 'em in de valley. He bus' dere hea'ts!" Tell em say, "He was herdin' lightnin's like sheep an' dey wuz too slow an' he picked 'em up an' sheared 'em an' sent 'em home." Dat's me, I'm de one you'll be talkin' 'bout. Fer why? 'Cause I cas' off ever'thing an' puts my trus' in myself an' nuthin' can't hole me. De mo' I says it de mo' I feels conference. I feels it a-wukin'.

LUCY. You goin' to wuk, Madison?

MADISON. Yes, indeedy. I got to wuk an' wuk ha'd. I can't shirk none.

LUCY. What wuk you goin' to do?

MADISON. I'm a stockbrokin' man. I goin' into de stock-brokin' business tomorrer.

LUCY. How?

MADISON. Buyin' an' sellin', dat's how an' which too.

LUCY. De Devil's wrastlin' wif you, Madison, an' you's per-ishin' fas'. Ef you keeps on in dis paf you'll lan' 'mongs' de rocks er mournin'. You's let somebody tu'n you roun'.

MADISON. Not me. Nobody can't tu'n me roun'. I dreamed it an' I dreamed it right, face fo'mos' an' on de run.

LUCY. How dream?

MADISON. Las' night an' day befo' yistiddy night an' night

befo' dat. I wuz layin' groanin', "O Lawd, how long,"
an' I heah a voice say, "Git up an' come a-runnin'."
Looks up an' sees a fine w'ite saddle hoss. Hoss say,
    "Ride me right an' I'll guide you right."
On I gits an' off he goes, slick as a rancid transom car.
Comes to high hill lookin' down on de sun an' moon.
Hoss stop an' say,
    "Brung you heah to give you noos
    De worl' is youahn to pick an' choose."
I ax him, "How dat?" Hoss say:
    "How is how an' why is why,
    Buy low an' sell high."
I say to him, "I got no money to buy. Wheah I goin'
git de fun's to buy low?" Hoss respon':
    "Trus' yo'se'f an' take youah own,
    Git de meat an' leave de bone,
    Bus' de nut an' fling 'em de shell,
    Ride an' let em walk a spell,
    Findeh's keepeh's, loseh's weepeh's,
    I hope dese few lines find you well."
I ax him who tole him all dis an' hoss say:
    "Ole hoss *Grab* will neveh balk,
    All dis heah is w'ite man talk."
Dat what de hoss say to me in my true dream ev'y night
dis week an' I'm a-goin' to bide by hit twell de las' er
pea time. 'Cause I'm er true dreameh an' my mammy
she wuz befo' me.

LUCY. What come of de hoss in de dream, Madison?

MADISON. Dat's all. Hoss went up in smoke an' I come
    down in bed.

LUCY. Hoss went up in smoke! No, hit went down in smoke
    an' fieh.

MADISON. Now look-a heah, woman. I'm goin' to make

you a good livin' f'um now on. I'm goin' into business
termorrer. I'm goin' in de specalatin' wu'k. I'm goin'
to buy low an' sell high.

LUCY. What kin you buy wif? You got no money.

MADISON. (*Hesitating but collecting his forces gradually*)
Oh, ain't I tell you 'bout dat? I got it in de dream.

LUCY. In de dream?

MADISON. Um Hmmm. You know dat hoss I tole you
'bout? Well'm, jes' fo' we pa'ted he prance up th'ough
a starry fiel' an' come to a gyarden fence. Oveh dat
fence he lep an', man, she was a fine gyarden. "Whose
patch dish yer?" I say to him. Hoss say:
        "If you asks me grab what you see."
Den he reaches down an' pulls up a tu'nip wif his teef
an' gives it to me an' say:
        "Dis gyarden truck will fetch you luck."
(*He watches* LUCY *furtively*) An' I takes an' sta'ts to
peel dis tu'nip an' what does I find? I finds she's a fine
fat roll er bills, dem tu'nip tops is greenbacks.

LUCY. So youah money is dream money?

MADISON. Well, no, not ezackly. De hoss whispeh sumpin'
in my eah, an' tole me how to make dat dream money
real money. An' I took de hint an' done it today. An'
on dat money I'll buy low an' gouge 'em all good.

LUCY. How much you got?

MADISON. Well'm—(*He hesitates*) I got a little an' den
some. I got erbout—fifty er so.

LUCY. Wheah you git it? (*She catches hold of him.*)

MADISON. Tu'n me loose, woman. I goin' to baid. I got
to make early sta't. (*He pulls off his coat.*)

LUCY. (*Wildly*) I ain' goin' let you stay in sin. (*She
snatches the coat from him*) I goin' take dis money an'

make you say wheah you got it. (*She begins hastily
searching through the pockets of the coat.*)

MADISON. (*Calmly regarding her with great good humor
and breaking into a laugh as she fails in her search*) Eh,
yah, yah, sea'ch an' look, sea'ch an' look.

LUCY. Oh, Madison, ain' yo' got no honin' ter be hones' at
all?

MADISON. Hones'! What kin' er fool talk is dat? I done
got my ear-string bus' now an' dem preachah wu'ds can't
fool me no mo'. You'll neveh fin' it, honey. 'Cause
why? 'Cause I'm got it in my pants an' I goin' to keep
it f'um a foolish woman.

LUCY. (*Running to him desperately*) You got to give it to
me.

MADISON. Gal, ef you don' tu'n me loose I'll git ugly. Now,
look heah. I wants to heah de las' er dis. I got new
ideahs. I got big plots an' plans. I done give you de
plankses in my platfo'm an' I'm a-goin' to stan' on hit.
When I makes a lot mo' money in de broker business
I'm a-goin' to give you all de gold you ap'un'll hold,
ev'y day er youah life, an' you won' have to wait long.
But till dat day an' to dat time I'm de treasu'eh er dis
lodge an' I'm de stakeholdeh er dis race an' dat money
stays in de pu'se in de hip er my ol' jeanses. (*He says
this last slowly and with growing emphasis and as he
ends, gives himself a resounding thwack on the hip
over his pocket. There is a moment's pause. He puts
his hand hurriedly in the pocket and then dazedly into
one on the other hip*) What dis? Wheah dat roll?

LUCY. (*Fearfully*) I ain' tech it. You know I ain' bin neah
you.

MADISON. (*Rushing to her*) Gimme de coat. (*He snatches
the coat and begins going through the pockets, from*

time to time searching and slapping the garments he is wearing) Didn't you git it? You mus' er tuk it.

LUCY. No, Madison, I ain' see nor tech it. You watched me.

MADISON. Oh, Lawd, he'p me look. (*He begins to run around the room, looking on the table, picking up articles and letting them fall, dropping on his knees and hunting under the table and chairs. As he searches he grows more frantic*) Oh, my Lawd, oh, wheah is it? I got to have it. Oh, I couldn' lose it, hit ain' mine ter lose. Stay by me, Lucy, an' he'p me fin' it, git down on youah knees, Lucy. Oh, wheah did I drop it? I'm gittin' old an' needs it. Ef I lose dis I lose all my push. I was jes' goin' into business an' we all wuz goin' to fly high. I got to fin' it. I ain' give up. Lemme think. Oh, I hopes some hones' puhson foun' it. Lemme come on down—Know I put it on dat side 'cause dat de side Mistah Long he wuz on—Oh, I'll go crazy—(*He strikes his forehead groaning.*)

LUCY. (*Starting*) Mistah Long! He's cashiah in de Dime Savin's! How he give you money?

MADISON. Oh, lemme see—he gimme de money an' I put it right in yere. (*He fumbles again distractedly in his pocket.*)

LUCY. (*Pursuing him desperately*) Onliest money at de Dime Savin's is *de* money. You couldn't draw *hit* out. You didn't do dat,—you couldn'—Tell me if you did fo' I'll fin' it out tomorrer—Oh, tell me true—you couldn' when it's in my name—tell me now fo' I'll find it out.

MADISON. Oh, I can't stand it.

LUCY. Ef you wan' me to he'p you den be free wif me. How you draw money from de bank? I give you no papeh. You *couldn'* draw *de* money.

MADISON. Wilson Byrd, he gimme de papeh.

LUCY. I give him no papeh.

MADISON. He write it fo' you.

LUCY. Oh, Gawd, dat w'ite man write my name. You drawed de money—I see it now. You had dealin's wif a fo'geh, Wilson Byrd.

MADISON. Spar' me an' he'p me. He tol' me ef I draw de money he'd take me into business wif him an' gimme de guitar besides.

LUCY. Did you spar' me? Fifty dollahs! You said fifty, didn' you? How could you do hit? More'n six months' ha'd slavin'. Six months mo' befo' I can resto' it back. I could 'a' bought de house tomorrer mo'nin' an' now it's six months off to pay in dat fifty. It *was* fifty, didn' you say? Maybe 'twuzzin' dat much. Tell me right. I'll fin' it out tomorrer.

MADISON. Dis yere'll kill me ef I can't think.

LUCY. How much did you draw? Tell me right. Look at me. Were hit fifty? (*She holds his eyes*) Less? Mo'? How much? (*She continues to hold his lustreless eyes, reading them*) A hunde'd? Two hunde'd? Eight hunde'd? (*A pause ensues as she reads the truth in his face*) All of hit! (*She sinks in a chair*) Twelve yeahs' labor sence I married you an' termorrer I wuz goin' to mek de payment an' we'd 'a' bin undeh owah own roof. I'm done. I could 'a' paid off pa't, mebbe fifty, but I won' las' twelve yeahs mo' at de same thing. But I thank thee, Lawd, dat it wuz stole f'um us all ef it had to be stole.

MADISON. Ef I could on'y think. Had hit in de bank—felt hit an' had it on Thu'd Street—slapped hit an' had it comin' up de alley—jes' fo' I clum' de hill—lemme see —went in th'oo Wilson Byrd's hedge fence—he gimme de guitar—scrape my back comin' out—(*His face shows gradual recollection, and suddenly brightens*) I know now! Dat's hit! In dat white man's yard wheah he gimme de guitar! I wuz jes' goin' to give him de money when somebody grabbed him f'um behin'. He give a squawk an' skeered me. I run out th'oo his hedge fence an' scrape my back. I scrape de pocketbook out. She's dere! In dat Wilson Byrd's yard. I'll git it yit. Watch me. (*He grabs his hat and runs excitedly toward the door.*)

LUCY. (*Rushing toward him*) No, sumpin' might happen. You might git mix up wif him ergin. Lemme go, but I mus' resto' dis guitar at Uncle Williams', as I go by his house. I'll slip it on his porch. Maybe he'll neveh know it wuz gone. Oh, if somebody had seen it heah! How could I have stood it? (*She puts on a shawl and takes up the bag but as she lays here hand on the door knob a loud knock is heard on the door. Both start back and wait. The knocking is repeated. She throws off the shawl, places the bag in a corner and returning to the door, opens it. She greets the visitor in a strained voice, almost with a shriek*) Uncle Williams! Step in, please. (*A man enters. The newcomer is old, with white hair and beard. He is probably of Moorish descent. He is so small and weazened as to be almost a dwarf, but his whole demeanor indicates great latent power. A strong personality, dominating the two others from the first instant.*)

WILLIAMS. Good evenin', Lucy. (*He seems to be unaware of the presence of* MADISON. *He comes forward with little mincing steps and an old man's gesture, then takes off his hat and looks about him. The others stand watching him, transfixed*) Ain' you goin' shut de do',

Lucy? I feels draf's. I'm gittin' old an' catches cold easy. Ain' you goin' take my hat? (*She reaches for it mechanically, watching him apprehensively*) No, de hat —not de stick—ol' pu'son like me always need good stout stick er club case er havin' faintin' spell—sumpin' to lean on. Now, wheah a cheer, bettah fetch me er cheer fo' feah I might set on sumpin' you wouldn' choose fo' me. (*She obeys dumbly and brings a chair to him*) Set it neareh. Dat's right. Now gimme youah shouldah an' ease me down. Ah—(*He leans heavily on her and sinks totteringly into the chair with a great show of feebleness*) Now take a cheer yo'se'f. I 'spize to see a lady standin' an' me takin' my res', old ez I is. (*She obeys, watching him with doubt and dread*) Set it dah, wheah I can see you good. (MADISON *is standing up by the wall, right, gazing at him as though paralyzed with fear*) Dah now. We kin be ca'm and have a nice talk. Does you know what business I come yere fo' to-night? (*He pauses*) You does, doesn't you?

LUCY. (*Almost beside herself with nervous tension*) You— come to see—ef—(*Recovering herself with a mighty effort*) Oh, yes, you come to look oveh de stove an' see ef you like to buy hit.

WILLIAMS. (*Musingly*) M-m. Well, I reckon—dat's hit. Yes, dey tells me y'all has a wahmin' stove to sell an' now katydid cease, fros' ain' fur off, an' I needs hit. Is dish yere de one?

LUCY. (*Rising and rushing toward door at side*) No, not dat. Hit's outside—ef you please to step out.

WILLIAMS. Well'm, I'll take'n look her oveh. (*She hastily lights a candle as he rises and totters in the wrong direction.*)

LUCY. Th'oo heah, th'oo heah. De stove's out in de wood-shed. (*She grasps and guides him.*)

WILLIAMS. Ah—well'm. Um hm. I always gives things er good lookin' oveh befo' takin' stock in 'm. You needn' come erlong. I lived so long in dis house befo' you wuz bawn dat I knows my way. Is de stove an easy wood eateh?

LUCY. Yes, yes. (*She gives him the candle and almost pushes him through doorway at side as she follows him out. MADISON, who has watched fearfully from a dark corner, darts forward and looks after them, listening. He then runs toward the door at back but hesitates before it and turns as LUCY comes swiftly in from outer room, closing the door softly.*)

MADISON. What he say? Do he know?

LUCY. (*Desperately seizing the bag and pressing it into his hands as she turns him again toward doorway at back*) Oh, I cain' tell. On'y resto' dis in case he don' know er case he do. Now's de one chance to be hones'.

MADISON. Huh. What erbout dat eight hundred dollahs?

LUCY. I don' know. Trus' Gawd an' be hones'.

MADISON. Huh uh. One of us has got to go look fo' dat money.

LUCY. One of us has got to take back de guitar.

MADISON. I'm goin' fo' de money.

LUCY. Den I'll take dis. (*She takes up the guitar and she and MADISON go toward door at back. Then she halts*) Oh, Madison, you can do bofe. One of us has got to stay wif Uncle Williams. But take back de guitar first.

MADISON. All right. I'll go. An' I ain't played on dis heah but twice. (*He takes the guitar from her.*)

LUCY. Go now. Can you fin' youah way to his porch in de
dahk?

MADISON. Will we find the money? Dat's de p'oblem I
wants de answeh fo'. (LUCY *opens door at back to go
out. MADISON is at her side. Both start back.
WILLIAMS stands before them in the open doorway.*)

LUCY. (*Haltingly, after a pause*) How—you like—de
stove?

WILLIAMS. (*Entering more vigorously than before*) Well'm,
befo' we goes any furder we betteh come neareh de real
p'int an' question. I didn' come fo' no stove dis night.
(MADISON *shrinks back into the shadows.*)

LUCY. (*Slowly*) Yo—don'—wan'——

WILLIAMS. No'm. To be sho', I might tek de stove one er
dese days, but dat ain' my erran' now. Hit's dis; does
you know when we mek de bargum about you buyin' dis
heah house?

LUCY. Twelve yeah ago.

WILLIAMS. Gal, you dreamin'! 'Tweren't but las' year.
'Twere de fus er Octobah las' year an' I say I gives you
de refusals fer one yeah. 'Membeh dat?

LUCY. Yassuh.

WILLIAMS. So fur so good. Now does you know what day
de month dis is?

LUCY. Fus' er Octobah.

WILLIAMS. Dat's true as preachin'. Well'm, time's up.

LUCY. What you mean?

WILLIAMS. I'm er man er my wuhd. Pay me de money an'
tek de house.

LUCY. Termorrer ——

WILLIAMS. No. Termorrer won' do.

LUCY. Why you push me so? Oh, please spar' me an' wait
—wait anutheh day.

"THE RIDER OF DREAMS".

WILLIAMS. No, I'm er business man. I kin sell de house fer mo' money termorrer but I hold'd to my wuhd ter sell it to you. I holds to it an' loses money, but it falls due dis day an' night an' I won' stretch it one jump er my hea't.

LUCY. You know—de bank—ain't open ——

WILLIAMS. Sign de check fer hit. You kin do dat, cain't you?

LUCY. I—s'pose—I—kin.

WILLIAMS. Den up an' do hit. Heah's er check, all wrote out but de signin'. (*She takes the check he produces*) An' heah's one er dese fountum pins. (*She takes the pen*) Octobah fus'—pay to Zek'l Williams—eight hundred dollahs. Des write "Lucy Sparrow." (*She mechanically turns to do so*) Looks easy, sho'. But de law allows hit; dis writin' out money. (*He pauses, then adds impressively*) Dat is, *ef* you got de money in de bank. Co'se ef de money ain' dah an' you writes de check fer hit de law puts you in State pris'm. (*She stops and stares at him. The pen falls from her hand and the check flutters to the floor*) What de matteh? You wants de house, don' you? (*LUCY's head sinks*) An' you got de money, ain' you?

MADISON. Dat's de question. (*He comes forward out of the shadow.*)

WILLIAMS. (*Seemingly observing MADISON for the first time during the evening*) Why, heighyo, Madison. I bin lookin' fer you dis very evenin'. Whah you bin?

MADISON. Bin home.

WILLIAMS. Sho'ly not, Madison, sho'ly not all evenin'? Has you?

MADISON. Yes.

WILLIAM. Well, ain' dat de whu'lygig? I wuz lookin' fer

you at Pratt's sto' at eight o'clock an' dey say you jes' lef' dah. You wuz dah, weren't you?

MADISON. No, suh.

WILLIAMS. Well, dere I am fool agin. An' who you think done fool me?

MADISON. Dunno.

WILLIAMS. Well, suh, 'twern't no one but—(*He pauses a moment*) Wilson Byrd.

LUCY. Byrd! (*Springing to her feet with the shock.*)

WILLIAMS. (*After watching the two a moment*) So you ain' got de money no mo', is you? (*They are speechless before him*) I knows you ain' 'ca'se I knows who *has* got hit.

MADISON. (*Involuntarily*) Who?

WILLIAMS. I has. (*He observes them and then chuckles softly*) I has de money an' de bargum's closed, fer de goods is bin delivered an' dey're right in dis room in dat corner. One guitar at eight hunderd dollahs. Insterments comes higher'n what dey did once but you would have it an' now you got it an' everybody's fixed.

MADISON. (*Groaning and bending over the table*) Oh!

WILLIAMS. Yassuh, de man what buys guitars at dat price su'tinly plays on de golden strings. Eight hunderd fer one guitar makes 'm mighty near twenty thousand dollahs er dozen. De cos' er livin' is shore gone up but ef you mus' you mus'.

MADISON. Oh!

WILLIAMS. Well, I cain' stay heah, I got er be amblin' on. I much erblige ter you to mek youah plans to move out er heah fo' I got ter sell de house befo' sundown. Well, so long, an' I hopes you gits all de good er youah high price music. (*He turns again with his feeble old man's step toward the doorway, putting on his hat*) I wish y'all good evenin'.

MADISON. (*Moving toward him with the threatening determination of despair*) Say, I've got to have dat money. I sees red. I'm gone bad an' I'll kill befo' I'll lose hit. (WILLIAMS *suddenly turns with a swiftness and agility astounding in so old a man. Starting forward he confronts* MADISON *with such dominance and fire that he seems suddenly to tower.*)

WILLIAMS. *You* kill *me! You* tek money away from *me!* Why, you po' grain er chaff, you don' know me. I'm a king in my own right. I got ways an' means er pertectin' myse'f dat you don' even dream on an' I don' need to lay a fingeh on you to do hit. Furdermo' I could brain you wif dis stick but ef you cross me I won' be dat easy on you. Ef you don' wan' wuss'n dat don' cross me no furder er youah troubles'll begin fer fa'r.

LUCY. Oh, please don' lay nothin' on him.

WILLIAMS. You po' sufferin' gal, I won' lay nothin' onto 'im but I'm a-goin' to tek sumpin' off'n you. I'm goin' tek de burding er dish yere pack er laziness off'n you. An' fus' I wants ter show you dish yere piece er papeh. (*He produces a folded document and opens it*) Does yo' know who wrote it? Answeh me. (*He shoves the paper under* MADISON'S *eye.*)

MADISON. It looks like dat Wilson Byrd's writin'.

WILLIAMS. Yassuh, an' what's mo' it is dat man's writin'. It's his confession dat he fo'ge Lucy Sparrow's name. I saw dat man steal my guitar an' follered him home. Dah I grabbed him, dah I foun' de purse wif Lucy's name inside an' dah I made dat thief write out his confession. Knowed so much of his meanness already dat he had to do hit. An' now I owns you. Does you undehstan' dat? Answeh me.

MADISON. Yas suh, no suh.

WILLIAMS. Well, I'll take'n cl'ar up de myst'ry fer you. I got dis confession outer Byrd an' I got other things ter prove hit an' I kin bring him an' you too, befo' de gran' jury.

LUCY. Oh, my sweet Jesus, save him. (*The old man stands watching the two before him for some time in silence.* LUCY *falls on her knees before him*) Oh, don't sen' Madison to de lawyers.

WILLIAMS. No, Lucy, I ain' wishful ter.

LUCY. You won't?

WILLIAMS. Mebbe not. But fus', les' put all dis talk aside dat I bin talkin' up to now. I bin puttin' on and pretendin' in ordeh ter try you bofe an' siff de chaff from de grain in you. I des bin playin' wif you ter see how good you is an' how orn'ry dish yere man er youah'n is. Yit I'll take an' give him er chance even so, an' I'll pluck him f'um de bu'nin' ef he follers de paf I p'ints out ter him. But we all got ter have cl'ar unde'stan'in' 'bout dat. Fus' an' fo'mos' youah money is all safe wif me. De house is youah'n.

LUCY. You means you sell it fer de money.

WILLIAMS. In co'se. You didn't speck I'd steal too, like a w'ite man, did you? I'll fetch you de needs fo' hit fus' thing in de mo'nin'.

LUCY. Oh, fu'give me. I was all mix up. But you won' sen' Madison to de gran' jury neitheh?

WILLIAMS. I say I ain' honin' ter.

LUCY. Oh, my Makeh, I thank Thee fo' Thy mercy.

WILLIAMS. But I shorely goin' to put dis man er youah'n

th'oo er tes' ter see whetheh he's fitten ter keep out er jail. Madison, will you tek er tes'?

MADISON. (*Humbly*) Yassuh. What is it?

WILLIAMS. A guitar.

MADISON. A guitar!

WILLIAMS. Yassuh, dat's hit, no mo' ner no less. I'm goin' give you dat guitar—but—dere's suhtinly goin' to be a string tied to it. You kin take dat guitar but you got to make somethin' outer yourself wif her or back she'll come to me. You kin give lessons an' learn folks music or you kin write down de music you make, but you got to do somethin' wif it fer Lucy. You got to wake up or I'll take de guitar. Which'll it be? Make youah choice.

MADISON. (*Crushed*) I'll—keep de guitar.

WILLIAMS. An' dat ain' all. You got ter quit runnin' wif Byrd an' Byrd wif you, you got ter be a better husban' an' you got to min' everything Lucy tells you. Will you do hit?

MADISON. Yassuh.

WILLIAMS. An' yo' ain' much of er temp'unce man neitheh, is you, Madison?

MADISON. I is a temp'unce man. But I ain' no frantic.

WILLIAMS. Well, suh, you got ter jine de frantics now. No dram drinking at all. Will you quit er go ter jail?

MADISON. I'll quit.

WILLIAMS. Well, dat's on'y a promise but I'll shore hol' you to hit er put you behin' de bahs. Why, look heah, man, does you know how you stan' 'pon top er dis yu'th? Does you know how you liken to er tree? 'Sposin' sumpin' wif er cool eye like er tree could see you an' talk. I cain' jedge you ca'm but er tree could. Tree would look at you an' say, "Does dat 'ere man wu'k?" Win' 'ud whispeh, "No." "Do he eat?" "Yas'n git fat," respon' de win'. "Who shines on him?" "His wife," win' say. "Do he put fo'th flower an' bless de wife?" say de tree. "No." "Do he give shade an' shelteh ter de wife?" say de tree. "No." "Well, chop'm down an' bu'n him befo' he rots," say de tree. "Dat's all." But mebbe I kin mek mo' of him dan dat an' so I'll try prunnin' him an' graftin' some good labeh onto him. An' I kin' er think hit'll save him yit. Well'm, I mus' be er goin' now. Hit's late an' I mus' git my res' fer I got to do a lot er bossin' termorrer an', Madison, you kin repo't to me at eight o'clock sha'p an' give my little boy a lesson on de guitar. You'll be dah, won't you?

MADISON. (*Meekly*) Yassuh.

WILLIAMS. Ready to whu'l in an' scratch.

MADISON. Yassuh.

WILLIAMS. Well den, les' all shek han's on de noo nes' an' de noo aig. (*They shake hands. He puts on his hat and turns to the door*) An' dat remin's me, Lucy, you better tell Madison to play on dat guitar a-plenty tonight because he'll need music fcr to stan' up undeh all de lessons I'm goin' to lay onto him. Well, I wish you good night. I'm er gittin' kin' er ole an' I cain' stay up late no mo' without bein' crosser in de mornin'. Good night den an' far' you well bofe. Eight o'clock, Madison. Good night. (*He goes, closing the door after him. The pair stand silent for a moment,* MADISON *with hanging head and in deep dejection.*)

LUCY. (*Throwing her arms around him*) Oh, my husban', I'll pray fer you. Don' sorrer now. Git youah res' tonight. We kin be hones' now. We've got de house at las' an' heah's de guitar.

MADISON. Yassuh, heah's de guitar. (*He plays it and*

fondles it.   Then his face assumes again its melancholy look.)

LUCY. What's de trouble?

MADISON. I don't undehstan' dis worl'. If I wants to make music why cain't folks lemme alone to make music? If I dream a fine dream why is it I always wake's up? Looks to me like somebody's always tryin' to crowd me out an' git me in a tight place.

LUCY. You wuz doin' all right till you git mix up wif dat white man an' his tricks. De trouble wuz dat dis dream of youahs wuzn't a good dream.

MADISON. Yes, but not all my dreams is bad ones. All I wants is room to dream my good dreams an' make my own music.

CURTAIN

RACKEY

A PLAY IN ONE ACT
By
ERNEST HOWARD CULBERTSON

CHARACTERS

"Mame" Frisbee, a young married woman
Jim Frisbee, her husband
"Mink" Hall, a friend
"Rackey" Foster, "Mame's" former lover

Scene: A Northern town: the cottage of the Frisbees, recent
migrants from the Lower South.
Time: An evening, supper time, in 1919.

First performance by a cast of Negro players
New York City, October, 1920.

RACKEY

(THE CURTAIN RISES *on the sitting room of* JIM FRIS-
BEE'S *cottage. It is small, but quite comfortably furnished—
though it presents a hodgepodge as far as the harmony of
the various pieces is concerned. On the whole it is rather the
worse for wear. Several crayon portraits, some small pos-
ters and framed photographs and engravings adorn the walls.
There is a door, left back, and beyond it, right back, a window. There is also a window, left center. Right center is
a door leading into an adjoining room. It is evening and a
lighted oil lamp sits on a small table, near center.*

*Shortly following rise of curtain a knock sounds on
the door, back. No one appears and it is repeated several
times. Presently the door, right center, opens and* MAME
FRISBEE *enters, hastens across and opens door, back. She
is a young, dark-brown negress of medium height—about
twenty-seven or eight, rather slender and frail. She is a
primitive, imaginative type with an eager confiding manner
when animated. In repose she displays a sort of pathetic
wistfulness. She walks with quite a perceptible limp.*

MINK HALL *enters. He is a tall, rawboned, lumbering
mulatto with a philosophic manner. He speaks with a rumbling drawl in ordinary conversation, but when roused his
voice rises to a booming crescendo. There is an undercur-*

*rent of marked geniality, wholesomeness and sincerity about
his manner. He wears a crinkled, gray suit, a trifle too small
for him, a white shirt and collar, but no tie. In his right
hand he carries a misshapen and dust-laden black felt hat.*

MINK. Howdy, Mame!

MAME. Hello, Mink! Come in! How is yo'?

MINK. Tol'able!

MAME. Set down. (MINK *sits in a chair and drops his hat
on the floor at his side.* MAME *sits down opposite him.*)

MINK. (*Glances about*) Whar's Jim?

MAME. Down to de sto'.

MINK. Business good?

MAME. Bes' evah. Niggahs in dis neighborhood ain' no
tightwads.

MINK. Not w'en it come ter fillin' dere gullets. (MAME
laughs) How he git started?

MAME. White man name Ames—gib him two hun'erd dollahs ter buy stock—an' pay six months on de lease.

MINK. Man day!

MAME. Taken no 'count grocery sto' an' make it inter some-
'fin dat boun' ter pay big. Wuk lik' a dog all de time.

MINK. Dat's de way ter git ahaid.

MAME. All he think 'bout is ter git 'nuff ter buy dis house.

MINK. Yo's lucky w'en yo' fotch up wid him.

MAME. Deed I was. (*A moment's pause. She stares wistfully into space*) Funny thing——

MINK. (*At length*) W'at?

MAME. I dream 'bout Rackey las' night.

MINK. Rackey Foster!

MAME. Yo' knowed him.

MINK. Sho' did! Lon' fo' I knowed yo' all.

MAME. Yo' hearn all 'bout him an' me?

MINK. (*Shakes his head*) Down in Norfolk w'en dat happen.

MAME. Taken me away from Jim yere—w'en I only seventeen. So many hard niggahs in our alley den—an' he could fight ——

MINK. Hard niggah hisse'f.

MAME. Hardes' in de worl'. I was scart a' him all de time —an' scart ter leave him.

MINK. Whar was Jim?

MAME. Beggin' me ter come back—but I'se too scart. Rackey drunk half de time. Guzzle booze like a cat lap milk.

MINK. Go long.

MAME. Breaks up de fu'niture—an' bust hell outer me evah few days. An' we move an' move—all de time— kicked outer dis place an' turned outer dat.

MINK. Nuffin' in dat.

MAME. Treat me like a dog. Aftah de baby's bawn I makes him marry me. Donc tore up de marriage license aftah dat. (*Shakes her head and speaks as though half to herself*) Big fine lookin' niggah—da'k brown—wid hair onliest a little crinkly. Somefin' in his eyes w'en he's sober dat makes yo' feel—oh—dat he could put yo' in one—a dem—um—ooly-mooly trances like—or cunjuh yo' ef he want ter git back.

MINK. Whar de chile?

MAME. (*With a catch in her voice*) Daid. (*Gets up and moves about*) Cripple me fo' life.

MINK. How come dat?

MAME. Knocks me 'cross de room. (MINK *grunts*) Yo' seen dat scar on Jim's cheek?

MINK. (*Nodding*) Yas.

MAME. Rackey cut him—w'en he gits me away. Nobody dat Jim hate like him. Swo' he gwine ter kill him!

MINK. Whar he now?

MAME. Don' know. Beats it aftah a fight wid "Hen" Carter. Las' I years he is in St. Louis—dat fo' yeres ago. (*Wistfully*) Kain't nevah seem ter git him outer mah haid.

MINK. You's crazy.

MAME. Devil have a hand in gittin' him yere. An' yet he so big an' strawn an' po'ful!

MINK. So is tigahs.

MAME. Dey's somefin' fetchin' bout tigahs.

MINK. W'en dey in a cage.

MAME. Yo' knows what I mean—like de charm what a snake has. Make yo' quivah an' tingle—an' scart ter dea'f—an yet—— (*Pause*) I allas felt ef he evah got sense in his haid he be de bes' ole lovah in de worl'. I nevah fergit de look in his face de fust time he seen Rackey—our lil' baby. (*The door, back, opens and* JIM FRISBEE *enters. He is a dark brown negro, of about thirty-five. He has an alert, self-confident, positive manner; is somewhat stoop shouldered. He impresses one as being a plodding, hard-working, prudent sort of a fellow. He is partially bald, and across his right cheek is a great ugly scar, as though made by the blow of a sharp instrument. He carries a document in his right hand and appears to be in a state of elation.*)

JIM. (*Exclaiming*) Hello, Mink! (*Taking Mame in his arms*) How is yo', gal?

MAME. Fine as si'k! (*Kisses him*) Mah ole buddy honey boy!

MINK. (*Rises and moves to door, back*) Jake Tucker 'roun ter mah house wid a cart a fish. Want's ter see yo'.

JIM. (*Half releases* MAME *and turns*) All right, Mink.
Be right 'round.

MINK. He ain' got long ter stay. See yo' some mo'. (*Passes
out, back.*)

MAME. Is yo' all mah baby?

JIM. Sho' nuff is!

JIM. (*Showing her the document*) Look!

MAME. (*Takes it and examines it with a wondering gaze*)
W'at——?

JIM. Don't yo' see?

MAME. (*Opening it up and examining it*) It ain' ——

JIM. It's de deed——!

MAME. (*With a cry*) De deed! Yo'—yo' mean—ter dis
house?

JIM. Sho' nuff! (*She stands for a moment—silent—quite
overcome with emotion, then thrusts the deed in her
bosom, and with an hysterical sob throws her arms
about his neck.*)

MAME. Jim! At las'—it all our own—oh, Gawd!

JIM. All *yo'* own!

MAME. It—it seem like a dream!

JIM. Dis w'at I been wukkin' fo'.

MAME. Nevah gwine ter move ag'in!

JIM. Not till I buys yo' somefin' bettah.

MAME. Mah, sugah baby buddy—an' den some!

JIM. Yo's niggah Irish!

MAME. Crazy in yo' haid!

JIM. One a yo' ancestors kiss some kin' niggah Blarney
stone—back in Africa.

MAME. Yo' ancestors was Kilkenny niggah Irish——

JIM. Keep on—yo' little ambulance bell——

MAME. Yo' fights like a Kilkenny cat—you' scratches w'en
yo' fights.

JIM. Bus' yo' in de mouf nex' time.

MAME. Wear a muzzle aftah dis.

JIM. Dog catchah sho' gwine ter git yo'—been lookin' fo' yo' long nuff, too. (*He gives her a kiss*) Suppah ready?

MAME. 'Bout.

JIM. Reckon I bettah wash up.

MAME. Sho' had. (*He removes his coat and throws it over a chair. As he turns his back to her, she spies his bulging hip pocket and just the tip end of a pistol protruding. In low, grave tones*) Jim———!

JIM. (*Turning and facing her abruptly*) W'at?

MAME. Yo' still totin' dat gun.

JIM. (*His manner undergoes a change. It becomes sinister, foreboding, tense*) I'se allas gwine ter tote dat!

MAME. No, no—honey!

JIM. Yo' know why———

MAME. Ain' no use takin' chances———

JIM. Ter hell wid chances!

MAME. Fo' mah sake!

JIM. I swo' I'se gwine ter make good—an' I'se gwine to—dat's all!

MAME. Fergit it all! Le's live now! What is pas' is pas'!

JIM. I'se gwine ter git dat niggah—even ef I goes ter de chair fo' it!

(*Pause. She covers her face with her hands and sobs.* MINK *calls—off stage, back.*)

MINK. Come on yere, Jim. Jake says he ain' got all night.

JIM. (*Hurries into his coat*) On de job! (*Grabbing up his hat and turning to Mame*) Be right back, honey. (*Passes out, back.* MAME *stands staring after him for a moment or two. At length she takes the deed from her bosom, examines it with loving care, then replaces it. A knock sounds on the door, back.* MAME *hurries*

across and answers the door. She opens it slowly.
RACKEY FOSTER *stands in the doorway. He wears a
soldier's uniform, with a Croix de Guerre on his breast.
He is a negro of medium height, rather powerfully
built, with broad shoulders, and he wears an expression
indicative of spiritual illumination*)

RACKEY. (*Staring down at her with an expression half of
awe and half of radiant admiration*) Mame!

MAME. (*Huskily*) Is—is it yo'?

RACKEY. (*Stepping in*) Yes—gal!

MAME. (*Tremulously*) Thought—thought yo' was daid.

RACKEY. I was—an' bin bawn ag'in!

MAME. How—how did yo' fin' me?

RACKEY. Seen yo' in de mahket. I tries ter catch up wid yo'
befo' yo' gits on a cah—but kaint make it. I takes de
nex' one. I stand on de fron' an' watch fo' yo' ter git
off. I seen yo' five squarc back—but w'en I gits yere—
yo' ain' nowhar in sight. Nobody know yo'—but a
lil' boy say dat a gal by de name of Miss Mame live
yere.

MAME. Lawsy! Lawsy! Yo' bin to war?

RACKEY. Yas. (*A moment's pause*) Who live yere wid
yo'?

MAME. (*With a quick apprehensive glance about*) Some—
some frien's—gal an' her husban'. (*Turning and searching his face*) Yo' look so differen'.

RACKEY. Bin ter de end of de worl'—an back, gal.

MAME. Fo' yeahs since I—I seen yo' las'.

RACKEY. Seem like fo' hun'erd yeahs! (*Eagerly*) Whar
lil' Rackey?

MAME. (*With a sob, as she turns her head.*)

(RACKEY *starts convulsively, stares fixedly into space*

for a moment, then allows his head to sink on his chest.)

MAME. (*Unable to account for his changed appearance and demeanor*) Ef it wasn't fo' yo' voice ——

RACKEY. I tell yo' I bin bawn ag'in!

MAME. W'at does yo' mean?

RACKEY. W'en I lef' yere I went ter St. Louis—lay in jail dere fo' six months. Den I wuks in a coal mine down in Missouri—give dat up an' bums mah way to de coast—drinkin' mahse'f ter dea'f evah time I gits a lil' money. I—I kills a man in San Francisco—but breaks jail an' gits away. Den I goes ter Japan on a ship—an' w'en I gits back from dere wuks mah way down inter Mexico— and meets up wid some of dem Mexicans. I fights wid dem fo' mos' a yeah—'till a greaser stabs me in de back in a pokah game. Aftah I gits well from dat —— W'ats de matter?

MAME. Nuffin'—only yo' change so!

RACKEY. (*Grabs her hand and impulsively draws her toward him*) Mame, gal! Mah own lil' baby!

MAME. (*Insistently*) Go on, go on! I wants ter year!

RACKEY. (*Collects his thoughts with an effort*) Aftah I gits well I wuks mah way no'f—an stop in Nashville. An' who I happen ter run inter—on de street one day— but young Marse George Fleming.

MAME. Law sakes ——!

RACKEY. Son ob ole Marse George Fleming—who own mah fawther. Young Marse George an' me use ter play togeder w'en we chillen. (*Halts for a moment and gazes down at her rapturously*) Ef yo' knowed how I bin dreamin' 'bout yo'! (*Continues with the story with an effort*) I hadn't et fo' two days—an' mah clothes was jes' hangin' on me. He buys me some new clothes, an' takes me out to his house—sets me down in de kitchen an' lets me eat mah haid off. Den he give me a hunderd dollahs an' gits me a job wid a frien' ob his who own a garage—an' I learns all 'bout runnin' automobiles. He kep' encouragin' me—makin' me see things an' think 'bout things I nevah bothered mah haid 'bout befo'.

MAME. (*Her eyes brighten momentarily, then a glance of apprehension sweeps over her*) Gawd, w'at a fine man!

RACKEY. Bes' in de worl'. De wah come on an' Marse George enlist right away. I enlist, too. He so big an' fine he make yo' feel yo' got to do w'at he do. I—I goes ovah dere—an'—an' no sooner I gits dere den dey sends our division to de front. Night an' day fo' mos' two months we fights—in de trenches an' out—an' eva' whar.

MAME. Rackey!

RACKEY. It ragin' hell—mos' de time. Some days up ter mah wais' in mud an' water. Wen' clean out mah haid onct an' lay out de sergeant flat. Big shells poppin' 'roun' like firecrackers——

MAME. Did yo' go ovah de top?

RACKEY. My Gawd, yes.

MAME. Mo'n once?

RACKEY. Fifteen I reckon.

MAME. W'ats dat medal fo'?

RACKEY. (*Indifferently, after a moment's hesitation*) Croix de Guerre. French medal.

MAME. Rackey!

RACKEY. I ain' botherin' 'bout dat.

MAME. (*With a catch in her voice*) W'at yo' do ter git it? Mus' bin somefin' mighty brave!

RACKEY. (*Shaking his head*) Noffin' much. Jes' seen mah
buddy go down. Dat set me crazy—an' I bus' out an'
puts a machine gun crew outer business. Hones' ter
Gawd, didn't hardly know w'at I was doin'.

MAME. All by yo' se'f!

RACKEY. (*Nods his head*) Few days aftah piece a shrapnel
hits me in de laig—yere. (*Indicates; then attempts to
take her in his arms. She draws back.*)

MAME. Not yere, Rackey—some—somebody liable ter
come—I—— (*He stares down at her with a puzzled
expression for several seconds, then goes on.*)

RACKEY. I was in de hospital free months. All de time I
lays dere I seems ter see yo' face—smilin' at me—sometimes in de night—reachin' out yo' hands ter me—an'
sayin', "Rackey—Rackey!" an' sometimes yo' had lil'
Rackey in yo' arms—— (*Pauses for a moment and
glances about*) I—I "come th'u'" here—like mah
Pappy did—back at de ole camp meetin' in Tennessee.
I seen an angel one night——

MAME. Go long!

RACKEY. Plain as day! Ridin' in de air—wid wings spread
out—in a cloud of sparklin' blue an' gold. Thought I
was gwine ter die——

MAME. No, no!

RACKEY. Sho' nuff! Den I look back—an' see how mah life
change—since dat day Marse George done took hole a
me. Seem like a great door done open in de back a mah
haid—an' I got a glimpse of what ole John Jasper use
ter call—"de lan' ob de spirit." Dere's gleaming rivers—an' wide valleys—an' green hills—all stretchin'
out—away ovah yondah—ter de lan' of promise. An'
back an' behin', Chris' an' his angels—an' sometimes I
kin year de flutterin' ob wings——

MAME. Rackey, boy!

RACKEY. (*He takes her in his arms, but she manages to wriggle free, wherefore he holds her tightly by both hands.*) It's yo' I come fo', Mame! I loves yo' bettah dan an'thing. It taken dese yeahs ter make me know!

MAME. But yo' see——

RACKEY. (*Impetuously*) Yo' fo'give me, don' yo'? Don' yo', Mame?

MAME. Yas, yas. I fo'gives yo'!

RACKEY. Yo'll come wid me now—won' yo, gal?

MAME. Rackey—I don' know—yo' see—yo' see yo' jes came back——

RACKEY. I'll makes yo' love me, gal! Dey ain' nuffin' I won' do! (*A knock sounds on the door, back.* MAME *draws back from him with a stifled cry of apprehension.*)

MAME. Who dat?

MINK. (*Off stage, back*) Me!

MAME. Come in! (MINK *enters, back. He stands staring at* RACKEY *for several seconds; then both advance and shake hands.*)

RACKEY. Mink!

MINK. I seen yo' comin' down de street!

RACKEY. Ain' change a bit!

MINK. Yo' lookin' fine!

RACKEY. Feelin' tiptop!

MINK. (*To* MAME) Want ter see him alone fo' a minute. (MAME *turns and passes out, right.*)

RACKEY. Didn' know yo' was anywhar' 'roun'.

MINK. Live down on de nex' cawner. (*Giving him a penetrating glance*) Bin ter war?

RACKEY. (*With a laugh*) Look like it—don't it?

MINK. (*Pointedly*) W'at yo' doin' yere?

RACKEY. Yere ter see mah Mame.

MINK. How long yo' been gone?

RACKEY. Fo' yeahs.

MINK. Kep' her in yo' haid all dat time?

RACKEY. She's de bes' li'l' gal in de worl'. I—I come back yere ter git her.

MINK. Whar d'yo' cal'ulate yo' take her?

RACKEY. Wharevah she want ter go!

MINK. Yo' ain' got nuffin'.

RACKEY. Won' take me long ter git it!

MINK. But yo' ain'!

RACKEY. W'at de hell difference it make to yo' anyway— Mink?

MINK. I'se her frien'.

RACKEY. Frien'—w'at do yo' mean?

MINK. She well fixed yere.

RACKEY. W'at she doin'?

MINK. Wukkin' hard an' mindin' her own business.

RACKEY. She mine—she belong ter me!

MINK. She belong ter de man who kin do de bes' by her!

RACKEY. (*Wildly*) Is yo' made a play fo' her?

MINK. Yo' crazy, man!

RACKEY. W'at do yo' mean? D'year me?

MINK. Dis is her house!

RACKEY. (*Glances about with a wondering gaze*) Her house!

MINK. Her husban' give it to her!

RACKEY. (*With a gasp*) Husband!

MINK. She's married!

RACKEY. Gawd! (*Eventually—and huskily*) Who to?

MINK. Jim Frisbee.

RACKEY. Jim—Jim Frisbee! (*Pause. He stares about in anguish. At length rushes to the door, right, and throws*

it open with a bang) Mame! (*She enters, right, tremblingly.*)

MAME. W'at yo' want?

RACKEY. Mink say yo' married!

MAME. (*Tremulously—after an interval*) Y-yas——!

RACKEY. Ter—ter Jim!

MAME. Y-Yas.

RACKEY. (*Breathing heavily*) Oh, Gawd! (*At this juncture the door, back, opens and* JIM *enters. He closes
the door, turns, discovers* RACKEY, *recognizes him after
an interval of scrutiny and gives a cry of rage.* RACKEY
recognizes him at the same instant. MAME *gives a
shriek of terror and dismay.*)

JIM. (*Whipping out his pistol*) Yo' black-hearted devil!
Now I got yo'!

RACKEY. (*Shouting*) Put it up!

JIM. Git down on yo' knees and say yo' prayers!

MAME. Oh, mah Gawd! Jim! Don'—fo' Chris' sake—
don'! (RACKEY *displaying the sang-froid of a man who
simply does not know the meaning of fear, grabs* JIM,
*with a twist or two wrests the pistol from him, then
with a whirling movement sends him reeling halfway
across the room.*)

RACKEY. Git outer yere! (JIM *stands in a semidaze.* RACKEY
*goes over, pushes him through the door, left, closes
door and locks it. With that he tosses the pistol in a
far corner of the room.* MAME *stands sobbing hysterically. She is in a half-fainting condition.* RACKEY
*takes her in his arms. He holds her there for a mo-
ment or two. Suddenly the deed—which has been in
her bosom—flutters to the floor. He releases her momentarily and picks it up. He examines it with great
interest. Hands it back to her at length, then impul-*

*sively takes both of her hands in his and stares down
into her face with an expression of anguished intensity.
At length he appears to pull himself together—as
though to act upon a tremendous resolve. He drops
her hands and steps back a pace or two with a wild,
uncanny laugh. He takes what appears to be an ordinary medicine bottle from his back pocket and pretends
to drink deeply of its contents)* Married, huh!

MAME. W'ats de mattah?

RACKEY. (*Feigning drunkenness*) Dat good gin, Mink—
bes' I had in a long time! (*Reels forward, leering at
MAME.*)

MAME. Rackey! W'at is yo' done?

RACKEY. Hic—mah—hic, li'l' Mame!

MAME. (*Angrily to MINK*) W'at yo' mean by givin' him
booze?

MINK. Didn't give him a drap!

RACKEY. Did so! Ha! Ha!

MAME. Yo's a damn fool, Mink!

MINK. I ain't got none ter give him!

RACKEY. (*Now assuming all of his old bestiality*) Yo' give
me half a pint—good stuff, too!

MINK. Yo's a liah!

RACKEY. (*Swaying toward him*) Hic—yo'—yo' call me
a liah!

MINK. Yas! (RACKEY *picks up a chair and throws it
across the room at him.* MINK *dodges it.* MAME
shrieks.)

RACKEY. I'll git yo'—yo' black hell-cat! (MINK *attempts
to grab* RACKEY. *The latter deftly eludes him, then
wheels swiftly about and deals* MINK *a blow that sends
him reeling across the room.*)

MAME. (*With a shriek*) Oh, Gawd! Stop! Police be yere!

MINK. (*Raging*) I'll git yo' fo' dat!

RACKEY. Yo' will——! (*He lunges forward. Grabs* MINK *by the throat and begins to slowly choke him to death.* MAME *rushes to right, unlocks door, and dashes out, with a wild yell. The moment she is out of the door,* RACKEY *straightens up, releases* MINK, *and is immediately his normal self once more. He moves leisurely over to door, right, and locks it again.*)

MINK. (*Half-choked, as he stirs groggily about*) Yo'—yo'——

RACKEY. (*Hurrying back to him and speaking rapidly*) Listen ter me, Mink—listen! I'se sober as de day I'se bawn! Ssh—now! Stop!

MINK. (*Utterly nonplussed*) W'at—w'at yo' mean?

RACKEY. I wanted ter make her think I wuz like I used ter be—understan'.

MINK. Like yo' used ter be——!

RACKEY. Hard—an' ornery—no 'count——

MINK. An' yo'——

RACKEY. I did dat ter make her sho' dat she ain' makin' any mistake in stickin' ter Jim.

MINK. (*Nodding*) Den—den dat lets yo' out——

RACKEY. (*Moves toward door, back*) Reckon I bettah be gwine.

MINK. Lawd, but yo' change!

RACKEY. (*With a half-hearted chuckle*) Reckon I has. (*At the door*) Mah fawther die w'en I'se ten—an mah ole mammy raise nine chillen. (*Twirls his decoration*) She didn' git no medal.

MINK. W'at dat?

RACKEY. Croix de Guerre! I'se gwine ter do somfin' now—

dat—dat's ten times harder dan w'at I did ter git dis.

MINK. W'at?

RACKEY. Go 'way widout Mame!

MINK. (*Eagerly*) I know whar dere's a job.

RACKEY. (*Indifferently*) Yo'—yo' do?

MINK. He want a niggah fo' it.

RACKEY. Jus' a niggah! Jus' a niggah—dat's all! (*Crying out*) Who—who want a *man* who—who kin see—night an' day—de lan' ob de spirit—who want a man who kin talk 'bout de vision—whar kin I go ter meet up wid dem dat's got w'at I got! I ain' *niggah*—I'se—I'se a man who sees de lan' ob de spirit——! (*With a cry he takes off the Croix de Guerre, throws it into a corner. He gazes about him for a fleeting moment with a wild, hungry look, then dashes out back.*)

CURTAIN

THE NO 'COUNT BOY

A FOLK COMEDY IN ONE ACT

By

PAUL GREEN

BELASCO CUP PRIZE PLAY, 1925, NATIONAL
LITTLE THEATRE TOURNAMENT
*Reprinted by permission from "The Lord's
Will and Other Plays" by Paul Green; Copy-
right, 1925, by Henry Holt and Company*

CHARACTERS

PHEELIE, a young Negro girl
ENOS, her lover
THE NO 'COUNT BOY
AN OLD NEGRO WOMAN

Place: Eastern North Carolina, near the Cape Fear River.
Time: Contemporary.

First performance by The Studio Players, Chicago Little
Theatre, December 6, 1924

Prize Winner in the National Little Theatre Tournament,
1925, awarded to THE DALLAS LITTLE
THEATRE PLAYERS

THE DALLAS LITTLE THEATRE PLAYERS IN "NO 'COUNT BOY"

THE NO 'COUNT BOY

THE SCENE *is the small yard immediately before a Negro cabin. At the right front is a thick lilac bush with a bench beside it, and to the left from this a clumpy china tree with a rocking-chair under it. At the left rear is a well, roughly boarded up, a chain and battered tin bucket hanging from a crosspiece above. In the back is the cabin. Rickety steps lead up to the door in the center. It is an afternoon in summer.*

When the curtain rises, PHEELIE, *a neat Negro girl of seventeen, is sitting on the bench by the lilac bush looking through a book. She is dressed in cheap clothes— a white dress, white shoes and stockings.*

Presently there is the sound of an approaching buggy in the lane off at the left and a voice calls "Whoa!" PHEELIE *listens a moment, and then without turning her head, goes on thumbing the leaves of her book.* ENOS *comes in at the left and stands watching her. He is a short, stocky Negro of twenty or more, dressed in a faded gray suit and black felt hat. His celluloid collar and scarlet tie shine out brilliantly against the black of his face.*

ENOS. (*In a drawling voice that now and then drops into a stammer*) Well, Pheelie, heah I is.

PHEELIE. (*Looking up casually*) I see you is, and you's 'bout a hour early.

ENOS. But ain't you all dressed up to go?

PHEELIE. I's dressed up, but I ain't ready to go.

ENOS. (*Dubiously*) Well, suh, now—I—I ——

PHEELIE. I des' put on dese heah clothes 'caze it was so hot
in de house wid my work duds on. (*He takes off his hat
and discloses his naturally kinky hair combed back in a
straight pompadour. He waits for her to notice it,
but she keeps looking straight before her*) Set down and
rest yo'se'f. (*Somewhat ill at ease, he sits down in the
rocking-chair and watches her.*)

ENOS. I drapped by a little early hoping—a—mebbe you'd
lak to take a small drive befo' church begun.

PHEELIE. (*In the same cold voice*) Thanky, I don't believe
I wants to take no drive. (*Absorbed in her book.*)

ENOS. (*Picking at the lining of his hat*) And I thought we
mought stop by Buie's Creek and git some ice cream.
(*He watches her narrowly.*)

PHEELIE. (*After a moment*) Dat'd be nice, I reckon, but I
don't want no ice cream nuther. (*She is silent again.
He pulls nervously at his fingers, making the joints pop*)
And I'd be much obliged if you'd quit poppin' yo' finger
j'ints.

ENOS. (*Jerking his hands apart and running his fingers over
his greased hair*) 'Scuse me, Pheelie. (*Somewhat timidly but with a hidden touch of spirit*) You—you don't
seem glad to see me much.

PHEELIE. You didn't have no date to come over heah a hour
befo' time.

ENOS. (*Worried*) I knows it. But whut's de matter wid
you? You ain't mad at me, is you?

PHEELIE. No, I ain't mad.

ENOS. Seems lak you'd druther look at dat old book dan talk
to me.

PHEELIE. Mebbe I had. (*He feels his tie, twirls his hat, and spits softly through his teeth off to one side*)

ENOS. Whut sorter book is it, Pheelie?

PHEELIE. Whut difference do it make to you? You ain't int'rested in no book.

ENOS. 'Speck dat's right. But you sho' seems mo' tuk wid it dan anything I ever seed you have befo'.

PHEELIE. It's a fine pitchture book.

ENOS. Whah'd you git it?

PHEELIE. Dis mawning I was up to Mis' Ella's helping her hoe out de gyarden, and she told me a whole heap 'bout de places she and Mr. Jack went when dey was merried. And she give me dis book dat showed a passel of things.

ENOS. Hunh, dey had money to travel wid and enjoy deirselves.

PHEELIE. She said one place dey went to was some sorter Falls or something lak dat, whah de water poured over in a great river and made a racket same as de world was busting up.

ENOS. Dat ain't nothing—mostly talk, I bet a dollar.

PHEELIE. (*Closing her book with a bang*) Dat's whut you allus says. You don't care a straw 'bout gwine off and seeing things.

ENOS. (*Sharply*) Ain't I done told you, honey bunch, we ain't gwine have no money to be traipsing round de world, not yit nowhow.

PHEELIE. Don't you honey me no mo', I tells you.

ENOS. (*Amazed*) Whut'n de name of Old Scratch ails you? Ain't I gut a right to honey you and you engaged to me!

PHEELIE. Engaged to you! It's you engaged to me.

ENOS. Aw right, I's engaged to you den, and you knows mighty drot'n well I's glad to be too. Dey ain't no put-on wid me.

PHEELIE. I reckon you is glad. But you mess wid me and you won't be engaged to nothing.

ENOS. (*Pleadingly*) Now, Pheelie, you better th'ow dat book in de far and come on and le's go foh a drive. It's stirred you all up. Come on, I's gut a mess of news to tell you.

PHEELIE. I ain't gwine on no drive. And I's 'bout decided not to go wid you to no meeting tonight nuther.

ENOS. (*Alarmed*) Lawd, don't talk lak dat. Heah I's been waiting all de week foh dis Saddy night, and you ain't gwine back on me, is you?

PHEELIE. (*Softening*) But, Enos, you's so samey, allus satisfied wid whut you has. You des' gits my goat.

ENOS. (*Humbly*) If you means I ain't tuk wid no wild idees or sich 'bout trips way off yonder to see folks making fools of deirselves, den I is samey. But you listen heah, chile, dey ain't no meracles and sich off dere lak what you thinks. Onct I spent a good five dollars gwine on a 'scursion to Wilmington, and dey wa'n't a thing to see, not ha'f as much as dey is on dis heah farm.

PHEELIE. You gut to have eyes to see things. Some folks is natchly bawn blind.

ENOS. (*Placatingly*) Well, mebbe when we's merricd we'll take a little trip to Raleigh or Durham and see de street cyars and big buildings.

PHEELIE. But I wants to go furder, furder, clean to de mountains, and right on den, mebbe.

ENOS. 'Y craps, must think I gut a can of money buried somewhah.

PHEELIE. I don't nuther. Us could hobo, or walk part de way, des' fool along.

ENOS. (*Laughing*) Hobo! Us'd hobo right into some white man's jail, dat's whut. And dey ain't nothing to dat walking business. We'd be a purty sight wid our feet blistered and somebody's bulldog tearing plugs out'n —well, you knows whut.

PHEELIE. (*Ignoring his reply*) Setting dere looking through dat book I gut plumb sick and tard of you and all dis farming and sweating and gitting nowhah—sick of everything. And des' looking at old lazy Lawrence dancing over the fields made me sicker'n sick.

ENOS. (*Eying her*) Honey chile, de last time I was heah you said you'd lak it working in de fields wid me and keeping de house and sich.

PHEELIE. I will, Enos, I reckons I will. But dat dere book set me to wanting to go off and git away.

ENOS. (*Moving his chair over to her*) Listen to me. I knows I ain't fitten to breave on you, but I's gwine do my best by you. And whut you reckon? Mr. Pearson done told me today dat he's having de lumber sawed to build our house. September she'll be done, den you'n me kin have business—kin see de preacher.

PHEELIE. Mr. Pearson's good to you awright.

ENOS. Ain't he! Dat's a man whut is a man. And it ain't all foh me he's building dat house. He laks you and says he'll be glad to have you on his place.

PHEELIE. (*With signs of interest*) Whut kind of house is it—des' a shack wid a stick-and-dirt chimley?

ENOS. (*Jubilantly*) Now, I was des' a-hoping you'd ax dat. No, suh, it ain't no cow shed you could th'ow a dog through de cracks—nunh—unh. It's gwine be a nice frame house wid a wide po'ch, and it'll be ceiled. And listen heah, it's gwine have wall paper. And, honey, Mr. Pearson said he wanted you to come up a-Monday and help choose de pattern. (*He looks at her delightedly.*)

PHEELIE. (*Her face brightening somewhat*) Oh, dat's so nice of you and him! (*She bows her head.*)

ENOS. Whut's de matter now?

PHEELIE. (*Looking up with tears in her eyes*) You's too good to me, Enos, and I hadn't ort to allus be so onsatisfied.

ENOS. Sho', never mind now. (*He puts his arm around her.*)

PHEELIE. (*Letting her hand rest on his hair*) Grannys alive! you done spent money to git yo' hair straightened.

ENOS. (*With a kind of shamed joy*) Yeh, yeh, I has. But it was to celebrate a little.

PHEELIE. Dat's th'owing away a dollar and a half. In a little bit it'll be kinky ag'in.

ENOS. Course it will, but I thought you'd lak it while it lasts.

PHEELIE. (*Laughing*) You sho' is a proud nigger. (*She kisses him quickly and stands away from him*) Nunhunh, I ain't gwine do it no mo'. (*He drops reluctantly back into his seat, and she sits again on the bench.*)

ENOS. (*After a moment*) You want to take dat little drive now?

PHEELIE. I mought, I guess.

ENOS. (*Slapping himself*) Hot dog, den le's go, honey!

PHEELIE. (*Brightly*) Lemme shet up de house and we'll be ready. Muh and Pap and all de kids is over to de ice cream supper at Uncle Haywood's befo' preaching. (*She starts up.*)

ENOS. (*Standing up*) Aw right, honey babe. I sho' laks to see you jollied up. And I's gut anudder surprise foh you.

PHEELIE. (*Stopping*) You has?

ENOS. (*Mysteriously*) Unh-hunh. But I'll tell you a little later.

PHEELIE. Naw, suh, tell me now—please.

ENOS. (*Anxious to tell it*) In course I cain't stand out ag'in you. Well, we ain't gwine drive behine no flop-yured mule dis time.

PHEELIE. We ain't! (*She starts towards the left to look out.*)

ENOS. Naw, suh, I's driving Egyp'.

PHEELIE. Mr. Pearson's fine hoss!

ENOS. (*Grinning*) Yeh, yeh, sho' is. I worked hard all de week, and dis mawning he come to me and axed me if I didn't want Egyp' to haul you wid tonight.

PHEELIE. (*Looking off*) Dere he is. Ain't dat fine, and is he safe?

ENOS. Safe! Safe as a cellar. But Lawd, he kin burn de wind!

PHEELIE. Goody-good. Now come help me shet de house.

ENOS. (*As they go off at the left rear*) Mr. Pearson knows I ain't gwine beat his stock and bellows 'em lak some de niggers. I tells you, sugar lump, if we stays wid him and do right, some dese days we gwine have money to take dem dere trips you wants to. (*They have hardly disappeared when a slender Negro youth of sixteen or seventeen, barefooted and raggedly dressed in an old pair of overalls, shirt and torn straw hat, comes in at the right front and stands staring after them. He is whittling a green walking stick. In a moment he pulls out a small mouth organ and begins playing a whirling jig.*)

ENOS. (*Coming around the corner*) Who's dat playing to beat de band? (*He and* PHEELIE *come back into the yard.* PHEELIE *stares at the boy in delighted astonishment. Suddenly he winds up on a high note. As he beats the saliva out of the harp against his thigh, he bursts into a loud, joyous laugh.*)

PHEELIE. Lawd, you kin play. Who is you?

ENOS. (*With a touch of authority in his voice*) Whut you want heah? I ain't never seed you befo'.

BOY. (*In a clear, childish voice, as he looks at* PHEELIE) You ain't?

ENOS. Naw, I ain't. Whut you mean walking up in people's yards and acting lak you was home?

BOY. I thought I mought git me a drink from de well dere.

PHEELIE. Help yo'se'f. (*He draws himself some water and drinks.* ENOS *and* PHEELIE *watch him.*)

ENOS. I bet he's some boy run away from home. Mebbe a tramp, I dunno.

PHEELIE. Dat boy a tramp! Hunh, he ain't no sich.

ENOS. Looks s'picious to me.

BOY. (*Coming back from the well and wiping his mouth with his sleeve*) I thought I mought git a bite to eat heah mebbe. (*He looks from one to the other, a lurking smile in his eyes.*)

PHEELIE. (*Uncertainly*) You mought.

ENOS. Lak as not de lady wants to know whah you come from and whut yo' business is befo' she 'gins to feed you.

BOY. (*Looking at* PHEELIE) Would you?

PHEELIE. Yeh. Whut's yo' name?

BOY. (*Laughing and blowing out a whiff of music*) Mostly I ain't gut no name. (*Beating the harp in his hand and scratching his leg with his toe*) 'Way, 'way back down dere (*Pointing indefinitely behind him*) whah I come from some of 'em calls me Pete, but mostly dey calls me de No 'Count Boy.

ENOS. Why dey call you dat for?

BOY. (*Laughing again*) 'Caze I don't lak to work in de fields.

ENOS. Unh-hunh, unh-hunh, I s'picioned it.

BOY. S'picioned whut?

ENOS. Aw, nothing. Anyhow dat's a good name foh you, I bet. Whose boy is you and whah'd you come from 'way back down dere, as you calls it?

BOY. (*Quickly*) Cuts no wool whose boy I is. As foh whah I come from, I cain't tell you, bo, 'caze I dunno hardly. (*Hesitating and pointing off to the right*) You see whah de sky come down to de earf—'way, 'way yonder?

ENOS. I sees it.

BOY. (*Grinning to himself*) Well, I come from miles and miles beyont it. (*A kind of awe creeping into his words*) Lawd, Lawd, how fuh has I come?

PHEELIE. You been all dat distance by yo'se'f?

BOY. Sho' has. And whut's mo' I walked it every jump. (*Again he draws the harp across his lips in a breath of music, all the while watching them with bright eyes.*)

ENOS. Whah you gwine?

BOY. Des' gwine.

PHEELIE. You mean you ain't gut no special place in mind— you des' hoboing along?

BOY. Dat's it, I reckon.

ENOS. How does you git yo' rations—beg foh it?

BOY. I pays foh it when I kin git 'em. Sometimes I goes hongry.

ENOS. (*Looking at him keenly*) You ain't gut no money, has you?

BOY. (*Cunningly*) Dat's aw right. I pays foh it des' de same. (*He stops and looks at* PHEELIE *with big eyes*) You's as purty as a pink, ain't you?

PHEELIE. (*Turning away her head*) Why you ax dat?

ENOS. (*Sharply*) You needn't be thinking you gwine git yo' supper on soft talk, hoss cake.

BOY. (*Still looking at* PHEELIE) Whut's yo' name?

PHEELIE. My name's Ophelia, but dey calls me Pheelie.

BOY. (*Staring at her admiringly and cracking his palm against his thigh*) Dawg-gone! des' lak me foh de world. I's named one thing and dey calls me anudder.

ENOS. (*With a hint of uneasiness*) Heah, I 'specks you better be gwine on up de road. Me'n Miss Pheelie's des' ready to go out foh our afternoon drive, and we don't want to be bothered wid nobody's no 'count boy.

BOY. (*His face falling*) I hates to hinder you, Miss Pheelie, and cain't I git nothing t'eat—a tater or anything?

PHEELIE. I 'speck I could give you a snack in yo' hand right quick.

BOY. No sooner said'n done, I hopes. And I pays you foh it too.

ENOS. (*Almost sarcastically*) Gut yo' pockets full of silver and gold apt as not.

BOY. Naw, suh, I gut something better'n new money. Heah she is. (*Holding up his harp*) I plays you a piece or two pieces or three, and you gives me a bite and whut you pleases. (*In mock seriousness he pulls off his hat and addresses them*) Ladies and ge'men, de fust piece I renders is called "De Dark-eyed 'Oman." It's music 'bout a 'oman whut had three little boys, and dey tuk sick and died one June night whilst de mocking birds was singing. And allus adder that dey said she had a dark shadow in her dark eyes. (*He clears his throat, spits once or twice and lays the harp gently to his lips. Closing his eyes, he begins to play.* ENOS *stirs about him as the notes flood from the boy's mouth, and now and then he looks questioningly at* PHEELIE'S *averted face. The boy's nostrils quiver, and he makes a sobbing sound in his throat. Tears begin to pour down his cheeks. He winds up with a flourish.*)

ENOS. (*Gruffly*) Lawd Jesus, dat rascal kin blow!

BOY. (*Looking at* PHEELIE *as he wipes his eyes*) I hopes
you don't mind. Every time I blows dat piece I cries.
(PHEELIE *glances up with moist eyes.*)

PHEELIE. I sho' don't mind. Whah you learn dat?

BOY. It's a made piece.

ENOS. Who made it?

BOY. Me.

ENOS. (*Ironically*) Hunh, you mought!

BOY. (*His face troubled*) You believes I made it, don't you,
Miss Pheelie?

PHEELIE. Dat I do.

BOY. (*His face clearing*) Aw right den. And I'll play you
anudder piece foh dat snack of grub.

PHEELIE. Dat one's enough to pay.

ENOS. You sho' you didn't git no rations down de road?

BOY. Not nary a chaw.

PHEELIE. Ain't you had nothing all day?

BOY. Nothing but some branch water and a little bitsy bird I
killed wid a rock and fried. (*His face takes on a sober
look, and tears again glisten in his eyes.*)

ENOS. (*Looking at him in astonishment*) You sho' is a
square fellow.

BOY. (*Staring up at the sky*) Dat little bird was singing so
sweet and ruffling his breast in de wind, and I picked
up a rock an des' th'owed devilish lak, never thought I'd
hit him. But dat's de way it is—when you thinks you
won't, you does, and I kilt him.

PHEELIE. And den you et him?

BOY. (*Wiping his eyes on his sleeve*) I was so hongry den,
and I built a speck of fire and baked him. (*Wretchedly*)
Won't it better foh me to eat him dan foh maggits to
git at him?

PHEELIE. 'Twas dat.

BOY. (*Mournfully*) But I sho felt bad 'bout dat little bird. I cain't git his chune out'n my haid. He sot on dat limb and would give a long call and den a short one (*Imitating on his harmonica*) des' lak dat.

ENOS. You's a mighty big fellow to be crying over a bird, seems lak to me.

PHEELIE. Enos, you quit dat making fun.

BOY. When I come through de creek back dere, a good-god was pecking in a high daid tree, and he turnt his haid sideways and whickered at me. I heah'd him say he gwine ha'nt me foh killing dat bird.

ENOS. I swear! (PHEELIE *gives him a cutting look, and he stops his laughing.*)

BOY. I've hearn dat dem good-gods is old women turnt to birds 'caze dey was weeked. And you see dey's still gut on little old red caps.

PHEELIE. Dey won't hurt you.

ENOS. Pshaw, dey ain't nothing but great big sapsuckers.

BOY. How you know? Des' de same dis'n scolded me foh th'owing dat rock. I could tell it in his talk and de way he looked at me.

PHEELIE. You didn't mean to do it nohow, and you was hongry too. Now play us some mo'.

BOY. I 'speck mebbe den it's aw right, I 'speck so. Now I plays you my udder piece to pay you plenty foh my eatings.

PHEELIE. 'Tain't dat, 'tain't dat. We laks to heah you. I'll feed you foh nothing.

BOY. Well, listen to dis, folkses. (*He again pulls off his hat and makes his stage bow*) Ladies and ge'men, dis is a talking piece I'se gwine render. It's 'titled "De Coffin Song," and tells 'bout a nice gal whut went away from home all dressed out in white and died, and dey sont her body back to her Muh and Pap. Dis heah's de Coast-Line coming down de track on a dark and rainy night wid her coffin on boa'd. (*He closes his eyes and begins blowing the choo-kerr-choo of a starting train. He intersperses his blowing with short speeches*) De rain is beating on de windowpanes and everybody is mournful. (*The choo-kerr-chooing takes on a sobbing note, and the speed of the train increases*) De old man and de old 'oman is at de station waiting foh deir daughter's body, her dey loved so well, oh, her dey loved so well. "Don't cry, honey, she gone to heaven," de old man say, "Lawd, Lawd," de old man say. Den he heah dat coffin-blow. (*A long mournful wail of the engine's whistle follows, swallowed up in the growing speed of the locomotive. He opens his eyes and begins to chant forth his bits of dialogue*) Now she's balling de jack 'cross de river trustle. (*He quivers and sings with the straining timbers of the bridge*) Heah she is passing by de gravelpit. How she goes by, how she goes by lak a great black hoss, a great black hoss! And now she's blowing foh de crossing. (*The whistle moans again*) Her Muh and Pap's on de platform at de station and dey feels deir hearts in deir moufs at de crying of dat train, Lawd, Lawd, de crying of dat train! (*Again he gives the coffin-blow, long and heartbreaking*) De train she slow up. (*The choo-kerr-chooing slowly stops*) Dey takes out de coffin and flowers and puts her in a huss, and dey all drives off slow, slow, lak dis—(*He plays a sort of dead march and stalks back and forth across the yard*) Den de next day dey takes her to de graveyard, de lonesome graveyard, and de preacher preach, and de people sing, shout—shout hallelujah—de preacher preach and de people sing, shouting glory to de Lamb. And den dey 'gin th'ow dirt in on her. (*He imitates the thump, thump of clods falling on the coffin*) Den de favver and muvver and sisters and bruvvers all cry out loud. Her Pap cries lak dis—(*He gives forth a long, deep groan*) And de sisters and bruvvers lak dis—(*A medley of weeping sounds*) And de muvver cry lak dis—(*A high, piercing shriek*) And den dey roach up de grave and de preacher make prayer—Lawd, Lawd Jesus, have mercy upon us! Den dey all go off and dey ain't nothing left 'cepting a crow in a high scraggly pine a-saying—(*He mingles his music with a raucous h-a-r-r-c-k, h-a-r-r-c-k*) Den adder dat when night come, dark and rainy night, de last thing is a small wind in de bushes lak dis—(*A trembling flutelike note rises, bubbles and disappears. He beats the harp against his hand and looks uncertainly at* ENOS *and* PHEELIE, *the tears wetting his cheeks.*)

ENOS. (*Presently*) I cain't deny you gut de world beat handling dat baby, but whut'n de name o' God makes you cry so much?

BOY. (*Watching* PHEELIE'S *bowed head*) When I plays dat piece I feel so lonesomelak I cain't help crying, I allus cries.

ENOS. I's seed folks cry when deir people died, but Lawd, I never seed no sich cry-baby as you.

BOY. You's hard-hearted. Look at Miss Pheelie, she's crying.

ENOS. Help my life! Whut ails you, Pheelie?

PHEELIE. (*Hurriedly drying her eyes*) Don't make no fun of me, Enos, I des' had de blues ag'in.

ENOS. (*Patting his hat anxiously*) Heah, don't you git to feeling dat a-way no mo', honey. Le's go on wid our drive.

Boy. You calls her honey!

Enos. Dat I do. She's my gal, dat's whut. And listen to me—I don't want no no 'count fellow come piddling by wid a harp and wild talk to git her upsot.

Boy. (*Unhappily*) I didn't know you was her man. I—I thought she was too purty and lak a angel foh dat. (Pheelie *looks at him tearfully, and he gazes back warmly.*)

Enos. (*Angrily*) Look out, nigger, mind whut you's up to!

Pheelie. Enos, you quit talking to dat boy lak dat!

Enos. (*Coming up to her and catching her by the arm*) Come on now and let dat fellow go on whah he's started.

Pheelie. (*Springing up*) Turn me a-loose. He's gwine stay right heah if he wants to, and eat and sleep to boot.

Enos. (*Hesitating a moment and then flaring out, his timidity and slowness gone*) De hell you say! (*He turns suddenly towards the boy and points off to the left*) You see 'way, 'way yonder in de west whah de sun is setting in de tops of dem long-straw pines?

Boy. (*Questioningly*) Yes, I sees it.

Enos. (*Moving towards him*) Well, I wants you to git in dat road and in three minutes start dere.

Pheelie. (*Putting herself quickly before him*) He ain't gwine, I tells you.

Boy. (*Emboldened by* Pheelie's *protection*) You means you wants to run me off befo' I gits any rations?

Enos. I don't keer whedder you gits any rations or not. I wants you to leave heah befo' you gits Pheelie all tore up wid you' foolish notions. (*Snapping*) You better git from heah!

Boy. (*Swinging his stick before him and smiling with weak grimness*) Ah—hah—I ain't gwine. (Enos *makes another step towards him*) Don't you come towards me.

I'll split yo' haid open wid dis heah stick. (ENOS *stops and eyes him cautiously. The boy holds his stick in trembling readiness.*)

PHEELIE. (*Getting between them*) I tells you, Enos Atkins, you ain't gwine harm nary a hair of dis boy's head. You do and I'll scratch yo' eyes out apt as not.

ENOS. God A'mighty! done hypnotized wid him a'ready, is you? (*In a wheedling tone*) Now, boy, cain't you see how 'tis wid me? We was des' ready to go off to church, and heah you pops up and sets yo'se'f in 'twixt us. (*He feels in his pocket and pulls out a dollar*) Heah, take dis dollar and go on. You kin buy enough grub wid it to last you a week.

BOY. (*Breaking into a loud, derisive laugh*) Ain't he a sight trying to har me off from his gal!

ENOS. Dem dere laughs is lakly gwine be coffin tacks foh you. (*The boy closes his eyes in merriment. With a quick movement* ENOS *snatches his stick from him*) Now see'f you don't strak a trot up dat road. (*He puts out his arm and pushes* PHEELIE *back.* EGYPT *is heard off the left pawing the ground and shaking his bridle.* ENOS *calls*) Whoa, Egypt!

BOY. (*Half-whimpering*) Don't hit me wid dat stick.

ENOS. I ain't gwine hit you if you lights a rag out'n heah dis minute. Scat, or I'll wring yo' neck. Make yo'se'f sca'ce, nigger.

PHEELIE. Let him 'lone, let him 'lone, I tells you!

BOY. You better go tend to you hoss, bo. I heah him trying to git loose.

ENOS. (*Looking appealingly at* PHEELIE) Egyp's gitting restless, Pheelie. You 'bout ready to be driving now? (*He steps to the left and calls*) Whoa! whoa dere, Egyp'! Come on, Pheelie, and le's go.

PHEELIE. (*Shaking her head determinedly*) I ain't gwine on no drive wid you, and dat's my last say.

ENOS. Oh, hell fiah! (*He lowers his stick. At the left he turns and speaks*) You des' wait heah, you little polecat, and I'll fix you yit! (*He hurries out.*)

BOY. (*Turning boldly back into the yard*) Hunh, dat nigger ain't nothing but bluff.

PHEELIE. And he ain't gwine make you leave nuther. You stay raght wid him.

BOY. He thinks you's gitting to laking me, dat's whut he thinks. (*He falls to staring at her intently.*)

PHEELIE. Why you look at me lak dat?

BOY. (*Shyly*) How old is you?

PHEELIE. Seventeen.

BOY. (*Joyously*) Is? Den we's des' de same age. Cain't—cain't I call you Pheelie?

PHEELIE. (*Looking at the ground*) Yeh, yeh, you kin.

BOY. I feels des' lak I knowed you all my life, and I ain't never seed nobody lak you in all my progueings, nobody —and I's travelled a heap too.

PHEELIE. And you's seed a monstrous lot whah you travelled, ain't you? Yeh, you has, I bet.

BOY. I has dat—Lawd, Lawd!

PHEELIE. (*Dropping into the rocking-chair*) Has you seed any big rivers and waters and sich?

BOY. Rivers! Lawd, yeh!

PHEELIE. Has you been by a place whah a great river pours over a steep hill roaring lak de judgment day?

BOY. (*Dropping on his knees and marking in the dirt as he ponders*) I dunno—Yeh, yeh, dat river was two miles wide and you had to stop yo' yurs in a mile of it.

PHEELIE. Go on, go on, tell me some mo'. Has you been in any big towns?

Boy. Has I? I's been in towns dat had streets so long dey won't no coming to de end of 'em.

Pheelie. Was dey many people dere?

Boy. People! People! (*He rolls over on the ground at the remembrance of it, and then sits up*) All kinds and sizes. People running, people walking, some wearing diamont dresses and gold shoes. Rich, my, my, how rich! Orty-mobiles as big as a house wid howns dat jar lak a earf-quake and b'iler busting all to onct.

Pheelie. (*A little dubiously*) Aw ——

Boy. Hit's so. And street cyars running wid nothing pulling or pushing 'em. And buildings so high dat de moon breshes de top. High! Lawd, Lawd, how high! And people hauling money wid trains, big train-loads whah dey keeps it in a big house wid a school breaking of folks to guard it.

Pheelie. I been looking at pitchtures in dis book, but nothing fine as dat. (*She brings the book and shows it to him.*)

Boy. (*Somewhat disturbed*) Yeh, I's gut a book lak dat. (*He begins picking his teeth meditatively with a straw*) It was give to me by a peddling man. (*Smiling wisely*) But dat was befo' I went out travelling foh myself. Lawd, Lawd, 'pared to what I's seed in New Yawk dat book ain't nothing.

Pheelie. You been New Yawk?

Boy. Dat I has. She's a long ways yonder too, mebbe two hundred miles, who knows? But, Pheelie, dat's de place to go, everything easy, people good to you, nothing to do but eat ice cream and mebbe now and den drink lemonade—and see people, people! worse'n de fair at Dunn. Never seed sich a mess of people. (Enos *is heard quieting his horse.*)

PHEELIE. How'd you travel so fuh and pay yo' way? Must take a lot of money.

BOY. I walked, dat's how, bum my way. And when I gits hongry I plays my harp.

PHEELIE. Whah you sleep?

BOY. You don't know nothing 'bout travelling, does you? I sleeps on de warm ground. Come sunset, I stops in a hollow and breaks down bushes and rakes up pine-straw and sleeps lak a log. And in de mawning I wakes and sees de jew on everything and heahs de birds singing, and I lies dere a while and practice on my harp. Den I's off down de road breaving de fine air and feeling des' as happy as I kin.

PHEELIE. (*Vehemently*) I done told Enos we could do lak dat. I sho' has told him time and ag'in.

BOY. You lak to live dat a-way?

PHEELIE. Unh-hunh, yeh I would.

BOY. (*Earnestly*) Why cain't you, Pheelie?

PHEELIE. (*Twisting her hands nervously*) I dunno—I wants to—I do wants to go and keep on gwine.

BOY. (*Leaning quickly forward*) Pheelie, Pheelie, come on wid me and go tromping through de world. You kin leave dat bench-leg Enos behine.

PHEELIE. (*Turning impulsively towards him and then dropping her head*) I cain't do it, I's 'fraid to. (ENOS *slips in at the left rear and listens.*)

BOY. I tell you we would have de best time gwine. Come on and go wid me.

PHEELIE. (*Hesitating*) I—mought do it—I's half tempted to do it.

BOY. (*Catching her hand*) I tells you whut—how 'bout me waiting out in de woods dere till dark comes down and den you put on a old dress and j'ine me?

PHEELIE. (*Pulling her hand unwillingly from him*) Dat'd be fine—fine, but wouldn't folks raise Cain?

BOY. Let 'em. Whut you'n me keer? We'll be splashing in de rain and shouting in de sun. And we'll step along togedder, and I'll hold you' purty little hand and you'll hold mine, and I'll teach you to sing songs. I knows a bushel of purty ones. And den I'll learn you how to blow my harp. And we'll slip down de roads at sunrise and sunset, singing and blowing de finest chunes dey is. Please'm say you'll go wid me.

PHEELIE. (*With shining eyes*) You have de purtiest talk of any man or boy I ever seed, and oh, I wish—wish— (*With sudden abandon*) Yeh, yeh, I will—I will—I'll go. (*Ecstatically he touches her arm and looks straight into her eyes.*)

BOY. (*Cooingly*) Birdie mine, birdie mine. (*He stands up by her chair.*)

PHEELIE. (*Her face a-light as she leans her head against him*) Oh, it makes my haid swim to think of all we's gwine see and heah. (*He timidly puts his arm over her shoulder.* ENOS *throws his stick behind him, springs forward and snatches the boy away from* PHEELIE.)

ENOS. Heah, you low-down rascal, trying to steal my gal, is you! Oh, yeh, I been heahing whut you said. (*His nostrils dilating*) And I's gwine give you a kick in de seat of yo' britches dat'll send you whah you's gwine.

BOY. (*Retreating behind* PHEELIE) I ain't trying to steal her nuther. She don't keer nothing foh you and wants to go on wid me.

ENOS. Dat's a lie, you little ficey fool, and you better look out befo' I gives you de lockjaw.

BOY. She much as said she don't love you, now den.

ENOS. You didn't say dat, did you, Pheelie?

PHEELIE. I dunno whah I loves you or not.

ENOS. (*Turning savagely upon the boy*) Damn yo' soul, I gut a notion to hamstring you. (*He makes a movement towards the boy, who darts over to the left, sees his walking stick, and seizes it*) You des' come heah rolling off yo' lies by de yard and tear up everything! Why don't you leave? Want me to bring out a fedder bed and wash yo' feet and sing to you and fan you and put you to sleep, does you? (*Jumping forward*) I'll put you to sleep!

BOY. (*Falling quickly behind* PHEELIE *and drawing his stick*) You make anudder move at me and I'll scrush yo' skull.

PHEELIE. (*Crying out*) Enos, stop dat, stop dat!

ENOS. (*Sarcastically*) Yeh, and who's you to order me—you lost every ray of sense you ever had! Wouldn't you be a purty fool running off wid dis heah wood's colt and sleeping in de jambs of fences and old hawg beds and scratching fleas lak a mangy hound! (*His voice rising high in wrath*) Dat you would. And in winter weather you'd have yo' shirt-tail friz to you hard as arn. You'd be a sight foh sore eyes!

PHEELIE. Shet up. Boy, I wouldn't let him call me no wood's colt.

BOY. (*Weakly*) Don't you call me dat.

ENOS. (*Taking off his coat*) Call you dat! I ain't started yit. I's gwine twist off bofe yo' yurs and make you eat 'em widdout no salt. Hell, you ain't gut no mo' backbone dan a ground puppy.

BOY. (*Trembling and clinging to his stick*) Pheelie, Pheelie, don't let him git at me.

PHEELIE. Don't you hurt dat boy, I tells you ag'in.

ENOS. (*Laughing brutally*) Hurt him! I's gwine crucify

him. (*He begins circling* PHEELIE. *The boy keeps on the opposite side.* ENOS *reaches out and pulls* PHEELIE *behind him*) Now, my little bohunkus, whah is you?

BOY. (*In desperation raising his stick*) Don't you come neah me. (ENOS *makes a dart at him. The boy starts to flee, but as* ENOS *clutches him he turns and brings his stick awkwardly down on his head.* ENOS *staggers and falls to his knees.*)

PHEELIE (*Looking on in amazement a moment and then screaming*) Lawd, you's kilt Enos! (*She stands uncertainly, and then runs and holds him to her.*)

BOY. (*In a scared voice as he drops his stick*) Muhcy, whut's I gwine do? Is—is you hurt, Enos? (ENOS *groans.*)

PHEELIE. Git out'n heah, you, you—You's murdered my husband. Enos, Enos, honey baby, is you hurt bad? (*He groans; she helps him to a chair.*)

ENOS. (*Twisting his head from side to side*) Hurt? Nothing but a little crack. Dat lizard ain't strong enough to kill a flea with a sledge hammer. (*He suddenly whirls around and runs his tongue out, snarling at the boy*) Ya-a-a-ah! (*The boy bounds backwards and, tripping over the bench, falls sprawling on the ground*) See dere, blowing my breaf on him th'ows him into fits. (*The boy lies stretched out still.*)

PHEELIE. Oh, my Lawdy, you—I believes he's daid or something!

ENOS. (*Trying to hide his fear*) Sho' nothing but de breaf knocked out'n him.

PHEELIE. (*Shrilly, as she bends above the boy*) He's hurt, I tells you. Po' boy. (*Turning towards* ENOS) Whut if you's kilt him?

ENOS. (*Rubbing his head*) Shet up, he ain't hurt bad.

PHEELIE. You hateful mule-beating rascal, he is hurt. (*Moaning over him*) Oh, my sweet honey boy.

BOY. (*Sitting up*) Jesus, dat fall jarred de wind out'n my stomach. (*Suddenly getting to his feet and eying* ENOS *fearfully*) Don't let dat man make at me.

PHEELIE. I don't reckon he will. You gin him a dost to last foh a while.

ENOS. (*Standing up*) A dost! Hunh, he cain't faze me wid no little tap on de skull. (*He begins rolling up his sleeves. There is a hail off at the right front*) And now I rolls up my sleeves foh de hawg-killing.

PHEELIE. You all stop dat rowing now. Yonder comes somebody. (*The boy reaches down and gets his harp out of the dirt.*)

ENOS. Who is dat? Some old 'oman in a steer cyart.

BOY. (*Looking up hastily*) Lawd Jesus, dat's—who's dat! Hide me, people, hide me quick so's she cain't git to me. (*He looks in terror*) Whah must I go?

PHEELIE. Why you skeered of her?

BOY. Pheelie, put me somewhah, civer me quick!

PHEELIE. Drap down on yo' knees, she's coming up de paf. Better git behine de house mebbe.

BOY. (*On his knees*) And if she axes foh me, don't you tell her.

PHEELIE. We'll tell her we ain't seed hair nor hide of you. But I cain't see why you so tore up. (*He crawls rapidly off at the left rear around the house*) Now, Enos, you keep yo' mouf closed. Dey's something up—dat boy 'fraid so.

ENOS. Dey is something up, and my s'picions is coming to de top.

OLD WOMAN. (*Calling off the right front*) Heigho.

PHEELIE. Heigho. (*A stout old negress, dressed in rough*

working clothes, comes in at the right. She carries a long heavy switch in her hand, with which she cuts at the ground as she talks.)

OLD WOMAN. How you all come on?

PHEELIE. Well as common, and how does you?

OLD WOMAN. Well, I thanky. I's looking foh my boy— seen anything of him?

PHEELIE. (*Slowly*) Whut sorter boy?

OLD WOMAN. Lawd, take me all day to gin you a pitchture of him. He's des' de no-'countest fellow ever was bawn. He goes round, playing a harp, and he's not des' right in his haid. He talks wild 'bout being off and travelling everywhah, and he ain't never been out'n Hornett County. Gut all dat mess out'n pitchture books and sich. (*A delighted grin begins to pass over* ENOS' *face.* PHEELIE *looks dejectedly at the ground.*)

PHEELIE. (*In a choked voice*) I ain't seed him nowhah.

OLD WOMAN. (*Watching her closely*) I whupped him t'udder day 'caze he so sorry, and he run off. And when I ketches him dis time I's gwine cyore him for good and all. You ain't seed him?

PHEELIE. (*Looking up*) Naw'm.

OLD WOMAN. (*Eyeing her*) Dat's quair. I thought I seed somebody lak him standing heah in de yard. Last house down de road said he passed dere a hour ago, and dey ain't no road to turn off.

PHEELIE. (*Persistently*) Naw'm, I ain't seed him. (*Unseen by* PHEELIE, ENOS *makes a signal to the woman that the boy is behind the house. Cunningly she goes on talking to* PHEELIE.)

PHEELIE. (*Looking off*) Mebbe he went by when we won't looking. (*The woman darts around the house and is heard crying out.*)

OLD WOMAN. Ah-hah, heah you is!

PHEELIE. How'd she find out he's dere? (*There is the sound of blows followed by loud crying.*)

ENOS. Listen at him cry, de baby!

PHEELIE. (*Who has started towards the rear*) Quit yo' laughing. (*She chokes with sobs*) You set her on him, dat's whut you done. And I'll help him out, she shan't beat him so. (*She meets the old woman coming in leading the boy by the collar. He is crying like a child.*)

OLD WOMAN. (*Yelling at him*) Dry up! (*He stops his sobbing and looks off ashamed*) Now, ain't you a mess to be running off and leaving me all de cotton to chop! (*Looking around her*) Well, we's gut to be moving, and I's gwine gin you a beating whut is a beating when you gits home.

ENOS. Whah you live?

OLD WOMAN. Down neah Dukes.

ENOS. Oh, ho, I thought mebbe from yo' boy's talk you was from New Yawk or de moon or somewhah.

OLD WOMAN. I be bound he's been lying to you. He cain't tell de truf. De devil must a gut him in de dark of de moon. (*She brings the switch across his legs. He shouts with pain*) Step on now! (*He struggles and holds back.*)

BOY. Pheelie, help me, cain't you?

PHEELIE. (*Raising a face filled with wrath*) Help you! Dat I won't. (*Coming up to him and glaring in his face*) You dirty stinking rascal, why you fool me so?

OLD WOMAN. (*Giving him another cut*) You put a move on you or I'll frail de stuffing out'n you. (*They move off towards the right front, he looking back and holding out his hands to* PHEELIE.)

Boy. Pheelie, don't turn ag'in me so. Pheelie! (*They go out.*)

Enos. (*Going up to* Pheelie) Honey, don't—don't be mad now. See, if it hadn't been foh me, apt as not you'd a-let dat little fool gut you to gwine off wid him. (Pheelie *bursts into wild sobs. He pulls her head against his breast, but she shakes herself from him. The loud voice of the* Old Woman *is heard outside.*)

Old Woman. You git in dat cyart or I'll Pheelie you!

Pheelie. I don't want—I ain't never gwine to speak to you ag'in. Oh, he's done gone! (*She runs to the right and calls down the road*) Heigh, boy! boy!

Boy. (*His voice coming back faint and high*) Pheelie— ee—ee! (Pheelie *falls on the bench, sobbing in uncontrollable grief.* Enos *stands looking at her with a wry smile while he gingerly rubs his bruised head. After a moment he goes over to her and puts his arms around her. They are still around her as the curtain falls.*)

CURTAIN

THE FLIGHT OF THE NATIVES

A PLAY IN ONE ACT

By

WILLIS RICHARDSON

Reprinted by permission from The Carolina Magazine, April, 1927

CHARACTERS

MOSE, a slave
PET, his wife
JUDE, an informer
TOM, a slave
SALLIE, his wife
LUKE, another slave,—a mulatto, evidently an illegitimate
   son
MONK, a slave lasher
JOHN, the white slave owner

Scene: A South Carolina slave cabin.

Time: 1860. A spring afternoon, towards sunset.

First performance, May 7, 1927, by the Krigwa Players,
Washington, D. C.

THE FLIGHT OF THE NATIVES

WE SEE *the interior of a crude candlelighted hut. There is no floor save the bare ground and no ceiling save the rough boards, shingles and rafters of the roof itself. At the right is a door which leads outside and above this against the same wall are bunks such as are used by steerage passengers. In the rear wall are two windows below which are two rough benches. On the left side against the wall are bunks similar to those on the right. At the center of the rear wall exactly between the two windows hangs an old quilt on a cord. The cord leads forward and fastens to one of the rafters so that when the quilt is pulled forward on it the hut is temporarily divided into two compartments, the one on the right for men and the other for women. It is the early part of the night and on each window-sill is a lighted candle. The quilt is drawn partly forward on the cord.* JUDE, *a small, narrow-shouldered man of thirty-five, is seated on the end of the men's bench with his elbows on his knees and his head in his hands;* TOM, *another man, is lying in a bunk; while* LUKE *is standing by the wall with the quilt pulled slightly aside at the rear end so that he can look through the window.* PET, MOSE'S *wife, is sitting on her bench sewing, and* SALLIE, TOM'S *wife, is lying in a bunk.*

SALLIE. (*Looking at Luke*) What you watchin', Luke?

LUKE. Ah'm watchin' the river and wishin' y'awl wuz men-

folks so's we could all make way from heah, same's
Slim.

SALLIE. Ah hope to God Slim gets away, but Ah ain't thinkin'
there's much chance.

PET. There ought to be much chance. He's gone.

SALLIE. Ah know he's gone, but dere's Marse an' his hound
dawgs right on his heels.

PET. Slim went fo' daybreak—and lessen de Lawd's ag'in
him, I reckon Marse John nevah ketch up wid him.

SALLIE. He mought have a chance, but ain't no man can
outrun dogs and horses.

PET. Who knows they went the right way? Slim left in
de dark and nobody ain't seen him go.

SALLIE. (*Knowingly*) Yes, somebody did see him go. Ah
seen him go. Ah know which a-way he went and Ah
know somebody else that knows which a-way he went.

PET. Who den?

SALLIE. Somebody done told Marse John the way he went.
Ah seen him. (*At this* JUDE *raises his head and listens.*)

PET. (*Interested*) Who told on Slim?

SALLIE. It wasn't nobody but Jude. Jude, that they lets
come tuh the big house. Jude, that they lets eat the
scraps off'n the table in the big house.

JUDE. (*Going quickly to the front end of the curtain*) You
talkin' about me, Sallie?

SALLIE. You the only one what's named Jude around here,
ain't you? Ah reckon your mammy named you Jude
'cause she knowed you'd be a 'trayer.

JUDE. You stan' there an' tell me Ah told Marse John de
way Slim went?

SALLIE. Yes, I say you tole him!

JUDE. Ah didn't!

"THE FLIGHT OF THE NATIVES"

SALLIE. You did! Ah heered you! An' Ah seen you with ma own eyes!

JUDE. It ain't true!

TOM. (*Who has risen in his bunk*) 'Tis true! If Sallie says it's de truf, it's de truf!

JUDE. (*More humbly*) Ah didn't tell him, Tom! Ah swear to de Lawd Ah didn't!

TOM. Ain't no use o' swearin' to a lie! You tole it and if Mose finds out you tattled on Slim he's goin' to beat the life out o' you!

LUKE. (*Who has been staring at* JUDE *ever since* SALLIE *accused him*) He'll half kill you, niggah, and he ought to!

JUDE. Mose ain't goin' to tech me! Marse John done said if Mose put his hands on me he'll sell him down the river.

PET. (*Indignantly*) So you been talkin' about Mose too, is you? You keep your mouth off Mose!

JUDE. Ah ain't goin' to say nothin' about him if he don't do nothin' to me.

SALLIE. If Slim gets away and dey don't catch him Ah won't say nothin'; but sho's you bawn if Slim gets caught Ah'm goin' to tell Mose on you!

TOM. Slim an' Mose wuz bosom friends and Mose was moughty glad when Slim got away. Now, if Slim gets caught 'count o' you, Mose'll half kill yuh.

PET. Don't you-all say nothin' to Mose, neither one of yuh. Ah don't want Mose to put his hands on Slim, 'cause they might sell Mose down the river sho 'nough, and if they done that Ah'd die. Ah 'clare to the Lawd, Ah'd die.

LUKE. We mought not tell Mose and Mose mought not do

nothin' to you; but Ah mought mahself. You can't tattle on none of us and get away with it.

SALLIE. You can't beat him up half as much as Mose can, Luke; and Mose is the one Ah'm goin' to tell if Slim gets caught.

PET. I done tole you, Sallie; don't you do it!

SALLIE. You reckon we'd let that big-house Judas 'tray Slim, and do nothin' to him?

PET. But Mose is ma husband! He ain't yo' husband, an' Ah don't want ma husband sold away from me, does I?

JUDE. You-all don't like me! Ah know you don't; you just want to get me in trouble!

SALLIE. You get yourself in trouble! If you had 'a' kept your tongue still in yo' mouth this never would 'a' happened. They never would 'a' found out the way Slim went!

JUDE. Ah doan' care what you-all likes, but the one that lays his hands on me'll be sold down the river. Marse done said so.

LUKE. Ah'd like to know what good that'll do you after you get busted to pieces.

JUDE. It might not do me much good, you white-man's trash, but it'll do one of you-all a lot o' harm. (LUKE *sneers at him to hide his discomfort.*)

SALLIE. All Ah hope is they don't catch Slim.

PET. Ah hope they don't neither.

TOM. (*To* JUDE) All Ah've got to say,—ef you cares fo' yo' hide, you bettah pray dey don't ketch Slim. (*Just then* MOSE, *a large, broad-shouldered man of thirty, enters.* PET *at once goes to him.* JUDE *slinks back to his seat.*)

TOM. (*After* MOSE *closes the door*) What's news, Mose?

MOSE. Marse is back and back swearin'. Slim must 'a' made it.

PET. Ah hope the Lord he's sho nuff gone lak de chillen ub Isreel.

MOSE. Lawd a-mussy, Ah hopes so. (*He goes on* PET'S *side and sits on the bench with her.*)

TOM. Haven't heerd de hound dawgs yet. Whah's dey at?

MOSE. Ain't back yit. Dey's on de udder side wid Bark's men.

PET. (*Hopefully*) Slim ought to be miles and miles away from hyah by now, oughtn't he, Mose?

MOSE. Yes, he ought to be out o' reach, way out o' reach. I reckon he's ketchin' his breath by now. Ah reckon there ain't nothin' in the whole world that's better'n bein' free.

PET. Ah reckon not. Just like heaven.

LUKE. (*Going towards the door*) Must be a moughty fine thing to be out wha you kin stretch yo' ahms and laigs and breathe the air deep, and know you ain't no mo' slave. Ah'm goin' out here and see how they're talkin'. (*He goes out.*)

MOSE. Ah'd give ten years o' ma life if Ah could live ten years a free man.

TOM. Ah'm a common dog if Ah wouldn't give the rest o' ma life for five years free.

MOSE. Sometimes Ah reckon Ah'd jus' like to break loose and make a dash for it. If it wasn't for Pet Ah'd 'a' done it long ago.

PET. Ah'd be willin' to go with you, Mose. Ah'd be willin' to go with you to the end o' time.

MOSE. Ah know you would, but the chances is too big. You couldn't never swim the river in no kind o' time, and then you mought get shot.

PET. When you talk like that Ah feel like Ah'm a millstone 'round yo' neck.

MOSE. You mustn't think that. If it hadn't 'a' been for you Ah'd 'a' been dead long ago. Ah take a lot o' things every day Ah wouldn't take if it don't be fo' you.

SALLIE. Mose, what you reckon ud happen if Slim got caught?

MOSE. It ud be a mighty bad thing, Sallie. There ain't no tellin' what they wouldn't do to him.

TOM. You think he's got a good chance, sho' nuff?

MOSE. Bes' he's evah had. He's done gone over twelve hours and he's a powerful good swimmer and knows the woods like a fox. Ah'm thinkin' it won't be long before Slim'll be real free and out o' danger and brushin' elbows with men.

TOM. Brushin' elbows with men—how Ah'd love dat. (*Here* LUKE *enters hurriedly and speaks with great excitement.*)

LUKE. Mose! Mose! For God's sake!

MOSE. (*Leaping up*) What?

LUKE. They done got Slim!

MOSE. Got Slim! How you know?

LUKE. That's what dey's sayin' out there! (JUDE *starts hastily towards the door but* LUKE *blocks him.*)

LUKE. No, you don't! You don't go nowhere, you dirty rat!

MOSE. What's the matter 'tween you-all?

SALLIE. He's the one that tole on Slim! He's done tole Marse John de way Slim went!

MOSE. You-all mean to say he done that!

SALLIE. Yes, he done it! Ah seen him! Ah heard him!

MOSE. (*Catching* JUDE *by the collar of his shirt*) You tole on Slim, did you?

JUDE. (*Frightened*) Ah didn't tattle on him! Ah didn't!

MOSE. I reckon you did! Ah can see it in your lyin' eyes! Slim was mah friend and you done tole on him and now he's caught! Ah'll break your neck! (*As he draws back his fist to strike* JUDE, PET *runs to him.*)

PET. (*Excitedly*) Don't hit him, Mose! Don't do it! He'll get you sent down the river! What'll become o' me if they sell you down the river? For God's sake, Mose, don't hit him! (MONK, *a short, ugly negro, enters with a whip in his hand.*)

MONK. Marse John wants Jude.

PET. Let him go, Mose! Let him go! Oh, it's the best to let him go! (MOSE *finally relinquishes* JUDE, *who hurries out where there is a great commotion.*)

MOSE. (*Sitting on the bench hopelessly*) They got him! They got Slim and Jude's the cause of it! Jude better look out for me when dis done blowed over!

PET. Don't you put your big hands on Jude, Mose; he's moughty dangerous!

SALLIE. Somebody ought to put de cat-er-nine-tails on him, dat's what.

PET. (*To* SALLIE) You doan' want Mose sold down the river, does you? Well den, take it quiet.

SALLIE. The master wouldn't never sell Mose. He's too good a worker 'round here.

PET. You don't know. Marse does mos' anything when he's in temper.

MOSE. (*As the commotion outside continues*) Lemme see what's goin' on out here. (*He goes to the door and opens it just a little.*) The dogs! They're tyin' him to a tree and Monk's goin' to lash him!

PET. Sho bad 'nuff, lashes on your bare back, but it's better'n bein' sold down the river.

Mose. No real man'd let hisself be tied to a tree and beat till the blood runs out o' him! (*Suddenly becomes infuriated*) Let me out o' yeah! (Luke *and* Tom *hold him back. Then comes the sound of* Slim *being lashed. The lashing is mingled with* Slim's *moans; each time he is struck every person in the room shudders. Finally when the lashing is over there is a sigh of relief from everyone.*)

Sallie. Lord, Ah'm glad it's over. Slim must be almost dead.

Mose. (*With determination*) And Jude'll be almost dead when Ah get ma hands on him!

Pet. Don't you lay your hands on Jude, Mose! They'll do you the same way they just done Slim!

Mose. Ain't no man goin' to whup me! (*Just then the door is thrown open suddenly and* John, *the slave owner, enters with the whip in his hand. He is followed by* Monk *and* Jude.)

John. (*To all save* Mose *and* Pet) You-all get out o' here! (*To* Mose *after they have gone*) Mose, Ah hear you been sympathizin' with Slim! And Ah hear you laid your hands on Jude for tellin' me the way Slim went!

Mose. Slim was ma friend

John. (*Scornfully*) Friend! What you doin' havin' a friend? You belong to me and Slim belongs to me and Jude belongs to me! All of you supposed to look out for what's mine and you ain't supposed to be glad when Ah lose it! You been a good worker, but for what you done tonight you goin' to be lashed just like Slim was!

Mose. (*In a determined tone*) Ah ain't never been lashed! Ain't no man goin' to lash me!

JOHN. They ain't, ain't they? (*With a motion towards the door*) Come on out o' here!

MOSE. (*Not moving*) Ain't nobody goin' to lash me!

JOHN. (*Handing the whip to* MONK) If you won't come out you'll be lashed right here! Lash him, Monk! Give him the same you just gave Slim!

MONK. (*Afraid of the task*) Ma arm's almost dead from lashin' Slim, Master John.

JOHN. (*Handing the whip to* JUDE) You lash him, Jude! You the one to lash him anyhow! He laid his hands on you! After you get through with him maybe he won't be so anxious to lay his hands on you next time!

JUDE. (*Whiningly*) Don't make me do it, Master John; Ah'm scared of him! He'd kill me soon as he got me by maself.

JOHN. (*Raging*) All of you scared of him? Give me that whip, Ah'll lash him! (*Taking the whip he starts towards* MOSE, *but at the same time* MOSE *starts towards him and he stops. He knows that a man as big and strong as* MOSE *is dangerous to strike under any circumstances.*)

JOHN. You threaten me!

MOSE. Ain't no man ever whipped me! Ah always done ma work and took a lot o' things Ah didn't want to take, but ain't no man goin' to whip me!

JOHN. Ah'll do worse'n whip you! Slim's just been whipped and he's goin' to be sold down the river in the mornin'! You won't be whipped, but you'll be sold down the river in the mornin' along with Slim! And Pet'll stay here on the plantation! (MOSE *shows no emotion save a slight shudder, but* PET *flies past him and falls on her knees before* JOHN.)

PET. Massa John! Massa John! For God's sake don't

sell Mose away from me! He's good! He don't mean nobody no harm! Please don't sell him away from me!

JOHN. Mose'll be sold down the river in the mornin' and you'll stay here! (*With this he goes out followed by* MONK *and* JUDE.)

MOSE. (*Lifting* PET *from the ground*) That's all right, Pet; don't worry. De Lawd'll git us out o' dis somehow.

PET. (*Fearfully*) But goin' down the river! Don't you know what dat'll mean? They'll kill you! They'll beat you to death!

MOSE. (*Taking her over to the bench*) Ah ain't goin' down no river.

PET. What you goin' to do? They'll make you go! They'll tie you and take you!

MOSE. Ah might start out from here, but Ah ain't goin' down no river.

PET. What you goin' to do?

MOSE. After dey gets started good, Ah'm goin' to jump in the river and swim for it.

PET. But they'll shoot you! They'll shoot you like a dog!

MOSE. Ah'll take the chance. If they shoot me Ah'll be gone to Glory, but if they miss me Ah'll be gone north for freedom. Freedom is wuth it, ain't it?

PET. Ah reckon it is; but what'll 'come o' me? What'll 'come o' me without you?

MOSE. Ah hear they're talkin' about war in the north— talkin' about war and whisperin' about freedom. If the war comes and the freedom comes Ah'm comin' back and get you, Pet. And if freedom don't come Ah'm comin' back and get you anyhow. Ah'll have a taste o' freedom then and Ah'll take you somehow or 'nuther.

PET. (*Hopefully*) Will you, Mose? Will you come back after me?

MOSE. Ah promise Ah will, Pet; Ah promise to God Ah will.

PET. (*Putting her arm around his neck*) Ah'll wait for you, then; Ah'll wait for you till Ah die. (LUKE *enters followed by* TOM *and* SALLIE.)

LUKE. (*After* TOM *closes the door*) What did they do, Mose? What did they say?

MOSE. They didn't do nothin' to me.

PET. (*Almost in tears*) But Marse John said he was goin' to sell Mose and Slim down the river in the mornin'.

SALLIE. (*Hardly able to believe it*) Sell Mose down the river?

PET. (*Angrily to* SALLIE) Yes, they goin' to sell him! Goin' to sell 'em both! Ah told you not to make Mose lay his hands on Jude!

TOM. Is that what they goin' to sell Mose for?

MOSE. No, it's cause Ah wouldn't stand up and let 'em whup me. Wouldn't Ah be a big ninny to stand up and let any man whup me? Ain't no man livin' goin' to whup me!

LUKE. But they'll do worse 'n whup you down the river, Mose.

MOSE. Ah ain't goin' down no river!

TOM. What you goin' to do?

MOSE. Goin' to make a break for it!

LUKE. (*Shaking his head doubtfully*) I dunno, Mose, as yuh could make it, but Gawd help yuh. (*In a sudden mood*) The Lawd help us all, fo' we needs deliv'rance.

PET. Amen!—But what we gwine to do wid'out Mose?

LUKE. We-all better go 'long wif Mose whichever way he's gwine; an' it don't much matteh. 'Sposin' we all made a

breakaway! (*They stand aghast*) Yassuh, I mean it—
ain't crazy, neither. (*They huddle round about him*)
Ah got a plan, I has. (*He ponders and then whispers.*)

TOM. These women can't swim no river.

LUKE. An' ain't goin' to—We's takin' the boat.

MOSE. What! What yer sayin'?

LUKE. I keep a' tellin' yuh, the boat.

MOSE. D'yuh think we ought make it that a-way?

TOM. We mought make it like a' that!

MOSE. (*Shaking his head and changing his tone at once*)
No, we cain't make it nowhere like that. Fust thing,
Jude'll be watchin' like a hawk to-night, an' we jes'
cain't make it together.

TOM. (*Pressing his point*) Jes' wait a minute, Mose! Le's
listen to Luke,—what he says 'bout it.

PET. Ah'm willin' to try anything, ef it's being wif' Mose.
Ah reckon Ah can swim de river——

SALLIE. (*Impatiently*) Let the men talk, Pet; let the men
talk!

LUKE. Jude's got to go ter the woodhouse shortly, ain't he?
Well, he ain't comin' out to tell no tales on nobody.
Mose kin sneak in behind him and fix him fo' sure.
(*Turning to* MOSE) An' be sho' an' lock de woodhouse
door, Mose—de keys is allus in Jude's back pocket. You
heah dat, Mose? Now that's ou'ah onliest chance!

MOSE. (*Elated*) Sho is—an Ah'm perticlar glad to go.

TOM. (*Detaining him*) No, Mose, you'd ruin it. Time Jude
set his eyes on you he'd holler murder and everybody
on the plantation ud be comin' round here. Let Luke
do it.

LUKE. Ain't likin' to go, mahself—but Mose sho' would
spile it. (*After a minute*) Ah'm a-goin'. An'—(*Hesitates*) Ah got a plan too. Dat's all right 'bout Mose

bein' the stronges' man on the place, but—(*Pointing to his forehead with his index finger*) folks, yo' jes' got ter use this sometimes.

MOSE. (*Grumpily*) Aw, go on den, an' hurry up.

TOM. (*After cracking the door stealthily and peeping out*) Da' Jude now. Mought a' been list'nin'. No. Ah reckon he goin' to the woodhouse now. (*Pause*) He be! (LUKE *goes out stealthily but with precision.*)

TOM. What we gwine do now?

MOSE. (*Rising to a sense of power*) Dat talkin', Luke! Ah got an ideah mahself! Got it clear as a whistle!

TOM. What?

MOSE. Luke an' me'll go steal out and hide fus', an' then you go tell Marse John we done run away—an' dat Sallie knows de way we went.

SALLIE. (*Surprised*) Me?

MOSE. Yes, can you lie?

SALLIE. Lie? Ah can do worse'n lie for a chance to get free!

MOSE. When Marse John comes to you to tell him the way we went you put him off an' tell him wrong—yah hear?

SALLIE. Ah won't never tell him!

MOSE. Yuh got to tell him sumthin'. Tell him we took a boat and said we was goin' up the river and cross at Moseby's Landin' and goin' north from there.

SALLIE. But you ain't goin' that a-way?

MOSE. No, we all goin' together and we goin' a different way.

TOM. Which a-way?

MOSE. When they take the dogs and the rowboats and go up the river lookin' for us on the other side, we'll take the flatboat and go south —— (*Proudly*) Now,—that Luke think he know so much!

TOM. Go south!

MOSE. Yes, we'll go down the river a mile or two and get out on this side and walk all around the plantation, then beat it north like the devil! That'll keep the dogs off our trail! We'll have the river between them and us.

TOM. By daybreak we ought to be a long ways off, oughtn't we?

MOSE. A long ways off.

TOM. Ah wonder how Luke's makin' out.

SALLIE. Ah hope to the Lord he makes out all right. (TOM *cracks the door and peeps out.*)

PET. If we can get away and get free it'll be just like goin' to heaven.

TOM. (*Suddenly*) Here he comes! Here comes Luke!

SALLIE. Is he runnin'?

TOM. No, and he don't want to be runnin'. Somebody mought notice him, moughtn't they?

PET. What about Slim?

MOSE. Po' Slim. We'll have tuh look after Slim! but he cain't travel none. (LUKE *enters and closes the door quickly.*)

LUKE. Ah got him! Got him good, gagged and tied! An' I found Slim in de woodhouse.

MOSE. Sho' nuff! Po' Slim—we cain't hardly make it,— but Ah don't see how he can. (*Pulling himself together quickly*) Now, you got to do your part, Sallie. Come on, Luke, we'll go hide! Ah'll tell you mo' 'bout it while we'se hidin'! Tom, you go and tell 'em we got away! (MOSE *and* LUKE *hurry out.*)

TOM. (*Earnestly*) Sallie, if you ever lied in your life, lie this time!

SALLIE. Ah'll lie, all right. I 'clar I will.

TOM. All right, Ah'm goin'. (*He hurries out.*)

SALLIE. Everything generally happens to a woman, Pet; but

this is goin' to be somethin' that ain't never happened to us before in our life.

PET. Ah know it ain't. They can say sickness is hard and bearin' children is hard; but ain't nothin' in the whole world as hard as livin' in slavery.

SALLIE. 'Deed it ain't. If Ah can only lie right and make the master believe what Ah'm sayin' Ah reckon Ah'll be doin' ma part.

PET. You will be doin' your part. Ah wish there was somethin' Ah could do.

SALLIE. You can do somethin'. Get in the bunk and make believe you're 'sleep and Ah'll do the same thing; cause the master'll be here in a minute ravin' like a thunderstorm.

PET. (*Getting into the bunk*) If things work out all right it won't be long before we'll be able to stop sayin' "Marsa," sho' 'nuff.

SALLIE. (*Getting into another bunk*) I 'clar Ah'll be glad of it. (*They hear the noise of running feet*) Shet up. Here they come, Ah can hear 'em comin'! (*Presently the door is thrown open suddenly and* JOHN *enters followed by* TOM.)

JOHN. (*To those outside*) You-all wait out there! Shut that door, Tom! (*Looking around*) Where's Sallie?

TOM. In the bunk, Ah reckon.

JOHN. (*Sharply*) Sallie!

SALLIE. (*Raising up*) Seh?

JOHN. Come here! (SALLIE *gets out of the bunk and goes to him*) Where's Mose and Luke?

SALLIE. (*In trembling tones*) Ah don't know, seh.

JOHN. (*Angrily*) Yes, you do know! Stop lyin'! You do know! Tom just told me you did!

SALLIE. Ah don't know where they went, Marse John; 'deed Ah don't.

JOHN. (*Turning to* TOM) Tom, didn't you just tell me she knowed where they went?

TOM. Yes, seh.

JOHN. (*Turning to* SALLIE *again*) Do you want to be sold down the river in the mornin'?

SALLIE. (*Pleading*) No, seh; for God's sake, Marse John, don't sell me down the river! Ah don't want to be sold down no river!

JOHN. Which a-way did they go?

SALLIE. Ah promised 'em not to tell.

JOHN. Either you tell me the way they went or you'll be goin' down the river yo'self in the mornin'!

SALLIE. They said—— (*She hesitates.*)

JOHN. (*Impatiently*) They said what? Hurry up!

SALLIE. They said they was goin' to take a boat and go up the river and cross at Moseby's Landin', and goin' north from there.

JOHN. If Ah gets ma hands on 'em they'll wish they wuz north, I'll tell ye! (*He hurries out.*)

SALLIE. (*To* TOM) Where's Mose? Where's Luke?

TOM. (*Going to the window*) Wait a minute, can't yah! Give 'em time to get out on the river! Mose and Luke's close by watchin' 'em, ain't dey?

SALLIE. Is they goin'?

TOM. Yes, dey's goin' down to the boats now.

SALLIE. All of 'em?

TOM. Yes, and takin' the dogs and guns. You-all better get some things together. But what we goin' tuh do 'bout po' Slim? (*The two women hustle about getting together the things they want to carry.*)

TOM. (*From the window*) Now, they're off! Mose and Luke ought to be runnin' in pretty soon!

SALLIE. Tom, is you glad?

TOM. Glad! You wait till Ah get away from here, Ah'll show you how glad Ah am!

SALLIE. Pet, is you glad? Ah ain't heard you say a word in Ah don't know when!

PET. Glad! Sallie, Ah'm jes' too scared ter talk! (*She cowers as* MOSE *enters.*)

MOSE. You folkses ready?

TOM. Yes, Mose. Wha's Luke?

MOSE. I knows wha' Slim is but I done los' Luke. He's a kind a' ondependable niggah, anyhow.

PET. Now, Mose, don't you talk 'gainst Luke. He fixed Jude, didn't he?

MOSE. Yas, Ah reckon so—but what's he doin' stayin' so long out dere? We got t' be gettin' away. Doubt's we get fuh anyway.

(*After several minutes of silent tension in the cabin, the door opens, and a lank figure dressed in planter's costume, with a broad-brim hat well down over his eyes, enters. They all cower, but* SALLIE *shrieks. The man springs forward and stops her mouth with his palm, and discloses himself. It is* LUKE.)

SALLIE. Oh, Gawd, I thought you was Massa John or someone! What you doin' ——

LUKE. (*Interrupting as they stand out in amazement*) Now folks, 'membah! You-alls my niggahs when we get away from heah. You understan'? (*They gradually come out of their stupefaction as the idea dawns on them*) An' you-all's—(*They begin to chorus "Yassuhs" in the intervals of his speech*) you-all's jes' been purchus', understand that?

ALL. (*Except* MOSE, *who turns sceptically*) Yassuh, Yassuh!

LUKE. An' we-all had to turn off de road after Slim, 'cause he run away—an' yo' helpin' me back with him. (*Grandiosely and making an effort to talk correctly*) You-all understand that?

SALLIE. Yassuh! An', please yo', what shill we call yuh?

LUKE. Marse John, of co'se! Ain't dese yeah Marse John's? (*Pointing to the clothes*) I done took Jude's keys. (*Drawing himself up proudly*) Ah told yo' I had plans. Does Ah look de part?

(*They all draw close to scrutinize him.* MOSE *surveys him suspiciously and spreads* LUKE'S *tie to hide his lack of a shirt.*)

SALLIE. Lawd a' mussy, you sho' does look like quality!—I hopes we makes it.

MOSE. Well, we'se got to try anyhow. (*To the women*) Don't you stan' there lookin' crazy like, come on! Come on, Ah tell yuh, ef you-all wants to be free. Ah'm not 'pendin' so much on Luke's foolin's, Ah'm goin' ta run, Ah am.

(LUKE *with a commanding gesture marshals them all out of the door and closes it.*)

CURTAIN

WHITE DRESSES

A FOLK TRAGEDY

By

PAUL GREEN

"Low is de way to de upper bright world. . ."
—NEGRO SONG

CHARACTERS

GRANNY MCLEAN, an old Negro woman
MARY MCLEAN, her granddaughter
JIM MATTHEWS, in love with Mary
HENRY MORGAN, a white man and landlord

Place: The home of Granny McLean in eastern North Carolina.
Time: The evening before Christmas, several years ago.

First production, Season of 1921, by The Carolina Playmakers, Frederick H. Koch, Director, Chapel Hill, N. C.

WHITE DRESSES

IN THE HUGE FIREPLACE *of a Negro cabin on a cold winter night a small fire is burning, lighting up with flickering flames the poverty-stricken interior of a comfortless room. Here and there on the rough-planked walls hang bright illustrations, striving in a crude way to beautify the place. A few chairs are in the room and a small eating table is in the center.*

GRANNY MCLEAN, *a big, bony, black, old woman comes in at the rear door, walking with the aid of a cane and carrying several sticks of firewood under her arm. She is dressed in a slat bonnet, which hides her face in its shadows, brogan shoes, a man's ragged coat, checkered apron, and dark-colored dress. After much straining and grunting, she puts the wood on the fire, and then takes the poker and examines some potatoes cooking in the ashes. Hanging her bonnet on the chair behind her, she takes out her snuffbox and fills her lip. In the firelight her features are discernible—sunken eyes, high cheek bones, and big flat nose. On her forehead she wears steel-rimmed spectacles.*

She sits down in the rocking-chair, now and then putting her hand to her head and groaning. For a moment she pats her foot nervously on the floor, and then gets up and opens the door. She stands looking out at the gathering dusk.

GRANNY. (*Muttering*) Why don' dat gal come on hyuh!

(She closes the door and looks restlessly around the room. Hobbling over to a chest, she rakes newspapers and catalogues to the floor, and taking a key from around her neck, opens the chest and lifts out a small black oblong box. Then she returns again to the fire and sits down, her fingers drumming on the lid of the box. She takes another key from the string around her neck and starts to unlock it. At that moment the door at the rear opens quickly and MARY McLEAN *comes in with a "turn" of collards and a bundle in her arms. She lays the collards on the floor near the door and puts the bundle on the bed. She is a light, cream-colored girl about eighteen years old, with an oval face and dark straight hair neatly done up. Her dress is shabby.)*

GRANNY. *(Suddenly springing up in confusion and then sitting back down with her hand to her hip.)* Oh—mah back! *(She hides the box under her apron.)*

MARY. How you feeling, Granny?

GRANNY. I's tuck in mah l'ins. *(She tries to straighten up.)*

MARY. You hadn't ought to jump so quick; I ain't going to bother you about that old box.

GRANNY. Yeh, yeh, and I dunno. I thought you wa'n't a-coming a good w'ile yet. He'p me up a li'l' bit. *(*MARY *catches her by the arm and raises her. She putters over to the chest, locks the box away, and returns to her chair.)*

MARY. *(Watching her)* Ain't you never going to let me see what you got hid in that box?

GRANNY. Hush it, chile! I done told you I'd let you know when de time come. *(Shaking her head)* And I's afea'd de time ain't fur off nuther.

MARY. *(Turning from hanging up her shawl)* What you

mean by that? All the week you been talking about something being not far off. What in the world is it?

GRANNY. Neveh you mind. Run on now and tell me why you stay up dere at Mis' Mawgin's so late.

MARY. (*Punching up the fire*) She had such a big ironing and a lot of cleaning up for Christmas, I couldn't get through no quicker.

GRANNY. And me setting hyuh dese las' two hours wid mah haid busting open, and being oneasy 'bout my gal off wukking so ha'd.

MARY. But look what I brought you. (*She opens her hand and shows her a five-dollar bill.*)

GRANNY. Five dollahs! Lawd he'p mah life!

MARY. (*Bringing the package from the bed*) And look what Mr.—Mr.—Morgan sent you. (*She undoes the package, revealing sausage, ham, and other cooked food*) He said as 'twas Christmas time, he sent you all these things and the collards there. (GRANNY *reaches impulsively for the food, but drops her hand and sits blinking at* MARY.)

GRANNY. Whah'd you git all dese things? (*Suspiciously*) Whah'd you git dat 'ere money?

MARY. (*Stammering*) They—they all sent it to you, I said.

GRANNY. (*Excitedly*) Mr. Mawgin ain't de kind to be making free wid his money. And dey ain't no past Chris'mus he was so good to me lak dat, and you knows it, him a-having his washing done raght up on Chris'mus Eve. (*Sharply*) Did Mr. Hugh gi'n you dat money?

MARY. He ain't give me nothing. It's every bit for you. When I was washing some of Mr. Hugh's shirts—and they was soft and shiny—he come out and handed me the money and said give it to you.

GRANNY. He'p mah soul and body, de boy said dat! He ain't fo'got his old granny since he gut to gwine off to school 'way yander.

MARY. (*Handing the money to* GRANNY *who takes it quickly*) He said maybe when he'd made a lot of money and got rich he'd send you more things than you could shake a stick at, like as not.

GRANNY. De Lawd bless his baby heart! Ain't he a sight to think o' me lak dat? He's a reg'la Trojas. Allus was a good boy, and he ain't changed since he growed up nuther. Mind me when I used to nuss him, he'd neveh whimpeh, no, suh. (*She rubs the bill in her hand.* MARY *sits down and looks into the fire.*)

MARY. (*After a moment*) I bet he was a purty baby, won't he, Granny?

GRANNY. De fines' gwine. (*Turning to look at her*) Why you ax dat?

MARY. I thought he must've been purty from—from the way he seems —— (*She looks at the fire without noticing the old woman's uneasy movement.*)

GRANNY. Listen hyuh. Don't you know you got no call to be talking 'bout a white boy lak dat?

MARY. (*Getting up hastily*) Time I was fixing your supper.

GRANNY. Didn't he g'in you nothing a-tall?

MARY. No'm, he didn't give me nothing. (*She suddenly sits down, stifling a sob.*)

GRANNY. Hyuh, putt dis money in de pocketbook. Don't mind whut I's saying. I 'spects I's too 'tickleh 'bout you, I dunno. (*Looking around*) What ails you, chile?

MARY. (*Wiping her eyes*) Nothing, nothing. (*She puts*

the money away, then lights the lamp. GRANNY
watches her perplexedly.)

GRANNY. (*Solicitously*) Mah po' baby's been wukking too
much.

MARY. I ain't neither. I feel fresh. You want me to fix
your supper on the table?

GRANNY. No, suh-ree. What betteh do I want'n dis hyuh
in mah lap? (*She begins eating greedily. Suddenly she
utters a low scream and puts her hand to her head.*)

MARY. It's your head again, ain't it? Now you rest easy.
(*And she comes over and begins rubbing her cheeks and
forehead.* GRANNY *becomes quiet and goes back to her
eating*) Set still while I git in a turn o' lightwood. It's
going to be a cold night and looks like snow. (*She goes
just outside the door and returns with an armful of
wood which she throws down near the fireplace.*) You
feel all right still?

GRANNY. Purty well. Dis hyuh victuals puts new life in
me.

MARY. Now you see that spell didn't last no time. And it's
like I keep telling you, you'll be well and back in the
fields with the hoe hands by spring.

GRANNY. (*Sharply*) No, suh, I ain't long foh dis world.
I's done my last washing and chopping and leading de
gang in de fields.

MARY. You're always talking like that, and you'll live to be
a hundred or more.

GRANNY. (*Licking her fingers*) Dese is good spar' ribs
and sa'sages sho' 'nough. (MARY *sits down again and
stares before her with her chin in her hand.*)

MARY. Don't it sorter make you feel lonesome and quare to
be setting here to-night just you'n me, and nobody in the

world that cares nothing for us? Up at Mis' Morgan's they're all having——

GRANNY. Whut's dat? Whut's de matteh?

MARY. Not much of nothing.

GRANNY. You's worried. Dey's sump'n on yo' mind, ain't dey? (*With misgiving*) Mr. Mawgin—he—ain't said nothing else 'bout us having to leave, has he?

MARY. No'm, no'm—he said—I don't think he's said no more of it.

GRANNY. (*Anxiously*) You sho' 'bout dat?

MARY. (*Stolidly*) Oh, he said to-day—he said maybe he'd let us stay right on here. (*Nervously*) Something like that.

GRANNY. (*Listening*) Talk louder, say dat ag'in.

MARY. He said it might be so we could stay as long as we pleased.

GRANNY. He did? (*Joyously*) Thank de Lawd! Bless His holy name! I knowed Mr. Mawgin gwine do it. I knowed it. (*Soberly*) But I been pow'ful skeahd he's gwine run us off—when Mr. Hugh gut to taking up foh us. Now I kin res' mah bones raght whah I wants to. (*Uncertainly*) How come he change lak dat and say we could stay on? How come?

MARY. I dunno—just did, I reckon.

GRANNY. (*Looking at her keenly*) Is you trying to keep de truf f'om me, hunh?

MARY. Shucks! It's going to be all right. Mr. Morgan didn't exactly say much about it. But Mr. Hugh, he said he'd look out for us, and he will too. (GRANNY *stops eating and sits in silence.*)

GRANNY. (*Harshly, after a moment*) Don' you say no mo' 'bout Mr. Hugh—heah me?—— You ain't even had nothing t'eat, has you?

MARY. Yes'm, I have too. They told me not to come off
without eating, and I et. (GRANNY *rakes a potato
from the ashes and begins peeling it.* MARY *turns restlessly in her chair. She goes over to the bureau, takes
out a piece of pink ribbon and begins arranging her
hair.*)

GRANNY. (*Noticing her movements*) Whut you dressing
up foh? Is Jim coming 'round to-night? (*She wraps
up the remainder of her food and puts it in the chimney
corner.*)

MARY. Yes'm, he'll be coming, I reckon. (*Scornfully*)
They ain't no getting away from him and his box.

GRANNY. (*Blowing on her potato*) Whut you gut ag'in
Jim? Dey ain't no betteh nigger'n Jim is. He's gwine
treat you straight. And it's time you's gitting married.

MARY. Don't start your talk about marrying. I ain't going
to marry, and you know it well enough.

GRANNY. Whut keeps gitting into you? When I was yo'
age, yo' mammy was a stropping young 'un pulling at
mah breas'. Yessuh, I wants you to git married. I told
you and told you. 'Tain't a good sign when a 'oman old
as you ain't thinking o' gitting her a home. I's lak to
nuss yo' li'l'-uns and sing to 'em 'fo' I go. Mind me
o' de old times.

MARY. (*Bitterly*) What's Jim Matthews for a husband with
his gab?

GRANNY. Well, he works ha'd and saves his money. (MARY
finishes her hair and powders her face. GRANNY *sits
silently peeling her potatoes.*)

MARY. (*Presently*) Granny, you ain't seen him since he
come back. He's as kind and good to me as he can be.

GRANNY. (*Looking at her questioningly*) Co'se he's kind
and good.

MARY. (*Softly*) And to-day he said 'twas a pity I had to work and wash like a dog for a living. He don't treat me like a—like a colored person. He acts same as if I was white.

GRANNY. (*Staring at her in troubled astonishment*) I knows it, honey, Jim's solid to de bottom.

MARY. (*Vehemently*) I ain't talking about Jim, I tell you.

GRANNY. Whut you mean! Who you talking 'bout?

MARY. Oh, nobody, like as not. (*Appealingly*) I don't look like a common nigger, do I?

GRANNY. Lawd bless you, you sho' don't. You's purty as dey makes 'em—lak yo' po' mammy whut's daid and gone, 'ceptin' you's—mebbe whiteh.

MARY. I been thinking a whole heap lately. If I was to go 'way off, the people there might think I was real white folks, wouldn't they?

GRANNY. (*Rising from her seat in alarm*) Gohd in heaben, chile! Whut's come oveh you?

MARY. I'm wore out with the mess of things, I am, I tell you! Didn't you never wish you was white?

GRANNY. Hesh, hesh, I says. (*Sitting down and turning her face away*) Po' thing, po' chile, yo' mammy used to talk lak dat. Don' you say no sech words to me. Lawd in heaben!

MARY. But they ain't no use of talking. (*Helplessly*) Talk won't change nothing. I cain't stand it no more!

GRANNY. (*Sternly*) Hesh dat! (*Kindly*) Honey chile, you listen to me. We's bofe niggehs, bawn niggehs and'll die niggehs. De Lawd He made us, and de Lawd He'll take us away and whut He does is raght. Now you trust in Him and rest easy.

MARY. No, no, I won't, I'll change it somehow, I will!
(*A sound of stamping feet outside and a knock at the*

door. MARY *brushes her hand across her face and calls out)* Come in!

GRANNY. Who's dat?

MARY. Sounds like Jim. (JIM MATTHEWS *enters. He is a young Negro of twenty-two or three and as black as his African ancestors. He carries a guitar slung over his shoulder, wears an old derby hat, tan shirt with flowing tie, a well-worn blue suit, the coat of which comes nearly to his knees, and shoes slashed along the edges to make room for his feet. As he comes in, he pulls off his hat and smiles genially, showing his white teeth.*)

JIM. Good evening, ladies. (*He lays his derby on the bed.*)

GRANNY. (*Turning in her chair*) Whut does he say?

MARY. He says good evening.

GRANNY. Ah-hah! Good evening, Jim. Take a seat. I's sho' glad you come 'round. Mary's been talking 'bout you. (*He smiles complacently and takes a seat between* MARY *and* GRANNY.)

JIM. Yeb'm, and I's sho' glad to be wid you-all. (*Gallantly*) I's allus glad to be wid de ladies.

GRANNY. Whut does he say?

JIM. (*More loudly*) I's glad to be wid you-all.

GRANNY. Ah-hah! (JIM *pulls out a large checkered handkerchief from his breast pocket, wipes his forehead and then flips the dust from his shoes. He folds it carefully and puts it back*) Any news, Jim?

JIM. Nob'm, any wid you?

GRANNY. None a-tall. Yo' folks all well?

JIM. Peart and kicking. How you-all come on?

GRANNY. Hah? I's purty feeble. (*She groans and rocks to and fro.*)

JIM. Still having dem spells wid her haid, Mary?

MARY. (*Lowering her voice*) You ought to know, you're

here 'most every night. Yes, she has 'em and will till
she's laid away for good. (*She goes to* GRANNY *and
begins rubbing her head again.* GRANNY *waves her off.*)

GRANNY. Ne' mind me now. You chillun go on wid yo'
co'ting. I's gwine peel mah 'taters. (JIM *looks sheepishly at* MARY *and strums his guitar. He moves his
chair nearer to her. She moves mechanically from him.*)

JIM. Uh—Mary, you's looking 'ceeding snatching in dat
pink ribbon. Glad to see you's 'specting me 'round.
Yeb'm, I tells all de gals you gut 'em beat to a frazzle.
(MARY *pays no attention to him*) F'om heah slam to
France and back I ain't seed nobody lak you, and I's a
old road niggeh and oughta know. (*He stops and
fidgets in his chair.*) Mary, I——

MARY. Jim, I done told you forty times over you needn't
come snooping around me. I ain't loving you, and I
ain't going to marry you.

JIM. Now—uh—Mary, honey, I knows des' how you feels.
And I ain't gwine give you up. I cain't heah you when
you says no. To-day I was talking to dat young Hugh
Mawgin, and he——

MARY. *Hugh Morgan!* Mr. Hugh Morgan, you mean.

JIM. (*Hurriedly*) Yeh, yeh, Mr. Hugh.

MARY. What'd you say to him?

JIM. I told him I was calling heah 'casionally, and he said—
he said—— (*He wilts before* MARY'S *eyes.*)

MARY. (*Eying him straightly*) Go on, go on.

JIM. He axed me if I's a-co'ting, and I told him I—uh—
mought be.

MARY. Did he seem glad that you was coming?

JIM. He said he 'spected to heah o' us being married some
dese days. (MARY *is silent*) He 'lowed as how you
was most too fine to be wukking yo' eyeballs out, and

you needed a man to look adder you. I tuk f'om his talk dat he thought I'd fill de bill.

MARY. Oh, yes, I reckon you thought that.

JIM. He's a eddicated boy, and he sees my worf. Dey teaches him to know a heap 'way out yander at dat college place.

MARY. (*Springing up*) Jim Matthews, you set there and talk like you owned the whole world and me to boot. Well, I tell you right now you don't! Before I'll marry a smut black nigger like you I'll die stone dead. (JIM *gasps in amazement.* MARY *goes to the window and looks out.*)

GRANNY. (*Looking up*) Whut ails you chillun making sech a racket? You ain't qua'lling, is you?

MARY. I'm just trying to get Jim to play a piece on his box. (*To* JIM *in a lower voice*) Play something for her.

GRANNY. Yeh, play us a piece, Jim, if you'n Mary's finished wid yo' corkusing.

JIM. (*Morosely*) I cain't play nothing.

GRANNY. Whut you say, Jim?

JIM. (*Shaking his head mournfully and strumming the strings*) I'll play you sump'n den. (*He plays a few bars and then begins singing, with ohs and ahs thrown in.*)

> Oh, whah you gwine, mah loveh?
> Gwine on down de road.
> Whut make you pale and weeping?
> I's carrying a heavy load.
>
> She th'owed her arms around me,
> And cast me silveh and gold,
> Sing, whah you gwine, mah loveh?
> I's a-gwine on down de road.

(MARY *comes back to her chair and sits down.* JIM *stops
    and speaks softly.*) Mary, why you want to cry lak
    dat? (*She makes no reply.*)

GRANNY. Whut de matteh wid you, Mary? You's same
    lak somebody whut's seed de dead.

MARY. (*To* JIM) Play her burying piece.

GRANNY. Yeh, yeh, play dat. (JIM *fits his pocketknife be-
    tween his fingers in imitation of the Hawaiians, clears
    his throat, and strikes another chord.*)

> Hearse done carried somebody to de graveyard.
> Lawd, I know mah time ain't long.
> Mary come a-weeping, Martha wailing.
> Lawd, I know mah time ain't long.

(*He sings louder, syncopating with his feet.*)

> Preacher keep a-preaching, people keep a-dying.
> Lawd, I know mah time ain't long.

(GRANNY *begins swaying with the music, clapping her hands,
    and now and then crying out, "Jesus, Lawdy mah
    Lawd!" She and* JIM *start singing, alternately, he the
    verses and she the refrain.* MARY *takes off her ribbon
    and throws it on the bureau.*)

> Hammer keep a-ringing on somebody's coffin.

GRANNY.

> Lawd, I know mah time ain't long.

JIM.

> Gwine a-roll 'em up lak leaves in de judgment.

GRANNY.

       Lawd, I know mah time ain't long.

MARY. (*Turning quickly from the window*) Yes, yes, roll 'em up like leaves in the judgment! (*Bitterly*) That's the time it's all made right, they say! (*With sharp insistence she sings, with unhappy mockery.*)

       Yea, yea, gwine a-roll 'em up lak leaves in de judgment.

JIM. (*Stopping his music before her shrill voice*) I dunno ezzactly whut you driving at.
MARY. They ain't no need of you knowing. (GRANNY *goes on swaying and singing a moment.*)
GRANNY. Le's don' stop de music, Jim. (*To* MARY) Jine in wid us and le's make 'er roll. (*There is a sudden banging on the door.* MARY *hesitates a moment, and then opens it. A look of fear spreads over her face as* HENRY MORGAN *enters. He is a heavily built man, about fifty years old. A week's growth of grizzled beard darkens his face. He wears a slouch hat, long black shabby overcoat buttoned up to his chin, big black boots, and yarn mittens. He carries a package which he throws contemptuously on the bed. He keeps his hat on.* MARY *closes the door and stands with her back to it.* GRANNY *and* JIM *offer their seats.* JIM'S *look is one of servile respect,* GRANNY'S *one of trouble.*)
MORGAN. (*In a booming voice*) Dad burn you, Jim! Still a-courting, eh? Set down, Granny, I ain't going to stay long.
GRANNY. (*Querulously*) Whut does he say?
MARY. (*Leaving the door and standing by her chair, as she eyes the package*) He says for you to set down. He ain't going to stay long.

GRANNY. (*Sitting down*) Ah-hah. . . . Oh, Lawdy, Lawdy!

MORGAN. How you getting on now, Granny?

GRANNY. Po'ly, po'ly, Mr. Mawgin. Ain't gut much longer down hyuh, ain't much longer.

MORGAN. (*Laughing*) Aw, come on, come on, cut out your fooling. You ain't half as bad off as you make out. (JIM *moves his chair into the corner and sits down.*)

MARY. (*Hotly*) She is sick too, she's bad off. (*She twists her apron nervously.*)

MORGAN. (*With a touch of anger*) 'Y God, I ain't talking to you right now, Mary.

GRANNY. (*Whining*) Mr. Mawgin, I sho' is in a bad condition. I hopes you'll neveh have to suffeh lak me.

MORGAN. Well, I may though. I'll send you some more medicine in a day or two.

GRANNY. Thanky, thanky, Mr. Mawgin.

MORGAN. Never mind the thanks. (*Turning to* MARY) Have you told her everything?

MARY. Not just yet. Somehow I couldn't just to-night.

MORGAN. Unh-hunh, I knowed it. I knowed I'd better come down and make sure. Durn me, you been crying, ain't you? (*Less brusquely*) What you crying over?

MARY. Nothing as I know of. I was just feeling bad or something.

MORGAN. (*Grimly*) Well, my young lady, you needn't be crying over what I told you to-day.

GRANNY. What does he say?

MORGAN. Keep quiet, cain't you? I'm talking to Mary.

GRANNY. Is it 'bout de package you brought? Is dat bundle foh me or her?

MORGAN. It's hers. Coming down here, I caught up with Zeke. Said he had a Christmas present for Mary. I took and brought it. Wonder what that nigger's giving her. (MARY *starts towards the bed. He clutches her arm*) No, you ain't going to see it now, gal. We got a little business to 'tend to first. (GRANNY *begins staring at the bundle on the bed, now and then glancing around to see if any one is watching her. She pays no attention to the conversation. MARY stands with head bowed*) Well, what you going to do about it?

MARY. (*Stammering*) I—I can't talk about it no more, Mr. Morgan.

MORGAN. Keep your mouth shet then, and I'll do what I said. That's all there is to it. (*He turns to* JIM, *who straightens up*) Jim, I've done my best to make a match for you and get things straightened out. (*To* MARY) Either marry him or take your duds and grandmuh and git from here. (GRANNY *steals across the room and picks up the package.*)

MARY. Oh, I dunno—I dunno—Mr. Morgan, she couldn't stand to leave here and you know it.

MORGAN. (*Angrily*) What'n the name o' God do you want me to do—lose money on you till the end of time? You ain't earned enough to keep you in clothes the last three years since Granny got down——

GRANNY. (*Crying out in a loud voice*) Lawd in heaben ha' muhcy on us! (*She stands by the bed holding a white dress up before her.* MORGAN *looks up in perplexity. She throws the dress on the bed and stares at* MORGAN.)

MARY. (*Running to the bed*) It's for me! It's mine!

GRANNY. Mr. Mawgin, Mr. Mawgin, you knows whut dat dress means! (*She sits down, rocking and mumbling.*)

MARY. He sent it to me! He sent it to me! I knowed he wouldn't forget.

MORGAN. (*Quickly*) Who sent it to you?

MARY. He did.

MORGAN. Who?

MARY. It was him and I don't care if you do know it.

MORGAN. (*Striding up to her and clutching her arm*) Him who? Who'n the devil you mean?

MARY. Your own boy, that's who. He give it to me.

MORGAN. God A'mighty, that's a lie! (MARY *goes to the mirror and holds the dress up in front of her*) It's a lie, I tell you. Zeke sent you that dress.

MARY. Mr. Hugh done it. He said he's going to remember me and give me something purty. And I knowed he would. After all I ain't been working all the whole year for nothing. He's got a heart in him if nobody else ain't.

MORGAN. (*Almost shouting*) Tell me, gal, what's the meaning of this!

GRANNY. (*Quavering*) You knows whut it all means, Mr. Mawgin, you knows. (*She groans and shakes her head.*)

MORGAN. (*Loudly*) Shet up, Granny! Mary, Mary, you put up that damned dress. Put it up, I say! (*She shrinks back from him, and he snatches the dress from her and throws it on the bed. Then he pushes her out into the room*) You listen to me now. We're going to settle it once and for all right now. Are you going to marry Jim?

MARY. Mr. Morgan, please—I cain't marry him. I'll work and hoe and wash day and night. I'll do anything.

MORGAN. Yes, you will! You've told me that time and again. You got to say one or t'other right here and now. Marry Jim, and everything will be all right. He'll take care of you.

MARY. I cain't do it, I tell you. I'd rather die. Look at

him, he's black, and I hate him.   I'll never marry no
nigger.

MORGAN. Black or white, that's got nothing to do with it.

MARY. I hate the ground he walks on.

MORGAN. (*Turning*) Granny——

MARY. Don't worry her, don't tell her.   I ain't going to see
her drove out in the cold like a dog.   (GRANNY *sits
rocking and gazing into the fire.* JIM, *lost in amazement, fingers his guitar*) Oh, what's the matter with
you!

MORGAN. Gal, I don't want to be too hard on you.   But
use common sense.   They ain't a man in this country
would have been as good to you all these years.

MARY. He wouldn't let you treat me so hard if he was here.
And he said he wouldn't let you run us off.

MORGAN. Who you talking about this time?

MARY. Mr. Hugh's got feelings, he has.

MORGAN. Damn Mr. Hugh!   Don't you mention his name
again.   Thank God he's not here and won't be.

MARY. He said he'd see that we was took care of.

MORGAN. The fool, he's got no more sense!   But he's gone
with a crowd of young folks to Charlotte, and when he
gets back there won't be no helping you.   I'll see to
that.

MARY. He said—he said he'd see me to-morrow and fix it
all.

MORGAN. Well, he won't.   And ain't you got no shame
about you, using my boy's name like a common nigger?
What's he to you?   (*Pleadingly*) Ain't you got no
sense, Mary?   Listen.   I'm going to talk plain.   Are
you planning to ruin his life?   You know what I mean
too, don't you?

MARY. (*Sobbing*) They ain't no use trying to change it.

(*Starting back*) But I won't do it. I won't be drove into it. Let us starve or freeze, I don't care what.

MORGAN. All right, is that your last word?

MARY. It is that. Beat me black and blue, I won't listen to you.

MORGAN. (*Turning to the old woman*) Granny, I got bad news for you. (*She makes no sign that she has heard*) Mary ain't got no more sense than she was born with, and you might as well get your fixings together and search another place.

GRANNY. (*Without looking around*) Mr. Mawgin, it don' matter whut you do to me now. You's done hurt me all you kin. Put me out and lemme die quick as I kin.

MORGAN. (*Turning to* MARY) Are you going to see her suffer for your craziness?

MARY. Yes, make me marry him then. They ain't nothing to be done about it. I thought it might be changed, but it won't. I'll marry him and raise more children to go through it all like me. No, no, they ain't no help nowhere. (*She sits dejectedly down in her chair.*)

MORGAN. (*Silent a moment and then speaking more kindly*) All right, Mary. That's sensible. I'll send for the license and preacher in the morning and have him marry you and Jim right here. Does that suit you, Jim?

JIM. (*Uncertainly*) Yessuh, yessuh, Mr. Mawgin.

MORGAN. (*Going up to* GRANNY) Well, Granny, things is going to be all right, after all. Mary and Jim's going to tie up. Don't worry no more. (*She makes no answer.* MORGAN *offers* MARY *his hand, but she keeps her head muffled in her apron*) Mary, I hated to push you along so, but it's all for the best. (*Embarrassed*) I could mebbe tell you something that'd make you understand what I mean—but—well, I cain't now. (*He *stands a moment looking at the floor, then goes out quietly. Presently* JIM *rises and lays more wood on the fire. He comes to* MARY.)

JIM. Mary, honey, don' take on so. (*He waits patiently, but she says nothing. He strums his guitar and breaks into a mournful song.*)

> Lying in de jail house,
> Peeping th'ough de bars,
> De cold rain a-falling,
> And—de——

Oh, don't worry no mo', Mary, please'm.

MARY. Leave me alone. I ain't going to have nothing to do with you. I promised, but I done took it back. (*Starting up*) And I'll run catch Mr. Morgan and tell him so. (*She moves towards the door*) I won't marry no Jim Matthews.

GRANNY. (*Calling loudly*) Hyuh, hyuh, chile! Don' you go out dat do'! Take dis hyuh key and bring me dat li'l' black box. (MARY *stops*) Bring me dat box, I say! (*Her threatening voice quavers high.* MARY *comes slowly back, gets the key, and brings the box from the chest and stands wiping the tears from her eyes*) I's gwine tell you de secret o' dis li'l' box. Yo' mammy said tell you if de time eveh come, and it's come. And when I tells you, you'll see why you got to marry Jim. She went th'ough sin and trouble, and I's gwine save you. (GRANNY *opens the box and pulls out a wrinkled white dress, of a generation ago, yellowed with age.* JIM *looks on with open mouth*) Listen hyuh, po' baby, I's gwine tell you now. Nineteen yeahs ago come dis Christmus dey was a white man gi'n yo' mammy dis heah dress, and dat white man is clost kin to you, and he don' live fur off nuther. Gimme dat udder dress dere on de bed. (MARY *gets it and holds it tightly to her.* GRANNY *snatches at it*) Gimme dat dress, I tells you.

MARY. It's mine and I'm going to keep it.

GRANNY. (*Glaring at her*) Gimme. (*She jerks the dress from* MARY. *Hobbling to the fireplace, she lays both of them carefully on the fire.* JIM *makes a movement to save them, but she waves him back with her stick*) Git back, niggeh, git back! Dis night I's gwine wipe out some o' de traces o' sin. (MARY *sits sobbing. As the dresses burn* GRANNY *comes over and stands looking down at her*) And when dey comes to-morrow wid de license, you go on and marry, and you'll live 'spectable. (*She lays her hand on her head*) I knows yo' feelings, chile, but you's gut to smother 'em in, you's gut to smother 'em in.

CURTAIN

IN ABRAHAM'S BOSOM

A PLAY IN ONE ACT

By

PAUL GREEN

"De blind man stood on de road and cried . . ."
—NEGRO SONG.

CHARACTERS

ABRAHAM McCRANIE, a Negro
GOLDIE McALLISTER, his sweetheart
COLONEL McCRANIE, a white man
LONNIE McCRANIE, his son
BUD GASKINS
LIJE HUNNEYCUTT }Negro turpentine hands
PUNY AVERY   for the Colonel

Place: A turpentine woods in eastern North Carolina.

Time: Noon on a summer day late in the Nineteenth Century.

First performance at the
Provincetown Playhouse, New York City,
December 28, 1926.

IN ABRAHAM'S BOSOM

THE SPRING *at the foot of a slope is in a cleared space, save for a spongy growth of grass and sickly ground creepers. To the rear a widespreading tangle of reeds, briars and alder bushes shuts around in a semicircle. At the right front the great body of a pine, gashed and barked by the turpentine farmer's ax, lifts straight from the earth, and to the left a log lies rotting in the embrace of wild ivy. Maples, bays, dogwoods and other small trees overrun by tenacious vines raise their leafy tops to shade the spot. Through interstices in the undergrowth one can see the pine forest stretching away until the eye is lost in a colonnade of trees. The newly scraped blazes on the pines show through the brush like the downward spreading beards of old men, the ancient gnomes of the woods, mysterious, impersonal and forever watchful.*

At the left front four tin dinner pails hang on a limby bush. The sound of axes against the trees, accompanied by the rhythmically guttural "han—n—h! han—n—n—h!" of the cutters comes from the distance, and one of the unseen laborers breaks into a high mournful song—

> My feet wuh wet—wid de sunrise dew,
> De mornin' star—wuh a witness too.
> 'Way, 'way up in de Rock of Ages,
> In God's bosom gwine be my pillah.

*Presently there is a loud halloo near at hand, and another
voice yodles and cries,* "Dinner time—mm—e! Git yo' peas,
ev'ybody!" *Voices are heard nearer, a loud burst of
laughter, and then three full-blooded Negroes shuffle in, carrying long, thin-bladed axes, which they lean against the pine
at the right. They are dressed in nondescript clothes, ragged
and covered with the glaze of raw turpentine. As they
move up to the spring they take off their ragged hats, fan
themselves, and wipe the streaming sweat from their brows.
Two of them are well-built and burly, one stout and past
middle age with some pretension to a thin scraggly mustache,
the second tall and muscled, and the third wiry, nervous and
bandy-legged. They punctuate their conversation with great
breaths of cool air.*

YOUNG NEGRO. Monkey walking in dis woods.

OLDER NEGRO. Yah, Jaboh progueing 'round and 'bout um.

LITTLE NEGRO. While us rest he roos' high in pine tree.

YOUNG NEGRO. Fall on Puny's back 'bout th'ee o'clock, git
um down. Hee—hee.

PUNY. Ain't no monkey kin ride me, tell you. (*They stand
fanning themselves.*)

OLDER NEGRO. Dat nigger tough, ain't you, Puny?

PUNY. Tough as whit-leather, tough 'y God! (*He gets
down on his belly at the spring*) Mouf 'bout to crack,
kin drink dis heah spring dry.

OLDER NEGRO. (*Slouching his heavy body towards the pool*)
Hunh, me too. Dem axes take water same lak a sawmill. (*He gets down flat and drinks with the other.
The water can be heard gluking over the cataract of
their Adam's apple. The* YOUNGER NEGRO *opens his
torn and sleeveless undershirt and stands raking the
sweat from his powerful chest with curved hands.*)

YOUNG NEGRO. (*After a moment*) Heigh, Puny, you'n Lije

Photo by Maurice Goldberg

THE WOOD SCENE FROM "IN ABRAHAM'S BOSOM"

pull yo' guts out'n dat mudhole and let de engineer take
a drink. (*With a sudden thought of devilment he steps
quickly forward and cracks their heads together.* PUNY
starts and falls face foremost in the spring. LIJE, *slow
and stolid, saves himself, crawls slowly up on his
haunches and sits smiling good-naturedly, smacking his
lips and sucking water from the slender tails of his
mustache.*)

LIJE. (*Cleaning his muddy hands with a bunch of leaves*)
Nunh-unh, not dis time, my boy.

YOUNG NEGRO. Haw, haw, look dere at po' Puny.

PUNY. (*Scrambling to his feet, strangling and sputtering*)
Damn yo' soul, why you push me, Bud Gaskins?

BUD. (*A threatening note slipping into his laugh*) Hyuh,
hyuh, don't you cuss at me, bo.

PUNY. Whyn't you 'pose on somebody yo' size? Better try
Lije dere. (BUD *gets down and begins drinking.*)

LIJE. (*Drawling*) Don't keer 'f 'e do. Ducking good foh
you dis hot weather.

PUNY. (*Helplessly*) Allus picking at me. Wisht, wisht ——

BUD. Heah I is lying down. Come on, do whut you wisht.
(PUNY *makes no reply but turns off, wiping his face on
his shirt sleeve, and staring morosely at the ground.*
BUD *gets to his feet*) Yah, reckon you sail on me and I
jam yo haid in dat spring lak a fence post and drown'd
you.

PUNY. (*His anger smoldering*) Talk is cheap, black man,
cheap! (*Suddenly afraid of his boldness in replying he
turns and looks at* BUD *in a weak pleading defiance.*)

BUD. (*Making a frightening movement towards him*) Mess
wid me a jowing and I knock yo' teef th'ough yo' skull.

LIJE. Hyuh, Bud, you let Puny 'lone. (*He moves over to
his bucket, gets it and sits down on the log at the left.*)

BUD. (*Turning for his bucket with a movement of disgust*) Sho' I ain't gwine hurt him—po' pitiful bowlegs. (PUNY *clenches his hands as if stung to the quick, and then beaten and forlorn reaches for his bucket, the weak member of the herd. He throws off his overall jacket, revealing himself stripped to the waist, and sits down at the pine tree.*)

LIJE. (*Laying out his food and singing*)
　　　'Way, 'way up in de Rock of Ages
　　　In God's bosom gwine be my pillah.

BUD. (*Looking at* PUNY's *bony chest*) Uhp, showing off dat 'oman's breast o' yo'n, is you? Haw-haw.

PUNY. (*In sheer ineffectuality answering him blandly*) Gwine cool myse'f.

LIJE. Me too, peoples. (*He loosens his belt, pulls out his shirt tails, undoes his shirt, and pats his belly*) Lawd, Bud, you sho' led us a race dis mawning on dem dere boxes. Musta sweat a peck er mo'.

BUD. (*Taking his bucket and sitting on the ground near the center*) Race? Hunh, wait till fo' o'clock dis evening, you gwine call foh de ca'f rope, sho' 'nough. (*Tickled at the tribute to his powers*) And po' Puny, de monkey have rid him to deaf.

PUNY. Ain't no monkey rid me, I tells you. Little but loud. Be raght dere when de hawn blows.

BUD. Mought, and you slubbering yo' work. I cawners my boxes lak de Colonel calls foh. You des' gi' 'em a lick and a promise. Ain't it so, Lije?

LIJE. (*Swallowing a hunk of bread*) Dunno, dunno. He do all right, reckon.

PUNY. Putt us in de cotton patch, and I kin kill you off de way a king snake do a lizard.

BUD. Picking cotton! Dat 'oman and chillun's job, no

reg'lar man mess wid dat. (*Waving his hand at the woods behind him*) Turpentining's de stuff. (*They fall to devouring their food, peas, side-meat, molasses poured in the top of the bucket lid from a bottle, bread and collards. The ax of a fourth hand is heard still thudding in the forest.*)

LIJE. (*Jerking his bread-filled hand behind him*) Whyn't Abe come on? Time he eating.

BUD. Let him rare. 'On't hurt hisself a-cutting. Gitting to be de no 'countest hand I ever see.

LIJE. Useter could cut boxes lak a house a-fiah.

PUNY. And hack! Lawd, dat nigger could hack.

LIJE. De champeen o' de woods and de swamps.

PUNY. Bedder'n Bud, bedder'n all. Knowed him to dip eight barrels many day.

BUD. Cain't he'p whut has been. Ain't wuth my ol' hat now. Colonel Mack say so too. And I heahd Mr. Lonnie talking rough to him over at de weaving house day 'fo' yistiddy 'bout his gitting trifling heah lately.

PUNY. Been gitting no 'count since two yeah 'go, de time when de white folks hang dat nigger Sampson on a telegram pole—him whut 'tacked a white 'oman, and dey shoot him full o' holes, ayh!

BUD. Dey did. And dat Abe got his neck stretched hadn't been foh de Colonel. Fool went down dere in de night and cut dat nigger down and bury 'im hese'f. Gohd A'mighty!

LIJE. (*Looking around him*) 'Twon't do to mess wid white folks and dey r'iled up.

BUD. (*Gently*) You said it, bruvver.

PUNY. (*Looking around him*) Won't do. Keep to yo' work, da's all.

BUD. Yeh, work, work foh 'em. Git yo' money and yo' meat,

push on th'ough, ax no questions, no sass, keep to yo' work.

LIJE. Nigger keep mouf shet, let white man do talking, he safe den.

BUD. Safe! You done said. No telegram poles, no shooting, no fiah burn um.

PUNY. Safe is best. (*They lapse into silence under the touch of worry, something undefinable, something not to be thought upon. They swallow their food heavily. Presently* LIJE *stops and looks at the ground.*)

LIJE. Abe ain't safe.

BUD. Ayh?

LIJE. (*Gesturing vaguely behind him*) Abe talk too much.

BUD. (*Nodding*) He do, talk too much to white folks.

PUNY. Cain't he'p it, I bet.

BUD. Kin too. Didn't talk too much 'fore dat boy wuh hung. Worked hard den and say nothing.

LIJE. Sump'n on he mind. Sump'n deep, worry 'im, trouble.

BUD. Trouble 'bout dat nigger, wanter rise up wid eddication,—fact!

PUNY. Hunh, rise him up to git a rope 'roun' his neck. Nigger's place down de bottom. He de mud sill. Abe git buried in his own graveyard, don't mind.

BUD. Raght on de bottom wid deir hands and hoofs, down wid de rocks and de shovels and de digging, dat's de nigger. White man on top.

LIJE. You's talking gospel.

PUNY. Abe say he gwine climb. I heah him tell de Colonel dat.

BUD. Fo' God! Whut de Colonel say?

PUNY. He ain't say nothing, des' look at 'im.

LIJE. Abe is bad mixed up all down inside.

BUD. White and black make bad mixtry.

LIJE. Do dat. (*Thumping on his chest*) Nigger down heah. (*Thumping his head*) White mens up heah. Heart say do one thing, head say 'nudder. Bad, bad.

PUNY. De white blood in him coming to de top. Dat make him wanta climb up and be sump'n. Nigger gwine hol' him down dough. Part of him lak de Colonel, part lak his muh, 'vision and misery inside.

LIJE. Ssh!

PUNY. (*Starting and looking around*) Colonel Mack he daddy, everybody knows. Lak as two peas, see de favor.

BUD. (*Bitingly*) Talk too much! Little bird drop de news in de Colonel's yeah and he fall on you and scrush you. Ain't nigger, ain't white whut ail him. Dem damn books he gut to studying last yeah or two. Cain't go to de woods widdout 'em. Look up dere on his bucket, foh Christ' sake! (*He points to the remaining tin bucket on the bush. A small book is lying on the top under the handle. Snorting*) 'Rifmatic I bet. Give a nigger a book and des' well shoot him. All de white folks tell you dat.

PUNY. (*Pouring molasses on his bread*) He sma't dough, in his haid. Dat nigger gut sense.

LIJE. Has dat. Gitting so he kin cipher raght up wid de Colonel.

PUNY. (*Looking at* BUD) Bet some day Colonel Mack putt him woods boss over us.

BUD. Ain't no nigger gwine boss me, hoss cake. Split him to de straddle wid my ax.

LIJE. (*Leaning back and emitting a halloo*) Heigho, you, Abe! Dinner! Gwine cut all day?

BUD. Gi' him de full title and he'll heah you.

LIJE. (*Grinning*) Aberham, Aberham McCranie.

PUNY. Yeh, you, Aberham Lincoln, you man whut p—d freedom on de nigger, you better git yo' grub! (*An answering shout comes out of the forest.*)

BUD. Trying to cut past time, mebbe us'll think he sma't.

PUNY. Don't keer whut you think, Bud. Gitting so he look down on you and de rest of us.

BUD. Damn yo' runty soul, whut you know 'bout it? Ain't no nigger living kin look down on me and git by wid it. Do, and I make 'em smell o' dat. (*He clenches his heavy fist and raises it to heaven.*)

PUNY. Jesus Christ! Dat Abe take you up in one hand and frail yo' behine to a blister.

LIJE. Whut make you two black-gyard so much?

BUD. (*To* PUNY) Keep on, keep on, little man. Some dese days you gwine come missing. (*He crams a handful of cornbread in his mouth.*)

LIJE. Try a little fist and skull and work de bile out'n yo' systems.

BUD. (*Spitting in scorn*) Ain't gwine bruise my fistes on his skull. Don't 'speck to notice him no mo'. (*He eats in huge mouthfuls*) But he bedder quit th'owing dat Abe in my face, I tells him dat.

PUNY. Don't see why dat make you mad.

BUD. It do dough. I don't lak him and his uppity ways, I don't.

PUNY. Hunh, and you wus one o' de fust to brag on him foh going on sho't rations so de Colonel buy him books and learn 'im to teach school.

BUD. Sho't rations. Ain't no sho't rations and dat Goldie gal bringing him pies and stuff eve'y day. Be here wid de bucket in a few minutes, I betcha. Fool love de ve'y ground he squats on! And he look down on her 'caze her ign'ant. And teach school! Been heahing dat

school teaching business de whole yeah. He ain't gwine
teach no school. Niggers 'on't send to him, dey 'on't.
Niggers don't want no schooling.

PUNY. Mought. Abe told me dis mawning dat de Colonel
gwine fix it wid de 'missioners or sump'n in Lillington
to-day. I know whut de matter wid you, Bud, hee-hee.

BUD. Whut?

PUNY. (*Hesitating*) Abe come riding by in two-hoss coach.
Us'll be bowing and a-scraping. Us'll pull off'n our hats
and be "Howdy, Mister Aberham." (BUD *turns and
looks at him with infinite scorn, saying nothing*) And,
Bud? (BUD *makes no answer*) Bud?

BUD. Whut?

PUNY. Dat Goldie business whut worrying you, hee-hee. She
love Abe and ——

BUD. (*Bounding up and kicking* PUNY's *basket and food into
the bushes*) Damn yo' lousy soul, 'minner mind stomp
you in de dirt! (*He towers over the terrified* PUNY
who lies flat on his back whimpering.)

PUNY. Don't hit me, Bud. Foh Gohd's sake! I des' joking.

LIJE. Go at it, fight it out.

BUD. (*Kicking dirt at* PUNY *and going back to his bucket*)
Done told him now. Ain't gwine say no mo'! Next
time be my fist rammed down his th'oat, and turn him
wrong-side out-ards. (ABE *comes in at the right, carrying his ax. He is a young mulatto of twenty-five or six,
tall and powerfully built, dressed much like the others
in cap and turpentine-glazed clothes. He puts his ax
by the pine at the right, pulls off his cap and fans himself, while he pinches his sweaty shirt loose from his
skin. His shaggy head, forehead and jaw are marked
with will and intelligence. But his wide nostrils and a
slumbrous flash in his eye that now and then shows itself*

suggest a passionate and dangerous person when aroused. From the change in the actions of the others when he enters it is evident that they respect and even fear him.)

ABE. What's the trouble 'tween you and Puny, Bud?

BUD. (*Sullenly*) Ain't no trouble.

PUNY. (*Crawling around on the ground and collecting his spilled food*) Ain't nothing, Abe, I des' spilled my rations. (ABE *gets his book and seats himself in the shade at the left. He begins working problems, using a stub of a pencil and a sheet of crumpled paper.*)

LIJE. Puny, I got some bread left you kin have. (*He pulls a harp from his pocket and begins to blow softly.*)

PUNY. (*Straightening out his mashed bucket and closing it*) I don't want nothing else, Lije. Et all I kin hold. (*After a moment*) Putt yo' bucket up foh you. (*He gets* LIJE'S *bucket and hangs it along with his own on the limby bush.* BUD *eats in silence, puts up his bucket, gets a drink from the spring, and resumes his seat, hanging his head between his knees and now and then spitting sharply through his teeth.* PUNY *goes to the spring and drinks.*)

BUD. (*Pouring snuff into his lip*) Don't fall in an' git drownded, Puny.

PUNY. Want some water, Lije? (*He goes to the log, curls himself up in the shade beside it and prepares to sleep.*)

LIJE. (*Stirring lazily*) Believe I does. (*He goes to the spring and drinks, returns to the pine tree and sits down.*)

PUNY. Ain't you gwine eat no dinner, Abe? (ABE *makes no reply.*)

LIJE. Call him again. (*Touching his head with his finger*) Deep, deep up dere.

PUNY. Heigh, Abe, bedder eat yo' grub.

ABE. (*Starting*) You call me?

PUNY. You so deep stud'in' didn't heah me. Bedder eat yo' dinner. Git full o' ants setting up dere.

ABE. I going to eat later.

BUD. Yeh, when Goldie come.

ABE. Hunh?

BUD. You heahd me.

ABE. (*Irritably*) Don't let me heah no mo'.

BUD. Hunh?

ABE. You heahd me. (PUNY *snickers from his log with audible delight.* LIJE *waits a moment and then lies down.* BUD *reaches out and tears a bush from the ground and casts it angrily from him*) I'll eat my dinner when it please me, you gentlemens allowing. (*There is a touch of anger in his voice which he apparently regrets on second thought, for he goes on more kindly*) Goldie said she going to fetch me sump'n t'eat to-day. I got to work dis problem. Been on it two days now. Cain't git it out'n my head. Ain't been able to sleep two nights. (BUD *sits staring and spitting straight before him. Presently* LIJE *begins to snore; then* PUNY *follows.* ABE *goes on with his figuring.* BUD *turns over on the ground and goes to sleep.* ABE *becomes more and more absorbed in the problem he is working. He mutters to himself*) How many sheep? How many sheep? (*He clutches at his hair, gnaws his pencil, and turns to the back of his book*) Answer say fifteen. Cain't make it come out fifteen, cain't, seem lak, to save me. Man must have answer wrong. Six go into fo'teen, three, no, two times and two over. (*His voice dies away as he becomes lost in his work. Presently his face begins to light up. He figures faster. Suddenly he slaps his knee*) Dere whah I been missing it all de time. I carried two 'stid o' one. Blame fool I is. (*He hits the side of his head with his knuckles. In his excitement he calls out*) Puny, I gitting dat answer. (*But* PUNY *is snoring away. In a moment he throws down his book with beaming face*) I got it, folkses, I got it. Fifteen! Dat white man know whut he doing. He all time git dem answer right. (*He turns expectantly towards* LIJE) Lije I got it. (LIJE *makes no answer. He turns towards* PUNY *again, starts to speak, but sees he is asleep*) Bud! (*But* BUD *makes no answer. The heavy breathing of the sleepers falls regularly upon his ears. His face sinks into a sort of hopeless brooding*) Yeh, sleep, sleep, sleep yo' life away. I figger foh you, foh me, foh all de black in de world to lead 'em up out'n ignorance. Dey don't listen, dey don't heah me, dey in de wilderness, don't wanta be led. Dey sleep, sleep in bondage. (*He bows his head between his knees*) Sleep in sin. (*Presently*) Time me to eat. (*He reaches for his bucket and is about to open it when* PUNY *springs high into the air with a squeak of terror, and begins rolling over and over in the leaves and briars.*)

PUNY. Come heah, folkses, come heah git dis thing off'n me! (*He clutches at his breeches.* LIJE *and* BUD *start up and out of their sleep.*)

LIJE. Who dat run-mad man?

BUD. Dat damn Puny, sump'n in he britches!

ABE. Be still, Puny, I git it out. (*He goes up to the frightened* PUNY, *reaches down his trousers and pulls out a mouse*) Nothing but a little bitty old field mice. (*He throws the mouse with a crushing plop against the pine tree.* LIJE *and* BUD *break into roaring laughter.* PUNY *sits down exhausted, fanning himself angrily.*)

JULIUS BLEDSOE IN THE CROSSROADS SCENE FROM "IN ABRAHAM'S BOSOM"

PUNY. Laugh, laugh, all o' you. Dat thing bite same as mud turtle. Yeh, funny, funny lak hell to you. (*He snaps his mouth closed and fans himself the more furiously. A loud shout comes from off left.*)

ABE. Stop yo' laughing, I heah somebody hollering. (*A second halloo comes down the hill.*)

PUNY. Dat's de Colonel and Mr. Lonnie!

BUD. Sound lak 'em. Da's who 'tis.

ABE. (*Going off at the left*) Heah we is, Colonel Mack, at de spring eating dinner. (*He comes back in*) Colonel Mack and Mr. Lonnie coming on down heah.

PUNY. Co'se. Gut to see how many boxes us cleaned up dis mawning.

ABE. He tells me 'bout de school now. (*He stirs around him in his excitement*) Mebbe dat his main business heah in de middle o' de day.

BUD. Hunh. Mebbe. Gut some special work he want done. Wanter hurry us to it, dat's whut. (*The sound of voices is heard approaching from the left, and almost immediately the COLONEL and LONNIE come in. The COLONEL carries a riding whip. He is a stout run-down old Southerner with all the signs of a moral and intellectual decadence upon him. Lechery, whisky, and levity of living have taken their toll of him, and yet his actions show he has retained a kind of native good-naturedness. His shirt front and once pointed beard are stained with the drippings of tobacco juice. There is something in his bearing and in the contour of his face that resembles ABE. His son, a heavyish florid young man of twenty-three or four, walks behind him.*)

COLONEL MCCRANIE. (*In a high jerky voice*) Snoozing, hanh?

ABE. Just finishing our dinner, suh.

PUNY. Us 'bout to wuk overtime to-day, Colonel.

COLONEL. Not likely, I reckon. Say, I want you fellows, all four of you, to get over to the swamp piece on Dry Creek. Boxes there are running over, two quarts in 'em apiece, prime virgin. (*They begin to move to their feet*) No, I don't mean to go right now. Gabe's coming by on the big road there (*Jerking his whip towards the rear*) with a load of barrels and the dippers in about a half hour. Meet him out there.

LONNIE. Yeh, we want to git the wagons off to Fayetteville to-night.

COLONEL. How you get on cornering this morning, Bud?

BUD. Purty good, suh. Us done 'bout all dat pastuh piece.

COLONEL. Fine, fine. That's the way. Puny and Lije stay with you?

BUD. Raght dere eve'y jump.

LIJE. Yessuh, yessuh.

PUNY. When he gi' de call us gi' de 'sponse eve'y time, suh. Yes, suh, us kept 'im crowded.

COLONEL. We got to git on, Lonnie. Want to see how the scrape's coming over on Uncle Joe's Branch. Be up on the road there in half an hour, you boys.

LONNIE. (*Stopping as they go out*) Got so you doing any better work lately, Abe?

ABE. (*Starting*) Suh?

LONNIE. You heard me.

ABE. Didn't understand you, Mr. Lonnie.

LONNIE. You understood me all right. (*Pointing to the book on the ground*) Let them damned books worry you still?

COLONEL. Come on, Lonnie.

ABE. (*Stammering*) I dunno—I ——

COLONEL. Still holding out on short rations, ain't you, Abe?

(*There is the least hint of pride in the* COLONEL'S *voice.*)

ABE. (*Somewhat in confusion*) I studying whut I kin. Slow go, slow go.

COLONEL. Stick to it. You the first nigger I ever see so determined. But then you're uncommon! (*The* COLONEL *moves on*) Come on, Lonnie.

ABE. (*Following somewhat timidly after him*) Colonel Mack, did di— you—what'd dey say over dere 'bout dat little school business?

COLONEL. Bless my soul, 'bout to forget it. I talked it over with the board and most of 'em think maybe we'd better not try it yet.

ABE. (*His face falling*) When dey say it might be a good time? I gitting right 'long wid dat 'rithmatic and spelling and reading. I kin teach de colored boys and gals a whole heap right now, and I'll keep studying.

COLONEL. (*Impatiently*) Oh, I dunno. Time'll come mebbe. Mebbe the time won't come. (*He moves on.*)

ABE. Cain't you git 'em to let me try it awhile? Reckon ——

COLONEL. I don't know, I tell you. Got my business on my mind now.

LONNIE. He's done told you two or three times, can't you hear?

ABE. (*His eyes flashing and his voice shaking with sudden uncontrollable anger*) Yeh, yeh, I hear 'im. Dem white folks don't keer—dey ——

LONNIE. (*Stepping before him*) Look out! None of your sass. Pa's already done more for you than you deserve. He even stood up for you and they laughing at him there in Lillington.

ABE. (*Trembling*) Yeh, yeh, I knows. But dem white folks don't think,—I going to show 'em, I ——

LONNIE. (*Pushing himself before him*) Dry up. Not another word.

ABE. (*His voice almost breaking into a sob*) Don't talk to me lak dat, Mr. Lonnie. Stop him, Colonel Mack, 'fore I hurt him. (*The other Negroes draw off into a knot by the pine tree, mumbling in excitement and fear.*)

COLONEL. Stop, Lonnie! Abe, don't you talk to my son like that.

LONNIE. By God, I'm going to take some of the airs off'n him right now. You've gone around here getting sorrier and more worthless every day for the last year. What you need is a good beating, and I'm gonna give it to you. (*He steps backward and snatches the whip from his father's hand.*)

COLONEL. Stop that, Lonnie!

LONNIE. Keep out of this, Pa. (*He comes towards* ABE) I'll beat his black hide off'n him.

ABE. Keep 'im back dere, Colonel Mack. I mought kill him! Keep 'im off.

LONNIE. Kill him! All right, do it. There, damn your dirty soul! (*He strikes* ABE *across the face with his whip. With a snarl* ABE *springs upon him, tears the whip from his hands and hurls him headlong into the thicket of briars and bushes. Then he stands with his hands and head hanging down, his body shaking like one with the palsy.*)

PUNY. (*Screaming*) You done kilt Mr. Lonnie! Oh, Lawdy, Lawdy!

COLONEL. (*Running to* LONNIE *who is crawling up out of the mud with his clothes and skin torn. He is sobbing and cursing*) Are you hurt? How bad are you hurt?

LONNIE. Let me git at that son of a bitch and I'll kill him

dead. (*Moaning*) Oh, I'll beat his brains out with one o' them axes.

COLONEL. If you ain't dead, you'd better keep your hands off'n him. I'll fix him. (*He reaches down and picks up the whip. Thundering*) Git down on your knees, Abe McCranie! Git down, you slave, I'm gonna beat you. (ABE *jerks his head up in defiance, but before the stern face of the* COLONEL *his strength goes out of him. He puts out his hands in supplication.*)

ABE. Don't beat me, Colonel Mack, don't beat me wid dat whip!

COLONEL. Git down on your knees! I've beat many a slave, and I'll beat you, you fool! (*He strikes him several blows.*)

ABE. (*Falling on his knees*) Oh, Lawd, have muhcy upon me! (*The* COLONEL *begins to beat him blow upon blow.* PUNY, BUD *and* LIJE *stand near the pine in breathless anxiety.*)

PUNY. De Colonel 'll kill 'im!

BUD. (*Seizing his arm*) Shet dat mouf, nigger!

COLONEL. (*As he brings the whip down*) Let this be a lesson to you to the end of your life!

ABE. (*His back twitching under the whip, his voice broken*) Muhcy, Colonel Mack, muhcy!

COLONEL. You struck a white man, you struck my son.

ABE. (*Raising his tear-stained face*) I yo' son, too; you my daddy. (*He throws himself down before him, embracing his feet. The* COLONEL *lowers the whip, then throws it behind him.*)

LONNIE. (*His voice husky with rage*) You hear what he say? Hear what he called you? (*He seizes the whip and in a blind rage strikes the prostrate* ABE *again and again.*)

COLONEL. (*Stepping between them with a shout*) Stop it!
Give me that whip. (LONNIE *reluctantly hands him the
whip*) Go on back out to the road and wait for me.
Trot! (*He threatens his son with the whip and finally
LONNIE goes off at the left nursing his face in his arms*)
Get up, Abe. Get up, I say. (ABE *sits up, hugging
his face between his knees. The* COLONEL *wets his
handkerchief in the spring, and with his hands on* ABE'S
head bathes the bruises on his neck and shoulders.)

ABE. (*In a voice grown strangely dignified and quiet*) Thank
'ee, thank 'ee, Colonel Mack.

COLONEL. (*Breathing heavily*) Thanky nothing. I had to
beat you, Abe, had to. Think no more about it. Dangerous thing, hitting a white man. But this is the end of
it. Won't be no law, nothing but this. Put some tar
and honey on yourself to-night and you'll be all right to-
morrow. (*The bushes are suddenly parted at the rear
and a tall sinuous young mulatto woman bounds through.
She carries a bucket in her hand. At the sight of the
COLONEL bathing ABE'S head and neck she rushes forward with a low cry. The COLONEL turns towards
her*) Now, Goldie, ain't no use cutting up. Abe been in
a little trouble. Nothing much.

GOLDIE. (*Moaning*) I heahd de racket and I 'fraid somebody being kilt. Is you hurt bad, Abe, honey babe?
(*She bends tenderly over him, her hand running over
his hair*) Who hurt you, honey, who hurt you?

COLONEL. (*Handing* GOLDIE *his handkerchief*) Look after
him, Goldie. (*He goes out at the left calling*) Wait a
minute, Lonnie!

GOLDIE. Whut dey do to you, Abe? Who hurt you? (*All
the while she is rubbing his neck, dabbing his shoulders
with the handkerchief, and cooing over him*) Whyn't

you kill dem white mens if dey hurt you? You kin do it, break 'em lak broomstraws.

ABE. (*Standing up*) Ain't nobody hurt me. I crazy dat's whut, crazy in de haid. Ain't nobody hurt me.

GOLDIE. (*Clinging to him*) You is hurt, hurt bad. Look at yo' po' neck and shoulders. Look at 'em, beat wid great whales on 'em!

ABE. (*Growling*) Ain't nobody hurt me, I tell you.

GOLDIE. Lay yo'se'f down heah and let me smoove off yo' forehead and putt some cold water on dat mark crost yo' face. Please'm, Abe.

ABE. (*Suddenly crying out in a loud voice*) I ain't nothing, nothing. Dat white man beat me, beat me lak a dawg. (*His voice rising into a wail*) He frail me lak a suck-egg dawg! (*He rocks his head from side to side in a frenzy of wrath*) Lemme git to him! (*He falls on his knees searching in the leaves and finds a stone.* GOLDIE *stands wringing her hands and moaning. He jumps to his feet, raising the stone high above his head*) Lemme git to him, I scrush his Goddam head lak a eggshell! (*He moves to left to follow the* COLONEL. GOLDIE *throws her arms around his neck.*)

GOLDIE. No, no, you ain't gwine out dere, Abe, Abe!

PUNY. (*Crying out*) Stop him, Bud! Lije, keep him back!

LIJE. (*Coming from the pine tree*) Hyuh, now you, Abe, stop dat.

BUD. (*Moving quickly before him and blocking his path*) Stop dat, fool. You gwine fix to git yo'se'f hung up on a telegram pole. Body so full o' holes it sift sand.

GOLDIE. (*Sobbing*) Don't do it, Abe, sugar babe. (*She throws herself upon his breast.*)

BUD. (*Reaching towards her*) Seem lak you mought take yo'se'f off'n dat man!

ABE. (*Pulling her arms from around him*) Lemme loose, lemme loose. (*After a moment he throws the stone down*) I ain't going to do nothing. (*He sits down on the log at the left, holding his head in his hands.*)

GOLDIE. (*Bringing her bucket*) Hyuh, eat sump'n, Abe, you feel better. I gut some pie and some cake in heah foh you.

PUNY. (*Stepping back and forth in senseless excitement*) Somebody gwine git kilt at dis heah mess, somebody ——

ABE. (*Pushing GOLDIE away*) I ain't want nothing t'eat, ain't hongry.

LIJE. Bedder eat, Abe. Git yo' stren'th back.

ABE. (*Savagely*) Ain't hongry, I keep telling you. (GOLDIE *falls on her knees beside him and dropping her head in his lap clasps her arms around him.*)

GOLDIE. (*Sobbing softly*) Oh, boy, boy, why dey beat you up so? Whut you do to 'em?

ABE. Fool, fool I is. Crazy, dat's it.

BUD. (*Sharply*) He gi'n Mr. Lonnie and de Colonel back talk. Cain't sass white mens and git 'way wid it. Abe orter know better. (LIJE *wanders over to the right blowing his harp softly and forlornly.*)

PUNY. (*Sitting down on the ground*) Cain't be done, Abe, cain't.

BUD. (*Stripping leaves from a bush and watching GOLDIE as she carries on over ABE*) Hyuh, 'oman, stop dat r'aring. (*Muttering to himself*) Neveh see two bigger fools. (ABE *puts his hands mechanically on GOLDIE's shoulders and begins stroking her.*)

ABE. Stop it, baby. Ain't no use to cry. (PUNY *sits with his mouth open in astonishment watching them.* LIJE

Photo by Maurice Goldberg

THE SCHOOLROOM SCENE FROM "IN ABRAHAM'S BOSOM"

lays himself back on the ground and blows his harp, apparently no longer interested.)

BUD. (*Jealousy rising within him*) Heigh, Goldie, git up from dat man's lap. He ain't keer nothing foh you. (GOLDIE'S *sobs die away and she is quiet*) He say you foolish many time. He look down on you.

GOLDIE. (*Raising her tear-stained face*) How you know? You jealous, Bud Gaskins. He better man dan you. Wuth a whole field full of you. (*Catching* ABE *by the hand and picking up her bucket*) Come on, come on, honey, le's go off dere in de woods and eat our dinner by ourse'fs. Leave dis low-down trash.

BUD. (*Coming up to her*) Hyuh, you stay out'n dat woods wid him, nigger.

ABE. (*Standing up*) Yeh, yeh, I come wid you. (*He moves as one in a dream and reaches out and knocks* BUD *behind him.*)

GOLDIE. (*Her face alight, a sort of reckless and unreal abandonment upon her*) I knows where dere's a cool place under a big tree. And dey's cool green moss dere and soft leaves. Le's go dere, boy. I gwine tend to you and feed you. (*She moves towards the right, leading* ABE *like a child*) We make us a bed dere, honey. (LIJE *sits up watching them*) Us fohgit de 'memb'ance o' all dis trouble. (*A kind of ecstasy breaking in her voice*) Dere de birds sing and we hear de little branch running over de rocks. Cool dere, sweet dere, you kin sleep, honey, rest dere, baby. Yo' mammy, yo' chile gwine love you, make you fohgit.

ABE. (*Wildly*) Yeh, yeh, I come wid you. I don't keer foh nothing, not nothing no mo'. You, des' you'n me.

GOLDIE. Ain't no worl', ain't no Lije and Bud, nobody. Us gwine make us a 'biding place and a pillah under dat

green tree. (*In sweet oblivion*) Feel yo' arms around
me, my lips on yo'n. We go singing up—up to heaben,
honey, togedder—togedder. (*They go off, her voice
gradually dying away like a nun's chant.*)

BUD. (*Breaking a sapling in his grasp*) Gwine off, gwine
off in de woods togedder dere lak hawgs.

PUNY. (*Bounding up, his body shaking in lascivious delight*) I gwine watch 'em—hee—hee —— I gwine
watch 'em.

LIJE. (*Snatching him back*) Bedder stay out'n dat woods.
Abe kill you.

PUNY. (*Standing up by the pine tree*) Kin see 'em, her
still a-leading 'im.

LIJE. (*Standing up and peering off to the right*) Dere on
de cool moss and de sof' leaves.

BUD. (*Stripping the limbs from the top of the broken sapling*) Ain't gwine look. Dey fools, bofe fools. (*Raging out*) Dere she go playing de hawg. Didn't know
she lak dat. (*He sucks in his breath with the sound of
eating something*) Wisht to Gohd I knowed she lak
dat. I de man foh her. Bud Gaskins. I tame her.
Gohddam her, I tame her down and take dat speerit
out'n her. (*He crowds out his chest and walks up and
down.*)

PUNY. (*Grasping* LIJE's *arm*) Cain't hardly see 'em no
mo', kin you?

LIJE. Kin hardly.

BUD. (*His anger and jealousy disappearing in physical emotion and curiosity*) Whah dey now?

LIJE. (*Pointing*) Dere, dere, dey crossing de branch now.

PUNY. (*Breathlessly*) I see 'em. I see 'em. He arm
'round her now, her head on he shoulder. (*He capers
in his excitement*) Lawd, Lawd!

BUD. (*With a loud brutal laugh as he slaps* LIJE *on the back*) On de sof' green moss.

LIJE. (*Laughing back and dragging his harp across his mouth*) Whah de leaves is cool.

PUNY. Cain't see 'em no mo'. (*He whirls about and turns a handspring*) Whoopee, folkses! Gwine run away wid myse'f!

BUD. (*His eyes shining*) Down whah de branch water run. (*He shuffles a jig among the leaves.*)

LIJE. (*Blowing upon his harp*) Singing raht up to heaben! (*He plays more wildly as they all drop into a barbaric dance.*)

PUNY. Heaben!

BUD. Jesus, Lawd, Fadder and Son!

LIJE. (*Singing loudly as they dance*)

> My feets wuh wet wid de sunrise dew
> De mawning stah wuh a witness too.
> 'Way 'way up in de Rock of Ages,
> In God's bosom gwine be my pillah.

(*They gambol, turn and twist, run on all fours, rear themselves up on their haunches, cavort like goats.*)

PUNY. In God's bosom—hanh!

BUD. In who bosom?

LIJE. In who bosom, bubber?

(*A loud halloo comes down from the hill in the rear, unnoticed by them.*)

PUNY. In Goldie's bosom.

BUD and LIJE. Haw-haw-haw! Hee-hee-hee! In God's bosom gwine be my pillah.

(*The halloo is repeated.*)

LIJE. (*Jerking up his head*) Hyuh, dere dat Gabe calling us. Better git, or de Colonel have dat stick on our back. (*They gather up their buckets and axes.* PUNY *clambers up the pine a few feet and drops to the ground.*)

BUD. Kin see?

PUNY. See nothing. Hee-hee!

LIJE. Gut to leave 'em now. Abe ketch it 'g'in don't mind out—he not coming wid us.

BUD. He done foh now. Dat gal gut him hard and fast. (*Snorting scornfully*) Books. Books! Rise 'em up, lak hell. Hunh, he gone to de bottom lak a rock!

LIJE. I done told you. Heart say dis, head say dat. Bad mixtry, bad. Crazy!

PUNY. (*Shouting*) Heigh, you Gabe! Coming! (*They move out at the rear up the hill, singing, laughing and jostling each other.*)

'Way, 'way down by de sweet branch water
In her bosom gwine be he pillah!
Hee-hee—haw—haw!

(*Their loud brutally mocking laughter floats back behind them.*)

CURTAIN

SUGAR CANE

A ONE ACT PLAY OF NEGRO LIFE

By

FRANK H. WILSON

OPPORTUNITY PRIZE PLAY, FIRST DRAMA PRIZE,
1926
*Reprinted by special permission of the author
and Opportunity, Journal of Negro Life*

CHARACTERS

PAUL, an old Negro farmer
MARTHA, his wife
"SUGAR CANE," their daughter
FRED, their son
HOWARD HILL, Sugar Cane's sweetheart
ORA, the baby daughter

Scene: Contemporary Georgia.

SUGAR CANE

Curtain Rises Showing: *Small room in an old-fashioned frame house, the wall hung with cheap wall paper, some of it hanging down in long strips. The wooden floor is covered with a torn and dilapidated rug. In the center of the room stands a small wooden table covered with cheap oilcloth. An old oil lamp sits in the center of table, shedding a faint glow throughout the room, two handmade wooden chairs sit at each end of the table. Back up against the wall, center, is an old couch, with broken springs—hanging up on the wall are several religious pictures and mottoes—over on the left side is an old bureau, cheaply covered and with many trinkets and glasses upon it. Down left front is the door leading into the spare room. Up right rear are steps leading upstairs to the rooms above. Down right the door leads out through the kitchen to the back yard. At the foot of the stairs is a small window, with a broken pane of glass in it. Cheap curtains hang from the top of the window. The whole room gives the appearance of honest, but poor people. There is a small cuspidor down alongside one of the chairs.*

Pause. Sugar *enters from spare room. She is a young dark brown-skinned girl about twenty-three years old, comely and well built. She closes the door quietly, as if not to disturb some one asleep therein; she then moodily crosses the room, and goes out through the kitchen door.*

PAUL *comes down the stairs as* SUGAR *is crossing the room. He is an old-fashioned Negro, about sixty-two years old, with gray beard, eyebrows and hair, walks and moves somewhat feebly from hard work. Watches* SUGAR *as she crosses room and goes out through kitchen.*

MARTHA *enters from kitchen, wiping her hands on her old apron. She is a small dark complexioned old lady of about fifty-five years, with kindly face and disposition.*

PAUL. What's de matter wid Sugar?

MARTHA. (*Coming in*) I doan know, why?

PAUL. She's bin actin' mou'ty funny dese las' few days.

MARTHA. Funny—how?

PAUL. Well, she's walkin' 'roun' hyer lak she's in a trance.

MARTHA. Mebbe she's think' bout dat Howard Hill.

PAUL. (*Angrily coming down from stairs*) Doan mention dat blackguard's name in ma house, I tole yer.

MARTHA. Oh, Paul, 'scuse me. I fergot yo' ain't got no use fer him.

PAUL. (*Coming down*) Ain't got no use fer him, nor fer anybuddy fum up North. (*Pause*) Dat's wot's de matter wid Sugar. Dat's why she's havin dem quiet spells, 'case she's worried 'bout her troubles. (*Going over to chair left of table*) All comes o' yo' lettin' dat Northern nigger stay hyer. I tole yo' I didn't want him in de first place.

MARTHA. (*Pleadingly*) Oh, Paul, be quiet and please doan go over all dat ag'in. I admit it was ma mistake, wot mo kin Ah do?

PAUL. (*Sitting in chair*) I know, but it makes me mad ebery time I think of it.

MARTHA. (*Timidly*) Goin' ter church ter-night?

PAUL. (*Taking out his pipe*) No.

MARTHA. Why not?

PAUL. 'Case I don't feel lak it.

MARTHA. Yo ought ter go ter church mo Paul. Mebbe yo'd feel better.

PAUL. Feel better nothin'. Think I'd go down there among dem ole gossipy an' backbitin' brothers? Dey done scandalize our name all over de town.

MARTHA. No, dey didn't.

PAUL. (*Lighting his pipe*) Doan tell me. (*Taking out another match*) De minnit dat Hill boy started stoppin' hyer dey started talkin' en' w'en he lef' an' dey heard about Sugar's baby, dey talkcd fer sho' den. (*Pause*) I wish yo' had taken ma advice an' not let him stay hyer. But you so hard-headed. Wouldn't lissen ter me.

MARTHA. Sugar says 'twarn't him.

PAUL. Sugar lies, who else could it be?

MARTHA. (*Her feelings hurt, goes back into the kitchen.*)

PAUL. (*Turns, sees that* MARTHA *has walked out on him, spits in cuspidor and grunts*) Humph!

FRED. (*Enters from kitchen. He is a husky young Negro about twenty-four years old. He is dressed in soft blue shirt, open at the throat, blue overalls, tan shoes, and black felt hat*) Hello, pop.

PAUL. (*Grunts*) Umph!

FRED. (*Coming in*) Jist met our fren'—Lee Drayton.

PAUL. Whar?

FRED. Goin' down de road towards his house; gwine ter pay his mother her usual weekly visit I reckon. (*Pause*) He goes away sometime and stays months.

PAUL. I reckon Miss Mary generally knows whar he is.

FRED. No, she don't.

PAUL. How you know?

FRED. She tole me so herse'f, she did an'—— (PAUL *grunts and continues to smoke his pipe.*) It's queer ter me how a good woman lak Miss Mary kin have sich a son.

PAUL. (*Spits again*) Yo des doan understan' him—dat's all.

FRED. How Ahm goin' ter understan' him, w'en his own mother don't?

PAUL. De boy's wile lak all yo' youngsters.

FRED. He's mo' den wile.

PAUL. I know he's a li'l' rough and gruff in his talk.

FRED. An' actions.

PAUL. But wot kin yer 'speck. His ole man befo' him was dat a-way. He ain't no worse den any of de res' ob dese white folks down hyer.

FRED. Oh, yes he is, Pop. Dere's some fine white folks down hyer I know. But Lee Drayton ain't one of em.

PAUL. (*Spits disgustedly*) He may not be all right ter people lak dat Hill boy fum up North,—who doan know how ter act w'en he gits in dis part ob de country, but ter we folks down hyer who understan's dese white folks,—Lee Drayton is all right. (*Puffs on his pipe.*)

FRED. (*Looks at* PAUL *for a minute*) Pop, yo' puts too much faith in dese white folks. (PAUL *gives him an angry look.*)

FRED. (*Taking a seat*) Yo's too willin' ter believe ebery-thing dey say. Yo' seems ter have mo' faith in dem den yo' hab in God.

PAUL. (*Quickly and angrily*) Wot if I has?

FRED. Yer ought ter believe a li'l' mo' in yo' own race—git a li'l' mo' race pride.

PAUL. (*Spits angrily*) Whar'd yo' git all dat foolishness? Fum dat Northern nigger—Hill, I reckon.

FRED. No, pop, I didn't git it fum nobody, but since I bin

gittin' a li'l' older Ahm trying ter think fer mase'f; these white folks bin thinking fer me long enuf.

PAUL. Yes, and if dey hadn't bin thinkin' fer yo' whar would yo' be now—runnin' 'roun' in Africa half naked, an yo' wouldn't knowed B fum bullfrog. (*Pause*) Who's got everything down hyer—white folks, ain' dey?

FRED. (*Reluctantly*) Yes.

PAUL. An who's got nothin'—we has, ain't we?

FRED. (*Shakes his head yes.*)

PAUL. All right—now we wants what de white man's got— or some of it.

FRED. (*Quickly*) We wants our share.

PAUL. (*Settling himself back in chair*) Well, how yo' goin' ter git it? Take it away fum him I 'specks?

FRED. (*Fails to find an answer to this question.*)

PAUL. (*Spits*) Yo' upstart youngsters know so-o-o much an' we ole folks dat libed fer years among dese people doan know nothin'. (*Pause*) If a man's goin' ter fight yo' and he's gotta gun, and yo' ain't got nothin'—what yo' goin' ter do?

FRED. (*Quickly*) Fight him.

PAUL. An' git killed, dat's wot de Indians done w'en de white man come ter dis country—fought him—dat's the reason Indians are so scarce now'days.

FRED. (*Anxiously*) But dey respec' him mo' fo' it.

PAUL. (*Impatiently*) I ain't lookin' fer no respec.' (*Pause*) I'm lookin' fer sumfin' dat's going ter feed me an' my family. (*Pause*) Dis house hyer whar yo' an' Sugar was born an' raised—it's mine ain't it?

FRED. (*Quietly*) Yes, sir.

PAUL. It may not be no palace, but it's *mine* jist de same. (*Points out window*) So is dat patch ob farm land out dere—all mine.   How yo' reckon I got it, by fightin' dese white folks down hyer?   Humph—I guess not.

FRED. But dey thinks dey better den we are, Pop.

PAUL. (*In exasperation*) Wot if dey does!   It ain't goin' ter hurt 'em ter think, is it?   (*Pointing his pipe at him*) As long as I can fool dese white folks outer dere money an' land, by lettin' 'em feel dat dey's better dan I am, dat's wot Ahm goin' ter do.   (*Spits*) Lissen, son—I got money an' I got property.   I could buy an' sell some o' dese white folks 'roun' hyer—but I ain't goin' ter let dem know it.   I could fix dis shack up and live in grand style if I wanted to—But de minnit I did dat dese folks would git curious, and wanter say dat I didn't know ma place, and dat I was tryin' ter act lak white folks—fust thing yo' know I'd have a lot ob trouble on ma han's—an' I couldn't stay hyer,—So I fools 'em.   Ah banks ma money, keeps ma mouth shut, an' makes-believe Ahm a poor ole nigger, and dat dey's de cock o' de walk.   And I kin git dere shirt.   I know 'em. An' I didn't learn dat in no school neither.   I ain't bin livin' in de Southlan' all dese years fer nothin'.

FRED. But, Pop, do you think dat's right ter ——

PAUL. (*Emphatically*) Yes, it's right.   Yo' all talk 'bout race pride, yo'd better get a li'l' race sense.   Dese niggers 'roun' hyer ain't got nothin' ter give yo'—nothin'. (*Imitating*) Niggers talk about "aw dey kain't do nothin'—*nothin'*—white folks got eberything."   Ahm going ter git some of it.

FRED. (*Rises despondently, and goes up to window.*)

PAUL. (*Takes a puff at his pipe*) Yo' bin gittin' all dese low-down notions fum Hill.

FRED. (*Turning quickly*) I ain't got no mo' use fer Hill den yo' has.

PAUL. (*Turning to him*) Stop lyin'. (*Pause.*)

FRED. (*Looks at his dad for a minute and then turns and looks out the window.*)

PAUL. I know wot yer bin doin', yo' bin 'round town shootin' off yo' mouth dat yo' was gittin' tired of de Souf, dat yo' wuz goin' up North ter live so yo' could get a education. Whar else did yo' git dat but fum Hill?

FRED. (*Looking down at* PAUL) Well, I do think I could truly stand a li'l' mo' learnin'—both me an' Sugar.

PAUL. (*Rising*) Well, if you wants learnin' yo'd better git it down hyer, 'case I ain't got 'nothin' fer up North ter do. Dis is ma home whar I wuz bred an' born, an' it's whar I truly wants ter be buried when I die—I doan care if I never see anybuddy fum up North—and if I ever lays ma han's on dat skunk Hill—I'll kill him.

PAUL. (*Stands glaring at* FRED.)

FRED. (*Does not answer.*)

PAUL. (*Exits into kitchen.*)

FRED. (*Takes letter from his pocket, then looks at it.*)

MARTHA. (*Enters from kitchen*) Fred, yo' goin' ter church wit' me ter-night ain't yer?

FRED. (*Still looking at letter*) Yessem.

MARTHA. I kain't git yer father to go.

FRED. I wuz jist tellin' Pop 'bout Lee Drayton.

MARTHA. Wot's the matter wit' him?

FRED. Pop says he's all right.

MARTHA. (*Kindly*) A man wit' sich a fine mother lak Miss Mary, must hab some good in him. Yo' know wot she say de odder day. She say, "Martha, I'm sick an' kain't git about so good, an yo'-all mus' come down an' see me often. We's all brudders and sisters in de sight ob de Lord. We got ter live tergether in Heaven, so we ought well git used ter it down hyer on earth."

FRED. Yeh, I know Miss Mary's all right, but dat ain't her son.

MARTHA. Oh, he's des young.

FRED. Umph! De only one dat seems ter think he's low down is me an' Hill. (*Shows* MARTHA *letter in his hand.*)

MARTHA. Wot's dat?

FRED. Dat's a letter fum Hill.

MARTHA. (*Surprised*) Howard Hill?

FRED. Yes, I got it yestiddy. He sent it ter me sayin' he wuz comin' down hyer ter make a surprise visit, an' ter see dat Sugar wuz home. I bin holdin' it secret, scared ter say anything. Yo' know how Pop is wid Hill.

MARTHA. Yes, Lord doan let him see dat—w'en is he comin'?

FRED. Ter-day I think. (*Looks at letter*) Yes, Sunday.

MARTHA. Mebbe he's comin' back ter (*Hesitates*) marry Sugar.

FRED. Do you know, Mom, I ought ter hate dat boy, but I don't.

MARTHA. (*Looking apprehensively toward kitchen*) I lak him, Fred. (*Lowers her voice*) He didn't do 'zactly right by Sugar w'en he ran off dat a-way. But we all makes mistakes.

FRED. I lak him, 'case he's got learnin'. But I wonder why Sugar protects him?

MARTHA. 'Case she loves him.

FRED. Wot do you think 'bout it?

MARTHA. He's de father ob Sugar's chile, all right. But Sugar's afraid ter admit it, for fear I'll git down on him. She knows her dad's on him already.

(SUGAR *enters from kitchen door*)

MARTHA. Whar's yo' father?

SUGAR. Sittin' out in de yard.

MARTHA. He's kinder cranky dis evening.

SUGAR. He's cranky every evenin'.

MARTHA. Fred, son, get dressed fer church.

FRED. Yessem. (FRED *goes upstairs.*)

MARTHA. (*Looks at* SUGAR *a minute, then speaks*) Fred jist got a letter.

SUGAR. From who?

MARTHA. Howard Hill.

SUGAR. (*Gives a slight start*) Wot does he say?

MARTHA. Fred said dat he wanted it kept fum yo'—but Ah reckon I'd better tell you.

SUGAR. Wanted wot kept from me?

MARTHA. The fac' dat he wuz comin' down hyer.

SUGAR. (*Greatly alarmed*) What?

MARTHA. Yes.

SUGAR. Wot's he comin' down hyer fo'?

MARTHA. Ter see yo'.

(SUGAR *stands in a daze*)

MARTHA. Ah'm frightened stiff. Yo' father threatened ter kill him on sight; now wot are we gwine ter do?

SUGAR. (*As if in a daze*) W'en is he comin'?

MARTHA. Ter-day—or ter-night de letter said. (*Calls*) Fred!

SUGAR. (*Quickly*) Doan call him.

FRED. What is it, Mom?

SUGAR. (*In a whisper*) Doan call him.

MARTHA. (*Looking at* SUGAR) Ne'mine gettin' ready fer church.

SUGAR. Wot shall I do?

MARTHA. Fergive him, Sugar. I'm sho' he'll make yo' a fine husband.

SUGAR. (*Almost to herself*) I wonder if he'll ever forgive me?

MARTHA. Fergive you'? It's him needs the forgivin'. Yo' ain't done nothin'.

SUGAR. Yes, I have.

MARTHA. Wot have yo' done?

SUGAR. (*Her voice choking with emotion*) I—I——

FRED. (*Coming downstairs, dressed for church*) Ready for church, Mom?

MARTHA. Yes, an' you had better come along, Sugar. (FRED *goes up to window and looks out.*)

MARTHA. Whar's Ora?

SUGAR. (*Points to door left.*)

MARTHA. Asleep?

SUGAR. Yessem.

MARTHA. She'll sleep until we get back. Come on.

SUGAR. I'm afraid dey church bell might frighten her. It's so near. When it rings she always wakes up. I'm goin' ter stay hyer.

FRED. (*To* MARTHA) Did yo' tell her?

MARTHA. Yes,—I thought it would make her feel kinder glad, but she's a gittin' scart.

SUGAR. Di'n yo' say dat Pop wuz goin' ter kill Howard if he came down hyer?

MARTHA. He'll be glad enuf ter see de man come back if he does de right thing.

SUGAR. I'm goin' ter stay hyer an' meet him.

FRED. Church time, Mom.

MARTHA. Well, if yo' won' go ter church, I'm goin' ter pray fer yo' both. Yo' and yo' father's goin' ter let people's tongues keep yo' outer heaven. (*Starts for door.*)

FRED. (*Goes out kitchen door.*)

SUGAR. (*Quickly*) Mom!

MARTHA. (*Stopping*) Wot's de matter?

SUGAR. Let Fred go ter church alone. I wanter talk ter ye.

MARTHA. (*Yelling off to* FRED) Fred!

FRED. (*Voice off*) Ma'm?

MARTHA. Go 'long ter church. I'll be there presently.

SUGAR. (*Stands looking piteously at* MARTHA.)

MARTHA. (*Coming back*) Talk fas'. I doan wanner miss dat sermon. Go ahead and talk.

SUGAR. (*Goes over, puts her arms about* MARTHA'S *neck and starts crying.*)

MARTHA. (*Caressing her*) Wot is it, Sugar?

SUGAR. Howard's comin'.

MARTHA. I know dat.

SUGAR. (*Now holding down her head*) But there is something else ye don't know.

MARTHA. (*Pointing toward room*) I know too much already.

SUGAR. No, Mom ——

MARTHA. Wot?

SUGAR. Dat ain't his chile.

MARTHA. Yo' still sticks ter dat story w'en we knows different?

SUGAR. Yo' de onley one I can trust, Mom. I've got ter tell yo' dis.

MARTHA. Tell me de truf den.

SUGAR. It wasn't Howard.

MARTHA. I ain't believin' you. Ain't it enuf ter bring disgrace down on your poor ole mother and father!

SUGAR. (*Goes over to chair, sits down and weeps.*)

MARTHA. (*Her heart softening*) Who's de guilty one, Sugar? Tell me. (*Goes over to her*) I laked Howard, and I wuz willin' ter stand fer dis, but fum no odder man livin'.   Tell me who de scamp wuz so I kin put him in jail.

SUGAR. (*Without looking up*) Lee Drayton.   (*Pause.*)

MARTHA. (*Stands as if petrified.*)

SUGAR. (*Sits afraid to move.*)

MARTHA. Wot's dat yo' said 'bout Lee Drayton?

SUGAR. (*Speaking slowly*) Lee Drayton is the father.

MARTHA. (*Frightened*) Stop, gal, shut yo' mout' ——

SUGAR. It's the truth, Mom.

MARTHA. How—w'en did it ——

SUGAR. W'en you sent me down there with Miss Mary's clothes ——

MARTHA. (*Forcefully*) I doan believe it.

SUGAR. He wouldn' let me go! He wouldn' let me go—he threatened the whole family in case I tole anybuddy, he said he'd bring the clan down on us—I feared fer yo', Pop, an' Fred—I didn't dare tell you the truth 'bout who it wuz.

MARTHA. (*Sinks helplessly in chair*) If you had oney spoken an' tole me ——

SUGAR. I wuz afraid, I wanted ter tell you dat Howard wuz innocent; but you might question me too close, and fine out the truth—Fred's so hot headed —— Wot am I going ter do? —— Howard's comin' ——

MARTHA. (*After thinking a minute*) I doan know—I'm goin' ter church, an' do the oney thing I kin do—pray— yo'd better come along wid us ——

PAUL. (*Enters from kitchen, goes toward stairs, stops and looks at them both*) Wot's the matter, you-all ain't gwine ter church?

MARTHA. Yes—come on, Sugar.

SUGAR. (*Shakes her head no.*)

SUGAR CANE 179

PAUL. (*Gives* SUGAR *a curious glance, then goes upstairs, and off.*)

MARTHA. (*Looks at* SUGAR—*tries to speak, words failing her, she goes on out.*)

SUGAR. (*Looks toward bedroom apparently listening, then comes slowly down and sits in chair.*) (*Pause.*)

HOWARD. (*Peeks in through window. He looks about room until he spies* SUGAR. *He then smiles, and leaves the window quietly.*)

SUGAR. (*Buries her head in her arms, leans on table, and groans.*)

HOWARD. (*Enters kitchen door quietly. He is a fine-looking, well-dressed young Negro about twenty-four years old, speaks with a clean and pure diction. He steals softly toward* SUGAR. *His straw hat accidentally drops from his hand.*)

SUGAR. (*Turns to him with a quick start.*)

HOWARD. (*Stands looking at her, smiling.*)

SUGAR. (*Rises from the chair, and quickly backs around to the other side of the table.*)

HOWARD. Celia—I wanted to surprise you. I sent word to your brother Fred.

SUGAR. (*Stands with a frightened look, staring at him.*)

HOWARD. (*Pauses, noticing her actions*) Aren't you glad to see me?

SUGAR. (*Smiling sickily*) Yes, Howard ——

HOWARD. You don't look it ——

SUGAR. (*Looks fearfully toward stairs*) Let's get outside. (*Starts toward kitchen door.*)

HOWARD. (*Unable to restrain himself, takes her in his arms*) Celia, I told you I'd come back after I graduated. Three years is a long time—but I'm happy now.

SUGAR. (*Struggles free from his grasp*) Please, Howard—don't—— (*Staggers weakly back against table.*)

HOWARD. (*Astonished*) Celia——

SUGAR. (*Leans heavily against table.*) (*Church bell is heard tolling near by.*)

SUGAR. (*A look of fear coming to her face, stares at bedroom.*)

HOWARD. (*Stands nonplussed.*)

ORA. (*Voice heard off in bedroom*) Mama!—Mama!

HOWARD. (*Looks toward bedroom door.*)

ORA. (*Enters quickly in her nightdress. She is a little brown baby, about three years old*) Mama!—I 'fraid—— (*Runs to* SUGAR *holding up her arms to be taken up.*)

HOWARD. (*Looks from* SUGAR *to* ORA.)

SUGAR. (*Frightened, holds baby close to her side.*)

HOWARD. Who—who is this——

SUGAR. (*Struggling to suppress her emotions, picks* ORA *up in her arms*) My baby!

HOWARD. (*Stands dazed at this confession.*) (*Pause.*)

PAUL. (*Comes quietly downstairs—sees Howard—a look of intense hatred comes to his face. His eyes riveted on Howard, he goes back stealthily upstairs again.*)

HOWARD. You—tell me this is your child?

PAUL. (*Comes downstairs quickly, looking at* HOWARD. *He has a shotgun in his hand*) Yo' dirty varmint! (*Points gun at* HOWARD)

SUGAR. (*Screams and rushes in between them holding* ORA *in her arms*)

PAUL. (*Angrily*) Git one side, gal, till I blow this snake ter hell——

SUGAR. No, Pop.

PAUL. (*Coming down with gun raised*) One side I tell you, you and his brat.

HOWARD. (*Steps out from behind* SUGAR)

SUGAR. (*Quickly steps in front of him*) No, Pop, you wrong; the chile ain't his, it's Lee Drayton's ——

PAUL. Wot ——

HOWARD. (*Looks at her at the name of* LEE DRAYTON)

SUGAR. Ora is Lee Drayton's chile.

PAUL. Yer lie, gal —— What are yer tryin' ter do, save him?—Come out fum behind there, nigger ——

HOWARD. Mr. Cain ——

PAUL. Mister nothin'—Sugar, move I tell yer.

SUGAR. (*Pleading*) No, Pop,—it wuz Lee Drayton, I tell yo' ——

HOWARD. (*To* SUGAR) Do you mean to tell me that this is—is —— (*Points at* ORA)

SUGAR. Yes, Howard, I ——

HOWARD. I'll get him—— (*Darts quickly out of room*)

SUGAR. (*Calling after him*) Howard!

PAUL. Runnin' away, eh—Well, I'll git him fo' he gits outer town ——

SUGAR. Pop ——

PAUL. (*Angrily*) Git outer ma sight, 'fo' I does yo' bof harm.

SUGAR. (*Crying, puts* ORA *in the bedroom, fearing* PAUL *in his frenzy might harm her. She locks the door taking the key herself.*)

PAUL. It ain't enough fer yo' ter disgrace me with that baby, but now yo' got that no 'count fool hangin' round. Well, he'll never go North agin' meddlin with us. I'll— Well maybe he'll git himself killed by somebody else! Serve him right!

(PAUL *fumes about the room aimlessly, while* SUGAR *wrings her hands hysterically.* SUGAR *finally goes out by the back-door looking for* HOWARD. *Presently* HOWARD *re-*

enters, SUGAR *clinging frantically to his left arm. In his right, he brandishes a revolver.* PAUL, *seeing this, lowers his gun which he has started to raise and points toward* HOWARD.)

HOWARD. Well, I got him!

PAUL. (*Sneering*) Got who?

SUGAR. You don't mean to say you killed him, Howard, do you?

HOWARD. Well, I dunno. I met him just as he was coming out, and he must have guessed I was after him. He ran back for this. (*Brandishes the revolver.*) But I cornered him in the kitchen, and——

SUGAR. (*Prayerfully*) Thank God! And what happened?

HOWARD. Dunno, exactly. I didn't shoot him—but he's on the kitchen-floor, and I don't expect there's much to him after the tussle we had. I'm done up myself.

PAUL. You mean to stand there an' tell me you done killed Lee Drayton, yer Northern fool! Yer know what that means, don't yer?

HOWARD. (*Starts to speak. There is a loud roar and a commotion heard from the direction of* DRAYTON'S *house. There is the noise of distant shouting and running about.*)

SUGAR. (*In a frenzy*) Oh, they're coming. The mob! They're coming after us! (*She snatches her father's gun from his hands*)

PAUL (*Quickly recovering himself*) Gimme ma gun—— You damned Northern nigger, come down here makin' trouble fer us—

HOWARD. (*Shouting to* SUGAR) Don't! (*Reaches for the shot-gun, and takes it*) Now, Mr. Cain, we've all got to face it. I'm going to fight—are you fighting with me or against me? (PAUL *is speechless with rage and*

fear.) Well, you better defend your family like a man,
—they won't be asking questions likely.

PAUL. (*In temper*) I'm aginst yo', tooth an' toe nail!
This gal's lyin' ter pertect yo', dat's all. An' now, look
whut yo' done. I opened ma door ter yo' befo' and yo'
done me dirt —— an' now yer come down hyer agin
an' stirred up dese white folks. Git outer mah house!

HOWARD. (*Tensely*) You try and put me out. (PAUL *turns
menacingly toward* SUGAR *for a moment until he sees he
is powerless in the situation. He then starts to go out.
HOWARD halts him with a threatening gesture, as the
noise outside grows louder. A red glow shines in
through the open window.* PAUL *noticing it, goes
quickly to look out*)

PAUL. (*Raising his hands in consternation and shouting*)
Fire! Miss Mary's house is on fire! (*Rushing toward*
HOWARD) You varmin, yo' done it!

SUGAR. (*In alarm*) Miss Mary's house on fire? (*She
points out the window, and* HOWARD, *in apparent bewilderment crosses over, watching* PAUL *carefully as
he does so*) I don't see an end to all this—I don't
know what ——

MARTHA. (*Coming in in the greatest excitement*) Paul!
Paul! Miss Mary's house is on fire!

PAUL. I know it —— and I know more than that, too.

MARTHA. (*Paying him no attention*) Fred's run down to
help Miss Mary ——

PAUL *and* SUGAR. Wot?

MARTHA. We saw the blaze fum de church. Fred rushed
right on down there (*Crying*) Oh, poor Miss Mary!
Wot can we do?

SUGAR. They'll kill him.

MARTHA. Kill who?

SUGAR. Fred. (MARTHA *raises her hands in bewilderment*)

PAUL. (*Pointing at* HOWARD) This man killed Lee Drayton and then sot his house a-fire. That's wot! And they'll get our boy for it! (*Rushes out as* HOWARD *is off his guard in his dilemma*)

HOWARD. I don't set no houses on fire. But I'm a man and I protect myself! (*A look of bewilderment comes over him and he leans out of the window. As he looks back, he is still evidently puzzled.*) We broke pretty much everything there was in the kitchen, but I don't just see how— Well, one thing (*As he tries to console the two women*) it doesn't matter much now what happens.

FRED. (*Voice off*) Mom! Mom!—(*In a little, he enters, followed by* PAUL) Mom!

MARTHA. Yes, sonny.

SUGAR. (*Somewhat relieved*) It's Fred ——

FRED. (*Rushes in—his clothes quite disheveled, his hands out*) Miss Mary's safe, Mom, Miss Mary's safe —— She wasn't hurt none—des frightened to death. She's carryin' on fearful 'bout Lee.

PAUL. Yas, I guess so. Poor woman, I'm sorry fo' her— an' that mo' an' I am fo' some other folks round hyeh.

MARTHA. (*Sees his hand*) Fred—son, yo's hurt ——

FRED. Just cut a li'l fum de winder-pane. (*Turns and sees* HILL) Oh, hello, Hill. Whyn't yer come down ——

PAUL. Yas, ask him. Ask the blasted murderer why he didn't ——(*His speech is cut short by a threat from* HOWARD'S *gun.*)

HOWARD. (*To* FRED) Are they coming? (*Starts to barricade the door*) I can hear them but I can't see them.

FRED. Oh, they're out back where Lee's body is.

HOWARD. Lee's body! (*Catching himself*) Yes, that's it. But wasn't there a gang coming down here?

FRED. (*Sitting in a chair while his mother dresses his hand*) No. Wot fer? They're too busy enough up there. The fire ain't quite out yit, an' they've sent for the sheriff.

PAUL. I jes' bet they have. (*Sneering*)

HOWARD. (*Directly to* FRED) Is Drayton living—can he speak?

FRED. Deadr'n a rabbit. Mut a' benn killed when the stove exploded, fo' the fyeh got to him good. But he's burnt too. I ain't so soory fer him, but I sho' am fo' Miss Mary. I'm glad she's safe.

HOWARD. Did you say he was dead, you sure?

FRED. Didn't I jes' tell you'? But I'm glad 'twas him had the accident 'stid o' Miss Mary. 'Twarn't like him to be at no cook-stove nohow. 'Spose he didn't know much about working it.

PAUL. He warn't at no cook-stove either. Lee Drayton was killed.

FRED. I 'clare you-all seem gone silly with the fuss. Sho' Lee Drayton's killed. Didn't I jes' tell you? But Miss Mary's safe all right, 'cept for grievin'.

HOWARD. (*Relieved but immediately tense again as he realizes the situation. He goes almost stealthily up to* PAUL, *covering him discreetly on the side away from* FRED *and* MARTHA.) Too bad Lee Drayton was killed —(*Gasps*) No, I don't mean that either,—but I mean it's too bad it had to happen. (*Glaring at* PAUL, *who returns his look menacingly*) You shut up. And stay shut up, if you know what's good for yourself and your family —— SUGAR, come here! (SUGAR *crosses to him in a daze. He kisses her.* PAUL *turns in aversion. He goes to the window in a sulky, depressed, but astonished manner and stands looking out.*) Well, I didn't come down here expecting trouble, and I don't want any either. I came down to marry SUGAR, and I'm going to marry SUGAR. (*They all register differently;* SUGAR, *amazed delight;* FRED, *gruff surprise;* MARTHA, *dismay;* PAUL, *sullen indifference.*)

MARTHA. Wait a minute, Howard. (*She rushes to* SUGAR) I would be happy, Mr. Hill, but you'd better have a little time to talk to Sugar 'bout it; you mought want a little time to—to talk.

SUGAR. HOWARD knows, Mom. 'Bout Ora. But—it's all right, I guess.

HOWARD. Yes, Sugar,—after what's just happened.

SUGAR. (*After a wild hug to* MARTHA, *rushes over to her father*) Pop! You see ——

PAUL. Don't bother me, gal! I tell yer, don't bother me —— I hope's you-all goes Nawth where you b'long!

CURTAIN

'CRUITER

A ONE ACT PLAY

By

JOHN MATHEUS

OPPORTUNITY PRIZE PLAY, DRAMA PRIZE, 1926

*Reprinted by special permission of the author
and Opportunity, Journal of Negro Life*

CHARACTERS

GRANNY, aged seventy-seven, a typical Negro "Mammy"
SONNY, her grandson, aged twenty-three
SISSY, his wife, aged twenty
A WHITE MAN, a recruiting agent for a Northern munitions
    factory

Scene: A Farm Cottage in Lower Georgia.
Time: Just after the entry of the United States into the
    World War.

'CRUITER

EARLY MORNING *and Spring, 1918, in lower Georgia. The rising of the curtain reveals the large room of a Negro cabin. The walls are the reverse of the outside weatherboarding. A kerosene lamp is on a shelf. At the end of the room looking toward the audience is a door leading to a bedroom, where the starchy whiteness of a well-made bed is visible. In front of the spectators, at the rear of the room, is a window without glass, half-closed by a heavy wooden shutter. Four feet from the window is a door, wide open, leading to a garden. Rows of collards are seen, an old hoe, and in the background a path to the big road.*

On the right is a wide, old-fashioned fireplace, where a big pine log makes a smoldering blaze. GRANNY, *her head swathed in a blue bandana, is bending over the fire, stirring the contents of a huge iron kettle. In the center of the room is a rough table. A hunk of salt pork is on the table and a rusty knife. Under the window is another table supporting a fifteen quart galvanized iron bucket. A gourd dipper is hanging on the wall between the window and the door. Under the gourd a tin washpan is suspended. Below the basin a box in which oranges have been crated. A backless chair is under the center table. A mongrel dog is curled under it.*

GRANNY. (*With her profile to the audience, stirring the kettle and singing*)

    Nobody knows de trouble Ah've seen,

    Nobody knows but Jesus;

    Nobody knows de trouble Ah've seen—

(*Stopping abruptly*) —Ah mus' put some mo' watah to dese plague-taked grits. (*Walks to the water bucket, takes down the gourd dipper and fills it with water. Returning to the kettle she slowly pours in the water, stirring as she pours and singing.*)

"Nobody knows de trouble Ah've seen"—dah now!

(*Hobbles to the open door and looks across the big road toward the east*) 'Pears like Sonny and Sissy ought to be hyar. It is (*Squinting at the sun*) it's mighty nigh onto six o'clock. (*A rooster crows lustily beyond the door. She claps her hands and stamps her feet*)—Skat! Skat, sir. Yo' honery rascal—bringin' me company so early in the mornin'. Ah ain't wantin' to see nobody wid all Ah got tuh do. (*A mocking bird sings.*) Jes' listen tuh dat bird. Hallelujah! Praise de Lam'. (*Sings*)

    Oh, when de world's on fiah,

    Ah wants God's bosom

    Fo' mah piller.

(*Goes to the table in the center of the room and begins to slice the bacon*) "Fo' mah piller." (*Voice is heard outside*)

SONNY. Whoa, mule, whoa, Ah say.

GRANNY. (*Putting the bacon in a large iron spider*) Ah knowed dey'd be a-gwine fum de field. (*Sound of two pairs of shoes is heard; the heavy tread of Sonny, the lighter tread of Sissy*)

SONNY. (*Wearing brogans and overalls*) Mo'in', Granny. Dat bacon sho' smells good.

SISSY. (*Enters, wearing a blue calico wrapper*) How yo' feelin', Granny?

GRANNY. Ah ain't feelin' so peart dis mo'in'. Mus' be needin' some spring tonic.

SONNY. (*Taking down the washpan and dipping water from the bucket into the pan*) Well, us done planted a haf'n acre co'n. (*Washing his face vigorously*) Ah don't know whut Ah'm goin' to do 'bout de cotton dis yeah, ef Ah don't go tuh wah.

SISSY. (*Dropping down in the doorsill*) Phew! Mah back is sho' breakin'—stoopin' an' stoopin', drappin' dat co'n.

GRANNY. Well, yo' know yo' po' pappy allus use tuh put in de cotton tuh pay Mistah Bob fo' he's rations fum de Commissary.

SONNY. But dere warn't nary a pesky ole weevil then neither. 'Sides Mistah Bob done tol' me de guv'ment wanted somethin' t'eat. Say dat de Germans ah goin' to sta've us out an' we mus' plant co'n an' 'taters an' sich. He lows, too, Ah got tuh gi' 'em all us maks dis yeah, 'scusin' ouh keep, tuh he'p him fo' not sendin' me to camp.

GRANNY. How come? He ain't no sheriff.

SONNY. Don't kere, he somethin' t'other wif dis here Draftin' Bo'd. Yo know dey done sent off Aunt Ca'line's crazy Jim?

GRANNY. Mah Jesus! Mah Jesus! Yo'se all Ah's lef', Sonny. Gi' it tuh him. Yo' sho'll git kilt ef yo' has to go off fightin'; like yo' gran'pappy bruder, Samuel, was kilt, when he jined de Yankee Army.

SONNY. But 'tain't his'n an' Ah jest as leef die a fightin'
dan stay heah an' tek his sass an 'uptiness an' gi' him all
Ah mak, lak Ah was on de chain gang.

SISSY. (*Coming in from the doorsill and throwing out the
dirty water in the basin*) Sonny, Sonny, don't yo' know
dese hyar whi' fo'ks?

SONNY. (*Wiping his hands on his overalls*) Don't Ah know
'em? Co'se Ah knows 'em. When Ah was in town
Sat'day didn't Ah see Mistah Bob 'sputin' wif ol' Judge
Wiley. Didn't Ah heah him say dis wah was raisin'
hell wid his business, takin' all de niggahs fum de plan-
tations?

GRANNY. Ah knowed dis here disturbance was comin', 'cause
Ah seed a light in de sky eb'ry night dis week.

SISSY. (*Washing her hands and wiping them on her dress*)
Where's dey takin' 'em to, Sonny? Do yo' think dey
goin' to take yo'?

SONNY. How does Ah know? Whatevah whi' fo'ks wants
o' we-all, we-all jes' nacherly got tuh do, Ah spose, but
Ah ain't ter gwine tuh give Mistah Bob all my wuk an'
Sissy's fo' tuh keep me out a wah. Ah ain't skeered.

GRANNY. Boy, yo' don't know whut yo' talkin' 'bout. Ah
done seed one wah. Men kilt, heads shot off—all de
whi' fo'ks in dey big houses, de wimmins, cryin' dey
eyes out an' ol' Gen'ral Sherman shootin' an' sottin'
on fiah evahthing waht 'ud bu'n. (*Mechanically takes
the spider off the fire, then the kettle of grits, dishing
up both on a large, heavy crockery platter*)

SISSY. (*Looking at* GRANNY *with tenderness. She and
SONNY exchange glances, showing appreciation of her.*)
Heah, Granny, lemme he'p yo' fix breakfas'.

GRANNY. Go 'way chile. Yo' got a heap to do he'pin'
Sonny all day in de field

SISSY. Oh, that ain't nothin'. (*Pulling out the backless chair, then bringing up the orange box and turning it lengthwise so that she and* SONNY *can sit upon it*)

SONNY. (*Patting* SISSY's *hand*) Po' chile, Ah ain't gwine to have yo' wukin' dis er-way. 'Tain't right.

SISSY. Hush, chile, Granny's askin' de blessin'.

GRANNY. (*Bowing her head*) Bress dis food we'se 'bout tuh receive fo' Christ's sake. Amen. (*She serves their plates generously of the bacon and grits and some gravy made with the bacon.*)

SONNY. (*Eating with his knife*) Er, ah, Granny—

GRANNY. Sonny, de co'n meal's 'bout gone. Dere's enough fo' co'npone to-day.

SONNY. (*Laying down his knife*) Sissy, don't lemme fergit to take some co'n meal when Ah goes tuh town to-morrow, Sat'day, ef us is heah.

SISSY. Ef us is heah? Whut yo' mean, Sonny?

GRANNY. He mean ef de Lawd's willin'. How come, chile yo' don't tek Him into yo' plannin'?

SONNY. (*Absent-mindedly*) No, Granny, Ah means jes' whut Ah say, ef all o' us is heah.

SISSY AND GRANNY. (*Looking at* SONNY *in amazement*) Wha' we gwine tuh be?

SONNY. (*Hangin' his head*) Ah don't know how to tell yo' 'bout it. Ah been a-thinkin' an' a-plannin' an' skeered to let on.

SISSY. (*Impatiently*) Whut's yo' talkin' bout?

SONNY. (*Doggedly*) Ah'm talkin' 'bout leavin' heah.

GRANNY. How we goin' tuh leave? Wha' to? Hit teks heaps o' money to git away.

SONNY. Yo' don't have tuh have no money, no nuthin'. Jes' git away.

SISSY. (*Incredulous*) How?

GRANNY. What's ailin' yo' boy?

SONNY. When Ah was in town las' Sat'day a whi' man done tol' me he was lookin' fo' wukers.

GRANNY. Whut whi' man?

SONNY. He said he was a 'cruiter. Lots a fo'ks ah talkin' 'bout him. Yo' all out heah in de country, yo' don't know nothin' 'bout whut's goin' on. Ah'm tellin' yo'. He sez tuh me ez Ah was standin' in de Gen'ral Sto', kin' o' whisperin' lak: "Do yo' wan' tuh mek some money?"

GRANNY. Be keerful o' dese heady fo'ks. Dey ain't out fuh no good.

SONNY. But, Granny, he talked hones'.

GRANNY. Ah know dey ain't no mo' wuk roun' heah dan whut we all is doin'.

SONNY. But dis ain' 'round heah.

SISSY. Wha' is ut, Sonny?

SONNY. Up No'th.

SISSY. (*Lighting up*) Up No'th!

GRANNY. (*With scorn*) UP NO'TH!

SONNY. (*Bubbling with enthusiasm*) Yes. Up No'th—wha' we kin be treated lak fo'ks. He told me he would tek us all, tek us an' put us on de train at River Station below town, 'cause a deputy sheriff done 'rested a pa'cel o' niggahs, whut was tryin' tuh follow some other 'cruiter.

SISSY. Wha' he now? When could he come?

SONNY. He say he wus comin' tuh see 'bout ut Friday, to-day. (*With hesitation*) Dat's why Ah had to tell yo' all.

GRANNY. Up No'th? Sonny, dey tell me it's too col' up No'th.

SONNY. No, Granny, de 'cruiter say us kin live ez wa'm ez

'CRUITER

down heah—houses all het by steam. An' Sissy won't
have to wuk in no fields neither, ner yo'.

GRANNY. But Ah done been down heah seventy-seven yeahs.

SONNY. (*Triumphantly*) But, Granny, Ah won't have tuh
leave yo' tuh fight de wa' 'gin dem Germans.

GRANNY. Who say so?

SONNY. De 'cruiter.

GRANNY. How he know?

SONNY. Oh—Ah jes' knows he knows. He sounds lak it
when he talks.

SISSY. Sonny, why wouldn't yo' have to go tuh wa'?

SONNY. He say somethin' Ah don't quite git de meanin'
ob, but Ah 'membahs dis. He say Ah could wuk in
some kin' o' a—a 'nition factory, wha' dey meks guns
an' things, tuh fight de Germans. Dat's why Ah
wouldn't have to go.

GRANNY. (*Looking off into space and tapping her foot
slowly*) But yo' can't believe dese whi' fo'ks. Dey're
sich liars.

SONNY. But he's tellin' de troof.

SISSY. Ah hope he's tellin' de troof.

SONNY. (*Emphatically*) He *is*. He's talkin' sense.

GRANNY. Eat yo' breakfus', chillun. Hit's gittin' col'. 'Spec
yo'll nebbah heah any mo' fum dat 'cruiter. (*They begin to eat.* GRANNY *gets up to get some hot grits, carrying the pot around and replenishing each plate.*)

SONNY. (*His mouth full*) We wuk—wuk—wuk. Whut
does us git fo' ut? Ouah victuals an' keep. De mules
git dat. We ain't no bettern de mules down heah.

GRANNY. Yo' ain't seen no slavery days, Sonny.

SONNY. Why, slavery days ah right heah now.

GRANNY. Dey can't sell yo'.

SONNY. But dey kin buy us. Ole Mistah Bob thinks he's

done bought us. Dey put bloodhounds on some po'
niggah who was tryin' tuh leave ol' man Popperil's plantation. Whut's dat but slavery?

SISSY. But, Sonny, Lincum done sot us free. Didn't he,
Granny?

GRANNY. 'Course he did. Sonny know dat.

SONNY. He ain't sot me free. (*An automobile horn is
heard at a distance.*)

SONNY. (*Jumping from the orange crate and speaking joyfully*) Dere now. Whut did Ah say? Ah bet dat's him,
de 'cruiter.

GRANNY. Comin' on Friday. No day to mek new business
on Friday. Bad luck's bound to follow yo'.

SISSY. 'Pears lak tuh me bad luck's been follering us. (*The
horn sounds near. They all go to the door to look.*)
There 'tis, comin' down de road lickity-split.

SONNY. Sho' nuf! Sissy, da hit is, an' hit sho' looks lak de
'cruiter's cah.

GRANNY. Looks say nuthin'.

SONNY. See. He's stoppin' right by ouah place.

SISSY. Sho' is. (*A brisk voice is heard*) Hey there!—
(*Steps sound. The* WHITE MAN *is seen coming down
the path. He stops in front of the open door, hat on
and wearing gloves. He talks rapidly and with finality.*)

THE WHITE MAN. This woman your wife?

SONNY. Yas, this is her, Mr. 'Cruiter, an' hyah is mah
Granny. (GRANNY *nods her head coldly*)

THE WHITE MAN. Well, everything is ready. I came
through the country early this morning to avoid other
cars on the road. If you say the word I will be back
here after you about eleven o'clock to-night. Don't
miss this opportunity, folks.

GRANNY. Yo' don't know whut yo're axin', Mistah 'Cruiter.

THE WHITE MAN. Why, Missus, I am giving this boy a chance to get out, to be a man, like anybody else, make plenty money and have time to enjoy it. (*Turning to* SISSY) What do you say? Don't you want to live like a lady and wear fine clothes?

SISSY. (*Grinning bashfully*) Yas, sir.

SONNY. 'Course, Mr. 'Cruiter, Ah sho' wants tuh go.

THE WHITE MAN. You know there are many jumping at the chance.

GRANNY. Honey, yo' can't tell him now. Whut yo' gwine tuh do wif yo' things?

SONNY. Us ain't got nothin' nohow, Granny.

THE WHITE MAN. (*Looking at his watch*) Well, I must hurry. Tell you what I'll do. I have to come down the road to-night anyway as far as the adjoining plantation.

SISSY. (*Turning to* GRANNY) Mistah Popperil's place.

THE WHITE MAN. I'll blow the horn three times. If you want to come I'll take you. Don't miss this chance of your lifetime. Good wages, transportation to Detroit straight, a good job waiting for you and freedom. (*He leaves hastily.*)

GRANNY. (*Sinks down on the steps.*) Huh! (SISSY *looks at* SONNY *expectantly.* SONNY *stands undecided, scratching his head. The automobile is heard leaving in the distance, down the big road.*)

GRANNY. (*Singing*)
Nobody knows de trouble Ah've seen,
Nobody knows but Jesus.
(SISSY *and* SONNY *stand looking on the ground.*)
'Twon't be right fo' tuh run dat er-way—widout tellin' nobody. 'Tain't Christian, Sonny.

SONNY. Ah ain't stud'in' 'bout Christian.

GRANNY. Yo' talk lak a po' sinnah, boy.

SISSY. Well, Granny, let us try it. Come on.

GRANNY. Ef we leave dis place dis a-way, we dasn't come back, even ef yo' didn't lak it.

SONNY. Ah wish Ah knowed whut tuh do.

GRANNY. Yo' ain't got no faith, son. Yo' ought tuh trust God, lak us did way back dar in slavery days. An' He heard ouah prayahs.

SISSY. Sonny prays, Granny.

SONNY. But Ah neveh gits no answer.

SISSY. Mebbe dis is an answer.

SONNY. (*Looking at the heavens*) De sun's risin'. Even ef we go we got tuh keep on wukin' to-day, 'cause ol' Mistah Bob's liable to come heah any time.

GRANNY. Sonny, Sissy, Ah can't leave dis place. Why, bress me, my mammy's died heah, ol' Missus is buried heah, yo' gran'daddy crossed ovah Jordan in dis ve'y house, yo' own po' mammy, atter yo' worthless pappy was kilt in de cotton mill, died heah too. Ah'm too puny to leave heah now, too far gone mahself.

SONNY. Granny, ain't Ah allus wuked and he'p to tek kere o' yo' evah sence Ah been big enough to hoe a row?

GRANNY. Yo' has been a mighty dutiful chile, Sonny. Ah ain't sayin' nuttin' 'gin yo' honey. Ah ain't wantin' tuh stan' in yo' light. But Ah can't he'p ut. Ah can't beah tuh leave heah, wha all mah fo'ks ah a-layin' an' go 'way 'mongst heathen people.

SISSY. But, Granny, you'd be happy wif us, won't yo'?

GRANNY. Yas, chile, Ah'd be happy all right, but Ah'm lak Ephraim Ah reckon, wedded to mah idols. (*Forcing the words*) Yo'-all go 'long an' lemme stay heah.

SONNY. (*Fiercely*) But, Granny, yo' know how Mistah

Bob's gwine tuh tek it, when he fin's us done gone. **Ah** nevah 'd feel safe leavin' yo' behin'.

GRANNY. Dat's a'right. Ain't Ah wuked fo' he's pappy?

SONNY. He ain't keerin' fo' 'at. He's liable to th'ow yo' out wif nuttin'.

GRANNY. Ain't dis mah cabin? (*Looks around tenderly*) Ain't Ah lived heah fo' fifty yeahs?

SONNY. But it's on Mistah Bob's lan'.

GRANNY. Yo' kin sen' me some money an' excusin' de asthma an' de misery in mah head Ah kin keep a youngah 'oman dan me pantin', when it come tuh wuk.

SISSY. Granny, yo' *mus'* come wid us.

SONNY. Ah can't think o' leavin' yo' behin'.

GRANNY. (*Getting up from the steps and walking wearily into the kitchen*) Don't pester me now. Mebbe—mebbe —Ah knowed trouble was comin', seein' dem lights in de elements.

SISSY. (*Whispers to* SONNY) She say "Mebbe."

SONNY. (*Whispering*) Ah wished Ah knowed what tu do.

GRANNY. (*Looking up and seeing them whispering*) Go long, chillun, yo' needn't be keepin' secrets fum yo' ol' Granny. Mebbe yo're right; mebbe Ah'm right. Dis is a cu'ios worl' anyhow. But dat whi' man ain't come back yit. Dey ain't tekin' niggahs on steam cahs fo' nuttin'. Whi' fo'ks *is* whi' fo'ks.

SONNY. Well, Granny, we'll see.

GRANNY. Ah'll fix yo'-all's dinner an' bring it down yander to de bottom tree.

SONNY. (*To* SISSY) Come on, Sissy, us'll put in one day more anyhow. (*They leave. As the sound of their footsteps ceases the rooster is heard to crow again.*)

GRANNY. (*Going to the door*) Plague tek yo' honery self. (*Picks up a spoon and throws in direction of the sound*)

Cl'ar out a heah—crowin' up company. Ah don't need
no 'cruiters. (*She becomes silent and then sings*)
Down in de Valley—couldn't heah mah Jesus,
Couldn't heah nobody pray, O Lord!——

CURTAIN

SCENE II

SAME PLACE: *Ten forty-five that night. The faint glow
of the kerosene lamp accentuates the desolate shadows.
GRANNY is sitting on the backless chair, her hands folded.
SISSY is packing clothes in an old dress suitcase. A big bag
with a string tied around it rests beside GRANNY. SONNY,
dressed in overalls and a gray coat, walks back and forth as
he talks.*

GRANNY. He ain't comin'.

SONNY. 'Tain't time yit. (*Looking at his dollar watch*)
It's only a quarter tuh 'leven.

GRANNY. He ain't comin', Ah say.

SONNY. Don't put a bad mouf on us, Granny.

SISSY. (*To SONNY*) Come heah, he'p me shet dis thing.
(*SONNY helps her close the stuffed suitcase.*)

GRANNY. Bad mouf, chile, Ah's been sittin' heah prayin' fo'
yo'-all. We ain't nuttin', but wif de ol' Marster we ah
pow'ful strong.

SISSY. (*Holding her head*) Mah head's turnin' 'round all
in a whirl.

SONNY. Ah yo' ready, Granny?

GRANNY. Reckon so.

SISSY. Do yo' think he's comin'?

SONNY. Sho'.

GRANNY. (*Shaking her head*) Can't keep fum thinkin' 'bout

yo' mammy, how she wouldn't wan' yo' tuh leab heah dis a-way.

SONNY. Ah believe she'd wan' us tuh go.

SISSY. Whut yo' all talkin' 'bout sich fo'? Yo' mak me skeert.

GRANNY. 'Tain't no use bein' skeert. Yo' got tuh face de ol' Marster some o' dese times.

SISSY. Oh, Ah ain't skeert o' no ol' Marster, but yo' mek me think o' ghos'es.

SONNY. Ah'm skeert o' de clutches o' ol' Mistah Bob. He don't mean us no good. Ah jes' know ef mammy an' pappy could speak dey'd shoo us on.

GRANNY. How yo' know so much?

SONNY. Ain't Ah done seed de way he looked at niggahs— wicked lak he could swallow 'em whole?

GRANNY. (Sighs)—Lordy! Lordy!

SISSY. Whut time is it, Sonny?

SONNY. (Looking at his watch)—Ten tuh 'leven.

GRANNY. (Singing)—O Lordy, Lordy, won't yo' ketch mah groan.

SONNY. Us ain't goin' tuh no funeral, Granny. Ah feels lak it's a picnic—a 'Mancipation Celebration picnic.

SISSY. Ah'm rarin' tuh go, too, 'specially sence yo' tol' me 'bout de schools up yander. Ouah chillun kin go tuh whi' fo'ks school.

GRANNY. Whi' fo'ks ain't goin' treat niggahs wif book learnin' any bettern we-all.

SONNY. We kin treat each othah bettah den. Ah kin treat mahself bettah. An' so kin mah chillun.

GRANNY. Yo' young niggahs ah sho' uppity, but Ah hope yo' ain't got no wool ovah yo' eyes.

GRANNY. We mought a sont ouah chickens tuh Sis Ca'line.

SISSY. She mought a tol' somebody, too, an' dere we'd be.

GRANNY. Yo' got dat box fixed for Berry?

SONNY. He's already in ut. He ain't used tuh bein' shut up lak dat, de lazy varmint.

GRANNY. (*Walks to the door and looks out*) The stars ah shinin'. (*Comes back and gets a drink from the bucket*)

SISSY. (*Excitedly*) SAKES ALIVE! Ah see de lights a-comin', 'mobile lights.

SONNY. (*Running to the door*) She is. We goin' fum heah.

GRANNY. (*Moodily silent. The glare from the headlights of the automobile lights up the room, shining in through the open door.* GRANNY *looks in wonder at the light.*) Ah, chillun, de Lawd is wif us. (*Sings*)

Shine on me. Let de light fum de lighthouse, shine on me.

(*The chug of the engine is heard and the grinding of the brakes, as the car pulls up. The horn blows three times.* THE WHITE MAN *runs down the walk.*)

THE WHITE MAN. Are you ready? We have no time to lose.

SONNY. We's waitin'. (*Gathers up bag, suitcase and hat and starts towards the door*)

SISSY. Don't forget Berry.

THE WHITE MAN. Who's Berry?

SISSY. De dog.

THE WHITE MAN. What do you mean? We can't take dogs on this trip.

GRANNY. Whut's de mattah wif yo', man? Think we're goin' tuh leave Berry?

THE WHITE MAN. See here. It is impossible to take any dog. He'll make too much noise and besides I can't be bothered looking out for him.

SONNY. Well, Berry 'll have tuh stay heah, dat's all.

GRANNY. Den Ah stays too.

SONNY. Whut yo' say?

GRANNY. (*Stubbornly*) Ah ain't goin' tuh leave Berry.

THE WHITE MAN. Ah, come on—cut the argument. We got to make that train.

SISSY. (*Worried*) He kin fend fo' hisself.

GRANNY. Go on yo' chillun, go on. Ah don't wan' tuh go nohow. Ah jes' been a-pretendin' tuh git yo' started. Ah kin git along. Ain't Ah got along wif whi' fo'ks fo' seventy yeahs an' mo'?

SONNY. (*Angrily*) Whut yo' wan' tuh act dis a-way fo'?

THE WHITE MAN. Well, come on or stay, people. Time's passing.

SONNY. Ah'm goin', Granny. Don't yo' see Ah can't stay heah? Ef Ah stay Ah'm goin' tuh git kilt fo' sassin' dese whi' fo'ks; ef Ah go tuh wa', Ah hastuh leave yo' jes' de same an' mebbe git kilt. Ef Ah go No'th and die, Ah'll be a dead free man. (*He puts down bundles and embraces* GRANNY.) Mah po' ol' Granny. Ah'm goin' tuh send yo' plenty a money an' Ah'll be back, come Christmas, mebbe to tek yo' atter we gits settled.

GRANNY. (*Frightened*) Don't, don't come back, not heah. Promise me dat, chile. Yo' know Mistah Bob. He git yo'.

SONNY. No, he won't. Ah'll show him.

THE WHITE MAN. (*Impatiently*) We must be going.

SISSY. Fo' God, Granny, come on.

GRANNY. (*Firmly*) Ah done said mah say.

SONNY. Den, good-bye, Granny. (*Gives her money*) Ah send yo' plenty mo' fust pay day an' Ah'm goin' tuh have a pay day ebery week.

SISSY. (*Kissing* GRANNY) Good-bye.

GRANNY. (*Her arms around them both*) Mah po' chillun.

Mah po' chillun. (*They tear themselves from her embrace.* THE WHITE MAN *leads the way to the car.* SONNY *takes up the suitcase, but leaves the bag.* SISSY *follows. The sound of the three pairs of footsteps dies away.*)

SONNY AND SISSY. (*Calling from the car*) Granny?

GRANNY. (*Standing in the doorway*) CHILLUN.

SISSY. Pray fo' us, Granny. (*The car is heard lurching ahead. The light disappears. The sounds die away.* GRANNY *stands for a minute in the deep silence, looking in the direction of the vanished car. A whining is heard. She looks out in the darkness.*)

GRANNY. Bress mah soul! Berry! (*She pulls in a crated box, containing the cur. She gets a poker and pries the box open. The dog is wild with appreciation*) Come heah, Berry. (*Pulls up the backless chair by the table and sits down, patting the dog*) Berry, you'se all Ah got lef' now. (*Rests her elbow on the table, shuts her eyes*) Lordy, Ah'm so tiahed, so tiahed. (*She sits up suddenly, listening attentively*) Who dat knockin' at mah do'? (*She gets up slowly and looks out. Nothing. Shuts the door and bolts it. Sits down again and buries her face in her hands. Again she raises up and listens*) Who dat, knockin' agin? (*Once more she gets up more painfully, unbolts and opens the door. Nothing. Closing it she totters feebly to the chair*) Berry, Ah'm tuckered out. (*Croons*) "Somebody knockin' at mah do'!" (*Stops. Listens*) Come in. (*Falls back in chair, her head rests on the table, her arms limp. She mumbles*) Come in, 'Cruiter. Reckon Ah'm all ready.

CURTAIN

THE STARTER
A COMEDY OF HARLEM LIFE
By
EULALIE SPENCE

OPPORTUNITY PRIZE PLAY, 1927
Reprinted by permission of the author and
Opportunity, Journal of Negro Life

CHARACTERS

T. J. KELLY
FIRST WOMAN
SECOND WOMAN
GEORGIA

Scene: Present-day Harlem.
Time: A summer evening.

THE STARTER

AT RISE: THOMAS JEFFERSON KELLY *is sprawled upon the bench, his straw hat on one side, his coat on the other. T. J. KELLY as he signs himself, is reading a copy of "The News." From time to time, he chuckles, mutters aloud, whistles or hums in a low baritone. T. J. KELLY'S face is the most important thing that ever happened to him. For the rest, T. J. is tall, dapper and in love.*

T. J. KELLY. Holy gee! What d'ye know 'bout that! (*He stares a bit, then turns the page*) Um! Some looker! Hello! 'Woman gives Birth To Four Healthy Sons'! Gee! A male quartet! Four! . . . 'Father Overjoyed!' Like hell, he is! (T. J. *throws the paper on the ground in disgust*) Gee! Suppose something like that was to happen to me! (T. J. *grabs his coat and hat and prepares for flight. Suddenly he stops short, laughing sheepishly. He resumes his seat. He takes his hat off and places it on the bench*) Reckon them things only happen to furriners. Sure! (T. J. *whistles a few lines from "'Tain't Gonna Rain No Mo'." Two tired looking women trudge into view. They stop short and look at* T. J. *in exasperation.*)

FIRST WOMAN. (*Mopping her face with a handkerchief*)

Any wonder we kain't find no place tuh set? Looka him sprawlin' on dat bench, will yuh? Gawd, it's hot!

SECOND WOMAN. (*Addressing* T. J. KELLY) Say, move up, will yuh? Yuh ain't go' no lease on dat bench. . . .

T. J. KELLY. (*With a provoking grin*) Reserved! (*He spreads both arms along the back of the bench.*)

FIRST WOMAN. (*With a snort*) Reserved! Kin yuh beat dat fer nerve, Mis' Clark?

SECOND WOMAN. Ah should say not! (*To* T. J. KELLY) Take yo' arms off dat bench, you loafin' nigger!

T. J. KELLY. (*Calmly*) Now, see here Angel face, and you too, Grape Nuts! Ah know you're both dying for a real live hug from an honest tuh goodness he-man. Well, come on an' get it. I won't charge you nothing.

FIRST WOMAN. (*Indignantly*) Kin yuh beat it?

SECOND WOMAN. (*Angrily*) Ah like yo' gall!

T. J. KELLY. (*Pleasantly*) They all do! You're not the only one!

FIRST WOMAN. A woman kain't walk tru dis park no mo', 'thout bein' insulted!

SECOND WOMAN. Aw, come on, Mrs. Henry! Ah would'n' set thar now ef he was tuh scrub de whole bench——

FIRST WOMAN. Me neither. (*They turn scornfully away and walk on.*)

T. J. KELLY. (*Hums audibly*)
    Honey! Say doan' yuh know
    Honey! Ah love yuh so—
    Yuh's cute, yuh's sweet
    Yuh's mighty fine—
    Sweeter dan de watermelon hangin' on de vine.
(*A pretty brown girl in a light dress comes along the path from the direction in which the women are walking. She merely glances at their angry faces and passes*

on. They stop and look back at her. As she approaches T. J. KELLY, *he rises, makes an elaborate bow and sweeps his belongings to one side. Then* T. J. KELLY *kisses the girl, Valentino-fashion. The women stand and stare.*

FIRST WOMAN. Brazen!

SECOND WOMAN. Hussy! (*They pass on.*)

GEORGIA. (*With her very first breath*) Say, T. J., did yuh see them ole hens stare?

T. J. KELLY. No. I couldn't see nothin' but you, then, Honey.

GEORGIA. Well, they sure did stare! Reckon they was jealous all right!

T. J. KELLY. Not a doubt of it!

GEORGIA. Say, yuh doan' hate yuhself, do you?

T. J. KELLY. Naw! 'Tain't no use hating the person you have to live with.

GEORGIA. Meanin' who?

T. J. KELLY. Meaning me—Thomas Jefferson Kelly—at your service.

GEORGIA. Oh! (*She moves away, the length of the bench.*)

T. J. KELLY. Say, what's the idea of moving down there?

GEORGIA. Yuh gets along pretty well by yuhself—doan' yuh?

T. J. KELLY. Sure, but I gets along better when you're around. (*He reaches out and draws her close to him.*)

GEORGIA. (*Leaning against his shoulder*) 'Twas a helluva day, T. J. (*She sighs.*)

T. J. KELLY. It sure was! Ninety in the shade! To see the way people shop in all this hot weather! I don't see how they do it! I have to stand there by that cage till I'm ready to drop! An' talk about dumb-bells! Why those birds can't read, some of them. They stand

by an elevator marked "down" an' expects it to go up
—and other way 'round! An' the fool questions they
asks! Gee! To think of all my education being lost
on those people!

GEORGIA. Poor T. J. Yuh's had too much schoolin'—that's
whut's the matter with yuh——

T. J. KELLY. (*Fully launched upon his grievances*) Two
terms in High School, and don't you forget it. . . .
Funny—me standing there in a Palm Beach suit with
brass buttons, an' a hat to match with more brass buttons! Sometimes a man gets to thinkin'—Here I am a
starter—a starter—just one step better'n the man who
runs the cage—Gee! *That's* a helluva job!

GEORGIA. It sure is! I'm glad yuh's a starter, T. J.

T. J. KELLY. (*Bitterly*) Yeh! But there's something about
the name that don't just hit me right. Starter! Starter!
It seems to get over into a man's life—somehow—
starter!

GEORGIA. (*Sitting up wide-eyed*) Gee! That's funny!

T. J. KELLY. Is it? Well, I don't just see the point—that's
all.

GEORGIA. Why T. J.—yuh knows Ah does sewin' doan yuh?
(T. J. *nods*) Well, Ah ain't never tole yuh 'bout mah
place 'cause it's so low-down. Eyetalians and Jews and
colored—all in tergether. It's a dump. Well, I'm
what they calls a Finisher. Finisher on dresses! See?
That's whut Ah meant—You bein' a Starter and me a
Finisher!

T. J. KELLY. (*Giving a loud laugh*) Holy gee! That's a
good one! Say, Georgia, we'd make a good team—we
would. (*He gives her a tight hug.*)

GEORGIA. (*Pleased*) Quit yuh kiddin'.

T. J. KELLY. No kiddin'. Y'know, kid, I bin thinkin'—
Say, why don't we get married? Huh?

GEORGIA. Ah dunno, 'cept yuh never mentioned it befo'.

T. J. KELLY. Well, I'm mentioning it now. See? Think it
over, kid. Well, what's the answer?

GEORGIA. (*Slowly*) Has yuh got any money, T. J.?

T. J. KELLY. (*With an injured air*) Money! Say! Have
a heart! That's a fine question.

GEORGIA. (*Slyly*) Fer a starter!

T. J. KELLY. (*Suspiciously*) Say—are you making fun of
me?

GEORGIA. Co'se not, T. J.!

T. J. KELLY. Well, you're taking your time 'bout answering
—ain't yuh?

GEORGIA. How much yuh got saved, T. J.?

T. J. KELLY. (*Frowning*) Ain't that a little personal,
Honey?

GEORGIA. Ah doan' think so—but co'se ef yuh doan' feel like
sayin' ——

T. J. KELLY. I have fifty-five dollars! That's not so bad
for ——

GEORGIA. Fer a *starter!* (*She draws away from him coldly*)
Yuh mean yuh ain't got mo'n fifty-five dollars an' you
wukin' steady?

T. J. KELLY. An' me dressing like a gentleman an' paying
dues in a club an' two Societies an' a Lodge? An'
taking you to the theatre twice a week ——

GEORGIA. *Movies*—an' doan' yuh ferget it!

T. J. KELLY. (*Angrily*) So, that's how you feel about it—
is it? Don't I take you to dances? Didn't we go to
Coney last week and a cabaret Monday night? How
the devil you expect me to have money?

GEORGIA. (*Coldly*) Nobuddy asked yuh nothin' 'bout mar-
  ryin'—you's the one mentioned it ——

T. J. KELLY. Sure, but that don't give you no right to ask
  'bout my bank account. Reckon you wouldn't say how
  much *you've* got in your bank.

GEORGIA. Well, sence yuh's dyin' tuh fine out ——

T. J. KELLY. (*Angrily*) Who—me?

GEORGIA. Sence yuh's dyin' ter know—Ah's got two hundred dollars!

T. J. KELLY. Whew! (*Almost immediately he recovers his
  air of superiority*) Well, that ain't so much!

GEORGIA. Mo'n you's got!

T. J. KELLY. (*Reflectively*) Two hundred dollars! Say,
  you know what, Georgia? That's enough money to
  start on. We could get a nice room—Why I've got a
  peachuva room. An' we could get new fixings—pay
  down a deposit, you know. I could arrange all that at
  the store. They know me—Two hundred dollars ain't
  so bad! Say! Say—many a man's got married on less!

GEORGIA. Yuh ain't sayin' nuthin' 'bout yo' fifty-five ——

T. J. KELLY. Fifty-five's all right—as a starter—but it ain't
  nothing for a man to talk about.

GEORGIA. An' whut 'bout a ring, T. J.?

T. J. KELLY. A ring! (*He looks the picture of dismay.*)

GEORGIA. (*Sarcastically*) Yuh ain't never heard 'bout that
  befo' has yuh?

T. J. KELLY. Sure—but—Well,—Oh, all right! I'll get
  you a ring—a beauty, too, get me?

GEORGIA. See here, boy friend! Ah'm a regular girl! An'
  Ah knows a Woolworth Special when Ah sees one!

T. J. KELLY. (*Indignantly*) Say, d'you think I'd put a Woolworth over on you? How d'you get that way?

GEORGIA. Reckon it's frum 'sociatin' wid them Jews an'
Eyetalians. Say, those folks sure wears diamonds.

T. J. KELLY. (*Incredulously*) To work?

GEORGIA. Sure!

T. J. KELLY. Fake, that's all!

GEORGIA. Fake nuthin'!

T. J. KELLY. Well, kid, what d'you say?

GEORGIA. Ah dunno, T. J. (*She sighs once more*) Ah
was reckonin' on that two hundred fer rainy weather—
(T. J. *whistles a bar or two from "'Tain't Gonna Rain
no Mo'"*) In mah business thar's plenty rainy weather.
Las' year Ah was outa wuk altogether four months.

T. J. KELLY. (*Aghast*) What? How come?

GEORGIA. Laid off. Nuthin' doin'—It's a reg'lar thing in
mah line—dull season—strikes—union dues ——

T. J. KELLY. But you could always find something else,
couldn't you?

GEORGIA. Naw. Wuk's slack every place. An' then's the
time Ah needs mah savin's.

T. J. KELLY. How 'bout waitress in some nice ——

GEORGIA. Nuthin' doin'. Ah ain't no hash slinger!

T. J. KELLY. You're mighty fussy ain't you?

GEORGIA. Ef we got married yuh would'n' mind mah stayin'
home when things was slow, would yuh, T. J. (T. J.
swallows painfully) Gee, it would be great tuh be able
tuh stay in bed mornin's. Yuh know, T. J., the thought
uh hittin' de chillies has driv' plenty into matrimony
befo' now. Gee! Tuh lie in bed on a cole winter
mornin' when de sleet an' rain er batterin' at de
winders!

T. J. KELLY. (*Impatiently*) Fer Gawd's sake, woman ——

GEORGIA. (*Startled out of her dreaming*) What the matter, T. J.?

T. J. KELLY. (*Irritably*) Say—all this talk 'bout cold and sleet—an' stayin' in bed—Gee! It's enough to give a man cold feet.

GEORGIA. Cole feet! Well, if yuh has cole feet, now's the time tuh say so! (*She rises.* T. J. KELLY *grasps her hand. He draws her down again.*)

T. J. KELLY. Say, it's a fine way to spoil a good night— talkin' 'bout winter mornings —— (*He kisses her*) Looka there, Honey!

GEORGIA. (*Reluctantly*) Whar?

T. J. KELLY. (*Pointing*) Over there. Going to be a moon to-night.

GEORGIA. Sure 'nuff.

T. J. KELLY. Not so bad! An' looka there Honey!

GEORGIA. Whar?

T. J. KELLY. (*Pointing*) Down there! All those lights an' those people an' this park— We owns the whole show!

GEORGIA. Quit yuh kiddin'.

T. J. KELLY. Gawd, Harlem sure is great! Looka them lights!

GEORGIA. Say, T. J.? (*She sits upright as though she has just remembered something.*)

T. J. KELLY. What you thinkin', Honey?

GEORGIA. Is we engaged?

T. J. KELLY. (*Annoyed*) Lawd! Do we have to go all over that? (*In a kindlier tone*) Keep yuh eyes on them lights, Honey an'—an' forget it. (*The park is very much darker now.* GEORGIA's *head snuggles up against* T. J.'s *shoulder. His arm slips about her waist. The Moon-man hangs his lantern in the heavens, and we do the only kindly thing we can think of. We draw the Curtain.*)

CURTAIN

JUDGE LYNCH

A DRAMA IN ONE ACT

By

JOHN WILLIAM ROGERS, JR.

BELASCO CUP PRIZE PLAY, THE NATIONAL
LITTLE THEATRE TOURNAMENT 1924
*Reprinted by permission of the Author and
Samuel French, Inc.*

CHARACTERS

Mrs. Joplin
Ella, her daughter-in-law
Ed Joplin, Ella's husband
A Stranger

Scene: The back porch of the Joplin farmhouse somewhere in the South just after dusk.

Time: The present.

First performance by the Green Mask Players, Houston, Texas. First New York performance, May 1, 1924, The Belasco Theatre, by the Dallas Little Theatre Players.

JUDGE LYNCH

SCENE: LOOKING INTO *the back porch of an unpreten-tious Southern farmhouse. A door in the center, with a window on each side, opens on the porch from the interior of the house. Against the left window is silhouetted a shelf built between two of the plain, unpainted posts that support the roof of the porch. On the shelf stands a water bucket with a dipper in it, and a tin basin. A rumpled towel is fastened to one of the posts beside it, and at the right from the eaves hangs a necklacelike string of red peppers drying. A large flat stone on the ground in front of the center of the porch serves for a step into the strip of yard between the porch and the audience. At the right in the yard lies a dis-ordered heap of logs sawed into lengths for stove wood. A few of these are split and the axe stands driven into one of them. A cane-bottom chair is on the porch, just by the step. In it is a pan with two knives, and beside it on the floor is a basket of apples.*

As the curtain rises, MRS. JOPLIN *opens the door and steps out of the lighted door on to the porch, carrying a teakettle which she proceeds to fill from the water bucket with the dipper. She is a tall, plainly dressed country woman about fifty-five. Hard work has left its mark, but she has an un-conscious dignity of manner which in spite of her lack of edu-cation commands respect. The monotonous years of trivi-*

alities and grinding daily tasks have never succeeded in killing an extraordinary emotional capacity.

While she is filling the pitcher, she stops abruptly, sets it down on the shelf and listens for something intently. The noise of someone moving a stove lid inside the house disturbs her.

MRS. JOPLIN. (*Irritable in her excitement*) Stop rattling that stove and be quiet a moment, will you? (*The noise stops and as she listens once more, her daughter-in-law, ELLA, appears at the door holding a lantern. ELLA is still rather pretty in a commonplace, colorless sort of way, but is without distinction—an everyday, unimaginative country girl.*)

ELLA. (*Coming out on the porch with the lantern*) What's the matter?

MRS. JOPLIN. I heard them hounds. Listen!

ELLA. (*After listening*) I don't hear nothing. You couldn't hear them this far.

MRS. JOPLIN. Yes, you could. When the wind's this way. It carries off them hills like a sound board. Maybe they've tracked him down the road, trying to get away, anyhow.

ELLA. (*Beginning to be alarmed*) Suppose he 'ould come here. He'd be desperate, I reckon. I don't think Ed ought to be stayin' off from home this time er night with a nigger like that loose in the woods.

MRS. JOPLIN. (*Cautiously*) Where's that gun?

ELLA. In yonder by the mantelpiece.

MRS. JOPLIN. Better bring it out here. I'll take that. (*She takes the lantern and hangs it on a nail in the right center post of the porch. Then she steps into the yard and listens intently until ELLA returns.*)

ELLA. (*Coming back*) Did you hear them again?

MRS. JOPLIN. (*Starting back on the porch and stopping before the chair*) Not yet . . . Here, take this knife. We might just as well finish these apples now. (MRS. JOPLIN *takes the gun from her, stands it against the right post, and hands her a knife; then seats herself in the chair, the pan of apples in her lap, and begins to peel.*) I'm shore I heard them hounds.

ELLA. I don't think Ed ought to leave us like this.

MRS. JOPLIN. Now, Ella, don't begin that again. You know ED 'ull be back as soon as he can. . . . Reach me that washpan for the peels and you can have this one. (ELLA *does so and seats herself on the edge of the porch, above the step*) We've got Pa's gun if anybody should come botherin' us. (*Moved*) They'll get that nigger, though. They always do. It'll be a terrible death he'll die, but he's brought it on himself. . . . It does look like niggers would learn, but I reckon they wouldn't be niggers if they did.

ELLA. I guess that nigger would do anything now. I wish Ed would hurry back.

MRS. JOPLIN. Ed's just out doing his duty with the rest.

ELLA. If there's a lynching, I don't suppose you can blame Ed for wanting to see it. He said there ain't been a lynching in this county for ten years. Not since they took that young nigger down at Dugger's Mills, and Ed warn't there that time.

MRS. JOPLIN. How men have got the heart, I never could tell. It don't seem right, but I guess there ain't no other way. Every now and then it looks like niggers is just obliged to have an awful warning to make 'em fitten to live in a Christian land.

ELLA. What do you reckon they'll do with him?

MRS. JOPLIN. Hang him, I reckon.

ELLA. You don't suppose they'll burn him? I seen in the paper where they burnt two down in Arkansas last month.

MRS. JOPLIN. Oh, pray God they don't do that.

ELLA. Maybe they'll ask Mrs. Tatum what *she* wants done with him. Squire Tatum lying there dead in his own blood, she might not be so particular about it. If a nigger was to slip up behind Ed and hit him with an axe handle, wouldn't you——

MRS. JOPLIN. Ella, don't——

ELLA. Well, if a nigger slipped up behind my husband in the barn and murdered him, I wouldn't care what they done to the nigger.

MRS. JOPLIN. Pore Mrs. Tatum—it was a terrible thing for her—coming on her husband like that, all unexpected—and her going down to the barn to look for hen-nests. If her brother hadn't been ploughin' down in the fields and come running when he heard her screaming, there ain't any telling what the pore thing would have done.

ELLA. They say her brother knowed right away it was the Jacks nigger who done it.

MRS. JOPLIN. I knowed that Jacks nigger when he was a tenant on Cousin Etty's place. I never would have suspected him of nothing like this. He always seemed a hard-workin' hand, and perlite and respectful as a body could want. Kinder timid-like, too.

ELLA. Well, they knowed it was him, all right—if Squire Tatum had words with the nigger yesterday and cussed him and give him until Saturday to get moved off the farm with his family——

MRS. JOPLIN. Squire Tatum did have a terrible temper.

ELLA. Yes, the last time I was up home, I heard Uncle

Photo by Maurice Goldberg

PAUL ROBESON AS "EMPEROR JONES"

Jimmy talking about it. He wouldn't stand nothin'
from no white man, let alone a nigger. Uncle Jimmy
said he saw him at the store one day when a crowd was
playin' dominoes around the stove. A tobacco drum-
mer that come in said something he didn't like, and
before anybody knowed what was happening, Squire
Tatum had run at the man and pushed him clean onto
the stove. He knocked the stove plum over, fire and
all. And the stovepipe came down, throwing soot all
over the place. Uncle Jimmy said the man hadn't really
said nothin' to him, neither.

MRS. JOPLIN. Yes, I always heard what a terrible tricky
temper he had. But he was a good man as he saw it,
and folks thought a heap of him when they come to
know him. Look at that watch the Odd Fellows give
him two Christmases back.

ELLA. I reckon that was the watch they say the nigger stole
out of his pocket. Nigger was a fool to take that watch
—everybody knows that watch. Remember, they had
a picture of it in the paper when it was give to him.
I saw the watch myself one Sunday when he was
a-showin' it before church.

MRS. JOPLIN. (*Resting her hands in her lap*) Well, I
reckon I must have been mistaken about them hounds,
and we ain't doing no good here. Ed'll be in soon,
wantin' to know whatever's the matter with supper.
(*Rising*) I'll take them apples. (*Pointing to woodpile*) You better bring in a armful of wood. Here,
before you do it, put these peelin's along of yours and
throw them over the fence where the pigs can get 'em
in the morning. (ELLA *comes down the step into the
yard with the pan of peelings and starts toward the left.
She gets almost to the side of the stage and is in the act*

of throwing them out, when she screams suddenly—
frightened.   She peers anxiously a moment into the
darkness and then turns about, almost running to the
porch.)

ELLA. Ma, there's somebody over there. I seen 'em move.

MRS. JOPLIN. (*Catching her alarm and coming into the*
yard—reaching for the gun by the post as she does so)
Where?

ELLA. (*Pointing, now thoroughly frightened*) Yonder.

MRS. JOPLIN. (*In a gruff voice, born of fear, halfway*
pointing the gun to have it ready)   Who's that out
there?   What do you want?

ELLA. (*After a tense moment, almost screaming*) He's
there, all right! See—he's moving! (*The two women*
draw away across the stage as the stranger enters
slowly.)

MRS. JOPLIN. (*With relief*) Why, it's a white man. (*She*
relaxes the gun and puts it against the post, stepping
back onto the porch as he speaks.)   (At first glance the
STRANGER *suggests a tramp, but a longer scrutiny re-*
veals that he may more probably be a respectable work-
man, disheveled and travel-stained from an indefinite
journey.   Over his shoulder is slung a battered brown
satchel.)

STRANGER. Good evening, folks.   Hope I ain't scared you?
Could you spare a passing traveler a bit of water to
drink?

MRS. JOPLIN. (*Hospitably offering him the dipper*) Why,
surely, here's some fresh drawed. (*She hands him the*
dipper.   He drinks with a show of gratefulness.)

STRANGER. My that's fine water, lady.   It's a fact—you've
got a good well there.

MRS. JOPLIN. We likes it.   The water always comes up

good cold. (*He hands back the dipper*) Will you have some more?

STRANGER. No, much obliged. It's getting late. I guess I'll start on the road again. (*He looks hard at* ELLA, *makes a false start at going, then turns as if on sudden impulse. He speaks to* ELLA) Pardon my speakin' of it, Ma'arm, but do you know I had quite a start when I first looked at you. You're that like my wife. I thought I was dreaming when I got a good sight of your face.

ELLA. (*Completely credulous*) Aw, really?

STRANGER. That's a fact, and say, my wife's one fine-looking woman. I wouldn't be down in this part of the world tonight if my wife hadn't sent me. I wanted her to come in my place this year, but she says to me: "You go. Folks wouldn't believe the truth if they saw me now, and I was to tell them." Well, say, when I think of her four years ago, I know she's right. It just seems like a miracle, that's all, a plain out and out miracle.

ELLA. (*Interested*) What happened four years ago?

STRANGER. (*Coming closer to her*) Lady, have you seen one of these here sickly women that gets all pulled down and don't nothin' do no more good? Up in the morning, back in bed before 'leven. Backache, headache—can't eat nothin', can't do nothin', weak as a fly. Payin' out enough money in doctors and drug store stuff to build a new barn. Always swallowing pills and making faces at a tablespoon. If I say it who shouldn't, that was a life-size picture of my wife. (*During this speech* MRS. JOPLIN *steps down from the side of the porch at the left and comes around down the stage to the box, where she seats herself during the* STRANGER'S *next long speech. Both women listen to him with interest.*)

MRS. JOPLIN. Pore thing!

ELLA. Sounds like Mrs. Pittard up on Dry Creek, don't it, Ma? Don't nothin' seem to do her any good at all.

MRS. JOPLIN. (*Laughing softly*) It shore do.

STRANGER. Well, folks, it run on until I just got plum discouraged. We kep' throwing our money to the drug trusts—and I guess we'd still be doing it today if my wife hadn't happened to hear of Nakomis and Korno. (*He pauses dramatically.*)

ELLA. (*Interested*) Who's them?

STRANGER. I'm glad you asked me that, lady. Korno is just about the most wonderful thing I ever heard of, and you'll agree with me. Some day the women of America are going to build a monument to Korno and old Nakomis. Korno, that's the greatest boon known to woman. Nakomis was the old Indian squaw that give my wife the secret. Look here—(*He opens the satchel and takes out two bottles of red liquid which he stands on the water shelf*) You've always heard how the Indians made the women do all the work. Folks, the Indians didn't make them—they couldn't keep 'em from it. Every Indian woman knowed about Korno. They took Korno and it kept them strong— they'd rather do the work themselves than fool with the men. Look at it, folks. (*He holds another bottle up so that it catches the light of the lamp*) Look how it sparkles with health. Korno, the great Indian secret. That's what put my wife on her feet again. That's what makes her able to do a week's washing and start out smilin' after supper to a church social. How do I happen to be here tonight? Listen. It all came to my wife in a dream. One night an Indian woman appeared to her in a vision holding up a bottle of Korno,

and the next day she says to me: "George, we've got
to give the women of America a chance to know about
Korno. I'll look after the farm, you go and tell them."
Well, folks, here I am. (*He takes four bottles out of
his satchel and stands them in a row on the water shelf*)
If I was a drug trust, I'd charge you five dollars a bottle.
After you've taken one bottle, you wouldn't be without
a bottle if you had to pay fifty. But I ain't no profiteer.
Now I'm goin' to let you have these six bottles ——

ELLA. (*Bursting out suddenly*) Ma, here's Ed! (*The
STRANGER'S spell is broken by the entrance of ED
JOPLIN. He is a healthy, smooth-faced farmer about
thirty-three—dressed in everyday working clothes and
carrying a shotgun. He has inherited some of the emotional capacity of his mother and is deeply moved by
what he has just witnessed—so deeply, he tries to appear indifferent with only partial success. From the
moment he comes on, the women forget all about the
existence of Korno. They crowd about ED in their
interest while the STRANGER stands apart on the right
listening. ED is too full of his news to notice him.*)

ED. (*After entering*) Well, we got him. (*He walks to
the center of stage and leans his gun against the left
post.*)

ELLA. What did you do with him?

ED. (*To STRANGER as he puts down gun*) Howdy.

STRANGER. Howdy.

ED. (*Still struggling to appear unmoved and stepping on
to porch, where he washes his hands in washbasin*) If
they ain't cut him down yet, I guess he's still hanging
to one of them trees in Squire Tatum's upper pasture.
He won't never bother nobody else. I didn't count

'em, but I reckon there's fifty bullet holes in him.   Let
alone buckshot.

ELLA. How'd you ketch him?   (MRS. JOPLIN *follows* ED
*on to the porch and stands in the doorway, handing him
the towel as he turns to reach for it.   He finishes, wipes
his hands and throwing the towel back to his mother,
steps down into the yard, giving his recital of the lynching in the center of the stage.   MRS. JOPLIN stands
listening by the water shelf, but as* ED *talks, in her intensity steps down from side of porch and comes to
stand by* ELLA *in the yard.*)

ED. That warn't hard.   I got over to the Squire's place
about the same time as Sim Butler.   He had picked up
Brother Williams and the Willard boys.   Mrs. Tatum's
brother met us and told us how the Squire had words
with the nigger yesterday and how they found the Squire
lying murdered in the hall of the barn.

MRS. JOPLIN. It must have been an awful thing.

ED. (*Coming into the yard again*) While he was talking,
they come bringing the nigger's wife up from her cabin.
She let on she didn't know nothin'.   She said the nigger
took his gun after dinner and said he was going squirrel
hunting up on the hill.   Sim Butler grabs her by the arm.
He shows her a big blacksnake whip and tells her if
she's lying—we wouldn't leave an inch of skin on her
brown body.   But she takes on and swears she didn't
know nothin' 'tall.   'Bout fifty of us there then. Looked
like the whole north end of Dry Creek County had got
there while we was talkin'!

MRS. JOPLIN. It don't take long for news of that kind to
draw a crowd.

ED. Sim Butler sort of took charge of things. "Well," he
says, "it don't look like there's but one thing to do—

find the nigger." We scattered out and we come on him down in the thick woods. The Williams boys just ahead of me seen him first and hollered to him to stop. We figured, havin' a gun, he was goin' to make fight and we was ready for him to start, but he was a foxy devil. He just stop and answer back perlite-like. He let on he didn't know nothin' 'bout nothin' and he'd shot a squirrel, pretending to be really out hunting. But Yancy Williams walks up to him and grabs his gun out of his hand. "Gimme that gun, you black—" (*Turning to* STRANGER)—and Yancy shore did cuss him. "Where the hell do you think you're running away to?" and he let his fist go up against the nigger's head.

ELLA. Where was the others?

ED. We hollered 'em up and they come running. . . . I never before seen a nigger so near the color of ashes. At first he kept sayin' he didn't know nothing at all about it. He'd beg and cry and call on God as witness. Some of them was for stopping his blasphemy with a rope right away. But Sim kept cool and held them back. "Men," he says, "I'm for law and order and justice. There's times when God-fearing, law-abiding citizens don't need no courts to help them do their duty. Squire Tatum lies down yonder murdered. We all know he had words with this nigger yesterday. And it don't take much to see who done the deed. But we ain't going to be hasty. There warn't any witnesses, so we're going to give this low-down black scoundrel a chance to tell the truth and confess his crime before we send his soul to hell—if the scrimey ape's got a soul." With that Walter Williams hauls off and knocks the nigger down, shoutin', "Confess, you black baboon, or we'll burn you alive." Sim kept Walter from hitting him again, but half a dozen of them began to yell. "Burn him—build a fire ——" The nigger was on his knees cryin' and pleadin'. For a minute I thought they was going to burn him, in spite of everything, but Sim didn't lose his head. "Wait a minute, men, hold steady. I agree with you, he don't deserve no consideration, but we'll be generous. We'll give him a chance. If he'll confess, we'll only hang him. If he don't— Well, boys, we'll give him a minute to make up his mind how he's going to die before we start gathering the wood." Then Sim turns to the nigger who was down on his knees hollerin' and beggin'. "Stand up," shouts Sim. Two or three that was closest grabs him by the collar and pulls him up. His eye was swelling where Walter had hit him, and he couldn't no more have stood than a tadpole, if they hadn't held him. He kept moanin' he hadn't done it, until at last Sim gets out of patience and shouts, "All right boys, 'tain't no use wastin' no more time. Git your fire ready . . ." Look like it took about half a minute for it to get through that nigger's head who was goin' to be burned. Then all of a sudden, it come to him. I thought he was takin' on before. He hadn't started. "Don't burn me, oh, Lawdy, don't burn me. Oh, boss, I don't know what it is, but if you say I done it, I done it, just don't burn me. I done it all."

STRANGER. (*Who has been listening to the recital much moved, breaking out surprised in spite of himself*) He confessed!

ED. (*Turning with a sort of scorn that it should be doubted*) He did that, and it wasn't three minutes before he was hanging from a tree, full er bullets as a rake is full er teeth. (ED *sits down on edge of porch and slips off shoes, standing up again in his sock feet.*)

ELLA. I reckon he would confess.

ED. I reckon he did. Mighty little good it would have done him, not confessing. Everybody knows he slipped up behind Squire Tatum in his own barn and murdered him with an axe handle. (*The* STRANGER *involuntarily turns away—on his face is written genuine horror and surprise. He tries to get hold of himself, but with difficulty.*)

ELLA. When are they goin' to have the Squire's buryin'?

ED. That warn't settled when I left. Sim said he'd stop by and let us know. He's going back tonight and set up with the corpse.

ELLA. Did they find the Squire's watch the nigger stole?

ED. No. Just before they put the rope around his neck, somebody thought of that and they stopped long enough to search for it. Sim tried to make him tell what he done with it, but shucks, that nigger was so scared, he didn't know his name.

ELLA. Hid it, I reckon. Maybe his wife's got it. (*The* STRANGER *looks about, anxious to go, but he is afraid to leave abruptly for fear of causing suspicion. The battle between flight and boldness is plain.*)

MRS. JOPLIN. Pore Mrs. Tatum, how was she?

ED. I didn't see her. Mrs. Williams and some of the women folks that come over when they heard the news was a-lookin' after her. They say she kept moanin' over and over, if the Squire only hadn't had such a terrible temper. She knowed all along something terrible would come of it some day. She knowed it was coming.

ELLA. He did have a powerful mean temper. (*The* STRAN-

GER's *face becomes dark and his fists clench slightly as though he remembered an insult.*)

ED. (*Picking up shoes and gun*) He has a nasty way with strangers, but when you got to know him, he was all right. . . . I'll just put up this gun. There's four mules and a passle of pigs that's got to be fed. I heard them pigs squealin' clean down on the road as I come up. (*He goes into the house followed by* ELLA. *The* STRANGER *stands eyeing* MRS. JOPLIN *irresolutely. His gaze shifts from her to the six bottles of Korno and he walks toward the shelf. She steps onto the porch and turns to him. He is not sure how to make the break of going.*)

MRS. JOPLIN. (*Interpreting his agitation*) I saw how you took it when Ed was a-tellin' it.

STRANGER. (*Alarmed*) Why, I don't know anything at all about it. I . . .

MRS. JOPLIN. Oh, I reckon I can understand how you feel, all right. *You* come from far off yonder where they don't have niggers. You can't make out how Christian men can do what you heard tell tonight.

STRANGER. (*Quickly*) I don't blame anybody.

MRS. JOPLIN. Well, I could see how you took it. Strangers always feel that way.

STRANGER. (*Anxious to have done and leave*) He confessed; he said he did it.

MRS. JOPLIN. I reckon there ain't any doubt about that.

STRANGER. (*Looks at her quickly and seeing that she is in earnest, is relieved*) No.

MRS. JOPLIN. You can't make out how my Ed and the rest of them could do what they done today. How they could hunt a human being and kill him like a wild animal.

STRANGER. (*Beginning to be out of patience*) I told you, lady, I don't blame nobody. (*He starts slowly to put the bottles on the shelf back into his kit*) I guess I'll be getting along. It's late.

MRS. JOPLIN. (*Walking to the edge of the porch and resting against the post*) You needn't keep pretendin'. Maybe you're just sensitive-like and easily affected. It's easy to read it on your face. (*He stops putting away the bottles and turns toward her*) But the right and wrong of it ain't as simple as you might think. I ain't never read it in no book and my Ed and the rest'll not admit it if you ask them, but it was being afraid that drove 'em to do what they done today. When the niggers were brought from that there African wilderness—they brung something along with them that folks didn't know was coming. Something that belongs to the wilderness—that ain't got no place in a white man's land, and never will. Niggers has got used to Christian clothes, they don't put rings in their noses no more, and some of them's ironed most of the kink out of their hair. But they ain't never got rid of that other thing, and civilization and laws ain't no good for it. Mostly it's asleep now, but you can't never tell when it's going to wake up—when it's going to lie waiting for you like one of them African animals they has in cages at the circus would. When it is awake, it don't know any language except what them animals knows. That's why no white woman dares go down a lonely road, or cross a field after dark. That's why Ed don't like to ride at night without his gun. It's fighting that wild thing, men are, when they do what they did today. Just like Ed hangs up a dead crow in a field.

STRANGER. (*Who has been fiercely occupied with his own*

thoughts) He had a terrible temper. They said just now he couldn't be civil to strangers.

MRS. JOPLIN. (*Bewildered*) What?

STRANGER. Him—the one—the nigger—*killed*.

MRS. JOPLIN. Squire Tatum?

STRANGER. His wife knew. She understood. She said he'd bring an end like that. Maybe he only got what was coming to him. (MRS. JOPLIN *stares at the* STRANGER, *unable to follow his words.* ELLA'S *voice comes from inside the house*)

ELLA. Ma, come here a minute . . . Ma, did you move Ed's other shoes when you were cleanin' up this—(*Lost to audience.* MRS. JOPLIN *goes into the house. As she disappears, the* STRANGER *swiftly puts the last bottle into his satchel. He hesitates a moment, then as he walks toward the woodpile he draws something from his pocket in a fashion that gets the audience's sharp attention, and stands examining it darkly six counts, when* ELLA'S *voice is heard inside*) All right, I'll tell him. (*The* STRANGER *looks up guiltily and starts forward at the sound. He stumbles over the wood and drops the thing in his hand down among the lengths of wood. His first impulse is to get it back, but he hears the voice of* ELLA *coming back and realizes he hasn't time. With sudden decision, he makes a bolt and exits swiftly to right.*)

ELLA. (*After four counts coming from inside the house*) Mister—we don't want—where—why, he isn't here. (*Calling*) Ma, he's done gone. He ain't here nowhere and he's took the bottles. (*Looking for him down in the yard.*)

MRS. JOPLIN. (*Entering from the house and following* ELLA *into the yard to look, then stepping back on the edge of the porch*) That's queer. Medicine men ain't usually so quick to go without having a sight of your pocketbook. He seemed kinder upset by what Ed said—Yankee, I reckon. Aw, Ella, just bring in an arm of that wood while you're out there and pick up a few of them little tiny pine splinters for in the morning. (*She holds the lantern up for* ELLA *to see and* ELLA, *who has been peering left into the darkness to see if she can discover the departing* STRANGER, *comes slowly over to the wood and picks up several sticks which she lays across her arm. Then she catches sight of something shining—the thing the* STRANGER *had thrown there. As she picks it up, she lets the wood slip from her arm in surprise.*)

MRS. JOPLIN. What's the matter? (*Brings lantern to yard to meet her.*)

ELLA. (*Bringing the thing over to the light*) Ma—Ma— here's a watch. (*Very slowly in her amazement*) It was lying down there among the wood, Ma—(*She pauses to examine it by the lamp—then looks at* MRS. JOPLIN. *Each word very slowly as her mind gradually grasps the full implication*) It's Squire Tatum's watch. (*With sudden comprehension but slowly, with intensity*) That nigger was here this afternoon. I told you Ed ought not to leave us alone. (*The two women stand staring at one another in horror at what they are both thinking.*)

CURTAIN

GRANNY MAUMEE

A PLAY FOR THE NEGRO THEATRE

By

RIDGLEY TORRENCE

CHARACTERS

GRANNY MAUMEE, an old Negro woman
PEARL, her great-granddaughter
SAPPHIE, her other great-granddaughter

Scene: A cabin interior in Lower Louisiana.
Time: Late Nineteenth Century.

First performance by The Stage Society, New York City
first performance with Negro cast, The Hapgood
Players, The Garden Theatre, New
York, April 5, 1917

GRANNY MAUMEE

SCENE: LIVING ROOM *in an old cabin with walls blackened by age. Red cotton curtains and red covers on the chairs and table. In left corner back, an open fire smolders in a great rough fireplace. There is a door at back leading out-of-doors. There are also doors left and right. A bed at left covered with a white counterpane. The room is neat and there are many growing flowers about potted in rude wooden boxes. Toward the right is an iron flower stand consisting of a basin mounted on a tripod. This stand is filled with a mass of bright red geraniums. A large chest against the wall at right is covered with red. A table near center bears candles. Beside the table in a high-backed chair sits* GRANNY MAUMEE. *She is seen to be blind. She is black and thin, with white hair and a face so seared by burns that it masks her great age. Her great-granddaughter* PEARL, *a girl of nineteen, is moving briskly about the room straightening chairs and rearranging flowers.*

PEARL. Seem kinder funny fer me to be fixin' up for Sapphie. Seem like I'm wukin' for her by the day. Mebbe she will tek'n hiah me now she's married. Seem kinder odd to be hiahed by a blood sisteh.

GRANNY. Spread my finespun sheets on de baid.

PEARL. I got the nex' bes'.

GRANNY. Fol' um up an' git out de fines'.

PEARL. Hit weahs um out so to wash um, an' Sapphie an'
that man of her'n aint used to such goodness. An' to
muss um up des for one night!

GRANNY. Hit's de night er all nights. Hit's de boy babe
wif 'em dat I wants de fineness fer.

PEARL. That's right, the baby. I keeps fohgitting hit. I'll
change 'm. I'll git the linun sheets on an' then I'll lay
the big covehled. (*She draws coverlid off, hauls box
from under the bed, and opening it takes out bedclothes
and remakes the bed.*) You'n me 'll have to lay in the
broke baid this night. You won't git no rest.

GRANNY. No mattah, heah's a good baid fer de babe an'
I'll soon git all my res'.

PEARL. I hopes Sapphie's husband ain't too hefty, for the
th'ee might break this heah'n same as the otheh'n is
broke.

GRANNY. De husban' shain't sleep da nohow. You c'n lay
him a bunk in de washhouse.

PEARL. What! You ain't goin' to leave him lay heah?

GRANNY. Dis baid my Sam bought fo' me. Onliest man kin
eveh lay in hit shill be Sam's own blood. De babe an'
his mother'll lay heah dis night erlone.

PEARL. Well, the babe'll have plenty room and softness.

GRANNY. We'n my Sam wuz er babe we laid on cotton sack.
We didn' have no baid, an' w'en he little shaveh he say,
"Mammy, I goin' git you nice baid w'en I git er man."
An' sho' nuff, w'en he grow up he took'n do hit, an'
mek pu'chus in de attehnoon an' de baid come nex' day.
But at midnight betwix' dee tuk'n bu'nt 'im.

PEARL. Now, Granny—

GRANNY. In de black dahk dee come on 'im, de bloody-
handed mens, an' wheah dee cotch 'im dah dee bu'nt

'im, de right man settin' de wrong man afieh at de i'un hitchin' pos'.

PEARL. (*Going to her*) Granny Maumee, don't leave yo'self go that a-way. Don't leave youah mine run on.

GRANNY. (*Rocking back and forth*) My Sam, my man babe-um.

PEARL. Hit git you all wuk up an' wore out. You won't look good to company.

GRANNY. Look! Has I looked fo' fifty yeah sence I rush in de fieh fo' my Sam, which hit de las' sight deze eyes seen? Oh, whuffo' dee drag me out an' hilt me back? I bo' one man an' him dee tuk'n bu'nt. An' 'e slep' right'n dis room w'en de man wuz shot w'ich dee 'cuze 'im er! Whuffo' dee drag me back f'um de fieh?

PEARL. Yu' sees the wisdom of Gawd in hit, Granny Maumee. Fifty yeahs ergo me and Sapphie's gran'pap been burnt and yet you was to live to git a new Sam.

GRANNY. W'ich 'e neveh come. Dee wuz all gals fum dat on, you an' yo' sisteh Sapphie an' yo' mammy an' yo' mammy's mammy, all down from my breas'; all gals.

PEARL. You fuhgits what Sapphie's fetchin' you.

GRANNY. Dat I don't, but not 'twell I sees 'im will Sam be cool off in my heaht.

PEARL. Granny, you can nurse the child but 'course you cain't espect to see him.

GRANNY. Deze eyes shill yit behole ——

PEARL. No, Granny Maumee, your eyes they're scorched and swiveled with the fire. But your arms ain't burnt, is they? An' they shall hold the baby! 'Tain't often old person live to heft a great-great-gran'baby.

GRANNY. Befo' my las' houah deze eyes shill look an' see ergin. (*She rises.*)

PEARL. Wheah you goin'?

GRANNY. Has you lay out my raid gown?

PEARL. Yes, it's all on the sofy.

GRANNY. Den I goes to primp up an' mek ready to receive.

PEARL. Yes, it's only perlite to put on ouah best to meet the husband.

GRANNY. I dresses fer none but de chile. (*She goes slowly out at left.*)

PEARL. (*Calling*) Betteh lay down fust; they won't be here for two hour yet. I'll be there pres'n'ly. (*She continues to bestir herself about the room and then starts to follow* GRANNY. *There is a faint tap at the door at right.* PEARL *stops and listens. The tapping is repeated. She goes and opens the door. A young woman, looking much like* PEARL, *and of about the same age, but gaudily dressed and carrying a baby, stands in the doorway.*)

PEARL. (*With a half-smothered exclamation*) Sapphie! (SAPPHIE *motions her to be silent and softly, fearfully enters the room*).

SAPPHIE. (*In a low voice*) Wheah Granny Maumee?

PEARL. She in the baidroom fixin' up. Wheah's youah husband?

SAPPHIE. (*After a pause*) He—didn'—come ——

PEARL. Oh, that's too bad, but it's good to see you,—and let's see the baby.

SAPPHIE. (*Drawing back with the swathed and veiled child*) Not yet.

PEARL. Oh, he's asleep, of course.

SAPPHIE. (*Pointing to doorway through which Granny passed*) Shut the door.

PEARL. (*Obeying wonderingly*) Well, hit do look good to see you ergin, Sapphie. Hit don't seem like er yeah sence you lef' home. Does youah husband tek you to pictuh shows?

SAPPHIE. Puhl, what's Granny Maumee like now; is she failed any? Is she fie'ce as eveh 'bout the burnin' and the w'ite mens?

PEARL. Why, of course she is. She don't neveh change f'um year ter year. Come on, let's see baby. What youah husband's name? You neveh sent us wu'd what youah new name was.

SAPPHIE. That's what I want to see you for before Granny Maumee comes out. Come here. (*She lifts the veil from the child's face.*)

PEARL. (*Peering eagerly forward and then starting back*) W'ite!

SAPPHIE. (*Breathlessly*) How'll she take hit? What'll she do? I'm scared of her.

PEARL. A light-head merlatter! So youah husband didn't come 'cause they ain't no husband. Who's the man?

SAPPHIE. You know wheah I work.

PEARL. Lightfoot!

SAPPHIE. He des would have his way.

PEARL. So, he took you off to town with him, did he? And that's how come you had the luck to go. I praise King Jesus he kept me f'um such luck.

SAPPHIE. How'll she take hit?

PEARL. Take hit! Does you s'pose we can take'n tell her? Thank my Makeh she's blind. It's the mussy of Gawd her eyes was swiveled in w'ite man's fire before she see the w'ite man mix with her blood. You—

SAPPHIE. Oh, I don't care what you calls me if you'll only help me and keep Granny Maumee off'n me and baby.

PEARL. It's only helpin' to keep us all from 'struction that I'll keep it from her.

SAPPHIE. What you think she'd do if she found out?

PEARL. I don't know. Sometimes when her mine runs on 'bout the burnin' she begins to work back'ards.

SAPPHIE. (*Fearfully*) What you mean?

PEARL. You knows what I means. Away from the love of Gawd, back to that Affykin devil stuff.

SAPPHIE. (*Starting with a cry toward the door at back*) Oh, she might 'witch me and the baby too.

PEARL. Don't be scared. She won't tech you 'cause she won't know the sinneh you been.

SAPPHIE. He des would have his way. (*A tap is heard outside* GRANNY'S *door.*)

PEARL. She's comin'. (SAPPHIE *shrinks back toward opposite side of room as door opens and* GRANNY *enters wearing a red dress with red apron and red silk cap on her head. She pauses just inside and listens intently.*)

GRANNY. Who bin talkin'?

PEARL. Me. (*She guides* GRANNY *to her chair.*)

GRANNY. Well, talk on. How I look? (*She straightens proudly in her chair.*)

PEARL. Good. The red ain't faded none.

GRANNY. Dat's good, fer I needs hit bright dis day an' night. De babe'll want tuh see hit. Red's de fus' coloh er baby notice an' red allers goes wif black. Red neveh go wif w'ite. Looks ghas'ly. I use allers tuh wrop my Sam in red—(*She pauses and her voice grows shriller*) an' red's de las' way I seen 'im.

PEARL. Now, Granny——

GRANNY. Dat's right, I mus' tek my mine off er dat sight now. But I'll tek'n wrop dis noo black babe in my red ap'un dat hilt my Sam. In red he shill be wrop an' black he shill shine. Royal black we is an' royal black we shill stay. Praise my Makeh, dey ain' no drop er

any yutheh coloh in 'im. All us wimens wuz hones',
all de way down, an' we kep' clean er de w'ite streak.
We kep' us clean, praise my King, an' we will ter de
en'. W'ite blood were 'stroyin' angel tuh my fambly
f'um de beginnin's, but hit never yit mix wif us. We
wuz save f'um dat las' pizen. (SAPPHIE *turns as*
though to go through the door at right with her child.
PEARL *motions her through side doorway at left. She*
goes out softly.)

PEARL. Hattie Lee she uz hones' an' her baby's w'ite. That
w'ite man tuk'n marry her with preacheh.

GRANNY. Married wif preacheh! Do dat change de trashy
blood? I wudn' have dat kinder mud pumpin' in er babe
er my blood, not ef de sevumty eldehs had j'ined a w'ite
man tuh you er Sapphie.

PEARL. W'ite blood no wus'n black blood.

GRANNY. 'Tis fer us! 'Tis fer dis house er sorrer. Hit's
bin fieh, hit's bin death, hit's bin de crawlin' stream er
hell fer me an' my fambly as fur as I knows, an' dat's
a hunderd yeah. But I lets all de yutheh go, 'case I
hates um ernuff fer dis one thing—— (*She goes to*
red-covered chest at right, lifts the lid and takes out two
half-charred sticks of wood.)

PEARL. Now, Granny, put um back——

GRANNY. (*Waving the sticks*) Deze w'ut I snatch f'um de
fieh undeh Sam. Deze is ernuff to mek us hate all er dat
blood an' keep hit fur f'um us.

PEARL. (*Going to her and taking the sticks*) Is this heah
makin' ready for comp'ny? Now ca'm yo'se'f. (*She*
lays the sticks on top of the chest.)

GRANNY. (*Seating herself and growing suddenly very still*
as though listening) Yo're right. Time's up, de houah
is heah an' de chile is neah. I feels hit. Run an' open

de do'. Sapphie mus' be comin' up de paf. Mek ready.
I feel my noo man chile neah me. (PEARL *goes out
doorway at left. After a moment she and* SAPPHIE
enter without the baby.)

SAPPHIE. (*Going forward hesitatingly to* GRANNY) Granny
Maumee.

GRANNY. Give 'im heah in deze ahms.

SAPPHIE. I lay him in yutheh room. I want to see you.

GRANNY. Fetch 'im.

SAPPHIE. Ain't you glad to have me back?

GRANNY. Fetch de babe, be swift! (PEARL *motions to* SAP-
PHIE; *she goes out to get the baby.*)

PEARL. Her man, he couldn't come with her.

GRANNY. No diffunce. I bless de man an' wish 'im well;
he's su'ved his puhpose, but he ain' none er ouah blood.
De boy babe's de chief un. (SAPPHIE *enters with the
baby.*) Give 'im heah, be swif'! (SAPPHIE *hesitatingly lays the child in* GRANNY'S *outstretched arms. As
she does so a strange reaction, like an electrical shock,
seems to overtake the old woman. She holds out the
child as though she would give it back. After a moment, however, she presses it to her breast, rocking back
and forth and crooning to it*) Babe, man babe-um,
er noo man, er puore-blood man raise' up atter all dem
gals. Sam kin res' now. 'Case w'y—(*She begins to
chant*) 'case er noo man bin raise up an' he shill lay
hol' er de stahs an' th'ow um down fer vingince. He
shill be er 'stroyin' fieh er heavum tuh roll ergin de
hell fieh w'ut dey lit fer Sam an' quinch hit out fuheveh.
De wrath er Gawd shill be wif 'im an' de w'ite blood
shill puhvail no more agin' 'im. De sun an' moon shill
rise no mo' on my house an' fin' on'y gals, 'case we got
er puore-blood man fer to gyard an' carry us on.

(*From time to time during her words she has paused and bent intently over the baby, striving to see it*) An' my King'll not keep de cuss on me now an' leave me go down to de grave wifouten sight er you, my babe-um. Dese eyes shill yit behole. (*She rises with the child in her arms*) Go on out er heah, Puhl an' Sapphie, lemme be alone now wif my babe. (*She waves them out imperiously.*)

PEARL. Whuffo'?

GRANNY. I wan' ter see dis chile befo' I dies.

PEARL. Why, Granny Maumee, your eyes is swiveled up with the fire. You couldn't see.

GRANNY. Go. I won't be long.

PEARL. (*To* SAPPHIE) Come on, don't cross her.

SAPPHIE. (*Whispering*) I'm 'fraid——

PEARL. You know she couldn't—— (*They go out doorway at left.* GRANNY *stands staring down at the child in her arms for some time. She then goes over to the bed and lays the child upon it, bending over it and striving to see. At last she turns, goes swiftly over to the red-covered chest and taking from its top the two charred sticks, turns, lights them at the fireplace, comes forward to the middle of the room and holding the flaming faggots before her face peers steadily at them.*)

GRANNY. (*Suddenly in a loud voice with upraised face*) Sam—ask Gawd tuh give back my sight dis night er all nights an' leave me look at de noo man w'ut bin handed down ter us. Fer we kep' de blood puore. Ask an' we shill receive—— (*In a still louder tone, stretching upward her hands*) Lawd, I believe. (*She suddenly sways, turns, drops the sticks on the hearth, puts her hands before her eyes and staggers forward. After a moment she takes her hands from her face and looks*

tremblingly about.)   Yes—he give hit back—I sees—
Oh, my black babe! (*She moves swiftly to the bed and
bends over the child. There is a moment's pause.*)
W'ut dis? Cain' I see yit? De wrong coloh. (*She
turns swiftly, seizes a white cloth from a chair and a
black one from another, holds them up and looks at
them alternately.*)   W'ite—black. (*Then turning to
the bed she stares again at the child. After a moment
she straightens and reaching her hands upward she gives
a cry.*) W'ite! Debbils! (SAPPHIE *and* PEARL *appear in doorway.* GRANNY *bends over the child with
clawlike fingers raised as though she were about to stran-
gle it.* SAPPHIE *darts forward and snatches the child.*
GRANNY *turns and looks at* SAPPHIE *and* PEARL *in
turn.*)

PEARL. She sees!

SAPPHIE. Granny Maumee, the babe'll be ouah'n an' we
can raise him right. He's a good baby and don't cry
none. I don't want to live'n town. I want to live here
with you and Puhl. Baby'll love you. And we won't
be no trouble to keep 'case I got money. Look—take
this. (*She draws from her bosom a crumpled handful
of bills which she stuffs into* GRANNY'S *hands.*)

GRANNY. Wheah you git dis? (*She stands immovably
staring before her.*)

SAPPHIE. He give it to me.

GRANNY. (*Shaking off the money on to the table*) W'ite
man money.

SAPPHIE. He des would have his way, but he's good to me
and he takes care of me. He's comin' heah to-night to
see me.

GRANNY. W'ut de name?

SAPPHIE. Young Lightfoot.

GRANNY. De gran'pap er dat man tetch off de fieh w'ut bu'n up my Sam.

SAPPHIE. But this'n ain't that a-way, Granny Maumee. He's always kind.

GRANNY. W'en's de man comin'?

SAPPHIE. He'll be here soon and if you'll only listen he'll sure talk you 'round.

GRANNY. (*Pointing to the baby.*) Hit wants out. Take it out an' come yere. (SAPPHIE *obeys, going through doorway at left.* GRANNY *suddenly turns to the flower basin mounted on a tripod. Seizing it she empties both flowers and earth in the fireplace, where she refills the basin with live coals. Then bringing it forward she places it upon its tripod.*)

PEARL. Granny Maumee, you're slippin' backwuds; please don't fuss with that conju'n foolishness; they ain't nothin' into hit an' hit des keeps you 'cited.

GRANNY. Debbils calls out debbils. (*She goes to several places where upon the walls are hung bunches of dried herbs. From several of these she seizes handfuls.*) Come, my seedin' Jimson, come, ole Rattlesnake-Marsteh, come, my Black-Ball, w'ut Pap Jack han' me up. (SAPPHIE *re-enters the room and stands watching* GRANNY *in terror.* GRANNY *closes all the doors to the room, then going to the red-covered chest on the right and opening it she drags forth several coils of blackened iron chain which she casts upon the table. She sprinkles a few of her handful of herbs on the fire in the brazier. A dense smoke arises.*)

SAPPHIE. (*With a scream*) Don't! Oh, don't conjuh me.

PEARL. (*Scornfully*) Don't fuss, Sapphie, she won't do no harm. What the chains for, Granny?

GRANNY. Dem's de chains w'ut bine Sam w'en dey tuk'n bu'n 'im.

PEARL. What you worry yourself by gittin' um out for?

GRANNY. I ain' worried no mo'. (*She throws more herbs on the fire in the brazier.*) Dem chains fer de w'ite man.

PEARL. What you mean?

GRANNY. (*Pointing to the door at left back*) W'en de w'ite man knock de do' shill be open an' dat shill be beginnin' er his trials.

PEARL. What you mean?

GRANNY. De smoke in dis room will strankle de man's will in his breas' an I'll use 'im den as I choose.

SAPPHIE. What you goin' do to 'im?

GRANNY. I goin' lead 'im out tuh de i'un hitchin' pos' w'ut dey fas'en Sam ter an' I goin' tuh chain 'im da wif dese chains an' I goin' tuh bring 'im tuh 'imself an' den I goin' tuh bu'n 'im lak he gran'pappy bu'n Sam.

SAPPHIE. (*With a scream*) You shan't!

PEARL. You s'pose we leave you do hit? (*The girls start forward toward the doorway at left back. As they near* GRANNY *she swiftly seizes a handful of burning herbs from the brazier and waves them smoking across the faces of the girls under their nostrils, so that they breathe the fumes. They take a few steps farther, staggering, and then stand motionless and silent. She takes them by the hands and leads them back. The fumes of stramonium, solanum and other herbs have produced catalepsis.* GRANNY *goes to the fireplace at back and from the mantel takes a wooden bowl, a short stick and a large dry gourd. She returns, gives the bowl and stick to* SAPPHIE, *causing her to beat rhythmically on the inverted bowl with the stick, a motion which* SAPPHIE *continues in imitative hypnosis.* GRANNY *gives the gourd to* PEARL, *causing her to shake it. The gourd gives forth a dry rattle from seeds or pebbles within it.* GRANNY *then places the two girls on either side of the tripod and they continue their drumming and rattling rhythmically. She then takes her place back of the tripod and casts more herbs upon the fire.*)

GRANNY. Sistehs, kin yo' heah me speak? Answer, Sapphie.

SAPPHIE. (*In a dull tone*) Yes.

GRANNY. Answeh, Puhl. Does yo' heah me?

PEARL. (*Also dully*) Yes.

GRANNY. Does yo' see?

BOTH GIRLS. Yes.

GRANNY. Den watch me mek my w'ite man Lightfoot outer Lightfoot money. (*She seizes the bunch of bills from the table and plucking strands of hair from her head she begins tying the money together; taking the candle from the table she holds it over the tripod until it is soft and then kneads it with the money until the whole grows into the rude semblance of a human figure. Stooping then to the hearth she takes up the two charred sticks of her son's pyre and with one of these she stabs the wax mannikin through the breast. Holding up the impaled figure she stands over her tripod and again speaks.*) Say dis atter me:— By de fieh at night, by de black boy down,

THE SISTERS. "By the fire at night, by the black boy down,"

GRANNY. By de skunt-off face an' de red on de groun',
(*The sisters repeat each line after her in unison, keeping up their rhythm with drum and rattle.*)
By de w'ip an' de rope an' de chain dat swung,
By de bloody mouf an' de bit-off tongue,
By de eat-up heaht an' de spit-out gall,

We scream, we beg, we whoop, we squall
Tuh git poweh, tuh git stren'th tuh put de trick on um
    all.
(*After this the remainder of* GRANNY'S *curse is spoken
by her alone. The sisters continue their sounds with
the drum and rattle.*) Let um git no res' in bed, er good
at vittals, er hope at wu'k, er he'p at home, er peace wif
fren's er kin, er tryin' tuh tek pleasuah, er in any place
dey kin go er hide.

    Th'ee fingeh Jack my Obi pap,
    He'p me, ole Marsteh.
    Keep de promise wif um all.
(*She lifts the mannikin on the stick and looks at it.*)
    Now, my Lightfoot, yore tu'n's come.
    Dis is Lightfoot, Ole Marsteh.
Let me slit 'im an' bu'n 'im an' was'e 'im an' cut 'im an'
choke an' weah 'im an' teah 'im as Sam 'uz slit an'
choked an' bu'nt an' was'e an' cut an' woah an' toah.
(*She waves the mannikin to the four points of the com-
pass.*)
    Fo' times fo' times fo' times fo',
    Fly an' call an' open de do'.
De chains is ready, de man is neah, an' almos' heah an'
de chahm shill hol'. Spile 'im as I spile 'im. (*She casts
the mannikin and the sticks with ferocity into the fire
on the tripod and then bends down staring intently into
the fire. There is a moment's silence and then she gives
a cry, as she looks into the fire.*) Sam! Is dat you in
da? You instid er he? W'ut dis? Is we bin trick?
'Tain't you—'tis you—Sam! Ah-h! (*With a cry she
snatches the blazing mannikin from the brazier and
folds it in her caught-up apron, staggering and beating
the air as though battling with unseen forces. Suddenly*

*a gust of wind blows open the door at the right and a
breeze fills the room, blowing the smoke and fluttering
the garments of the women. The drum and rattle cease
and fall to the floor. Immediately* GRANNY *raises her
face in awe, seeing a vision. She stretches out her arms
toward it, speaking brokenly.*) Sam! Yes, I sees yo'.
I heahs yo'. Yes, my babe-um——Talk on—Tell me.
—W'at? (*She pauses, listening intently, with eyes
fixed on the unseen.*) Leave 'im go!—Oh, how kin I?—
Gi' me stren'th. (*She pauses again and bows her head.
After a moment she again raises her face to the vision.*)
I knows.—I fuhgot. I'll do hit.—I des wen' backerds
but I'm wif yo' now.—Yas—Ez we fuhgives utehs—
yas—I knows—we'll do hit.—We will be tuhgetheh.—
Ez we fuhgives utehs. (*A knocking is heard on the
door back, at left of the fireplace.* GRANNY *turns her
head and listens. After a pause the knocking begins
again more imperatively. She turns, seizes the tripod
brazier, casts it into the fireplace, and staggers toward
the door, taking her stand beside it. The knocking
pauses.*) Go back, w'ite man. Roll back, w'ite wave er
de fiery lek. Once you lit de fieh an' bu'n me. Once
you po' de blood an' pizen me, but dis time Sam an' me
we's de stronges' an' we leaves you go, we leaves you
live tuh mek yore peace wif Gawd. We're puore bloods
heah, royal black—all but one an' we'll do de bes' we
kin erbout 'im. He shill be name Sam. Go back, w'ite
man, an' sin no mo'. (*She pauses and listens. There
is no further sound from without.* GRANNY *staggers
over to the sisters and shakes them, saying in a faint
voice*) Wake up, Sapphie; come tuh, Puhl. (*As she
does so she looks upward again and cries out:*) Sam,
we done hit, an' we stays tuhgetheh! (*She sinks down*

*slowly to the floor. The sisters have stirred and looke[d]
about stupidly.* PEARL *now sees* GRANNY *and ben[d]
over her.*)

PEARL. Granny!—Sapphie, come hyeh, quick! (*With [a]
cry*) Ah—Granny Maumee's dead. (*She runs terro[r]
stricken to the door at back, crouching beside it.* SA[P-]
PHIE *then, after gazing intently at* GRANNY, *sudden[ly]
runs toward the door, and dragging it open rushes ou[t]
followed by her sister.*)

BOTH GIRLS. (*Outside*) Granny Maumee's dead! Gran[ny]
Maumee's dead! (*Their voices gradually die away [in]
the distance, the door blows shut. The body of* GRAN[NY]
MAUMEE *is left alone in the room.*)

CURTAIN

THE BIRD CHILD

A PLAY OF THE SOUTH

By

LUCY WHITE

*Reprinted by special permission of the author
and The Howard Players, Washington, D. C.*

CHARACTERS

EZEKIEL BURROWS, a country lawyer
RANDALL, his secretary
MARY, his youngest sister
HALLIE, a mulatto
SILVY WILKINS, Hallie's mother

Scene: A Mississippi Valley town, in the early nineties.

THE BIRD CHILD

THE SCENE *is the library at the residence of* EZEKIEL BURROWS, *which, after the manner of country lawyers of his section and period, he uses also as a reception room for his clients. The room is large, light, and the hangings and furnishings stuffily old-fashioned, but the room betrays some distinction and culture on the part of the owner. It has the appearance of having been allowed to become shabby in order to be more comfortable. At the right corner rear is a large circular bay window, on the right toward the front of the stage is an open grate in which a fire is burning. Between this and the window at center right is a door leading to* BURROWS' *private study and bedroom. At center rear are folding doors, leading to the sitting room, at left a door leading to a hallway which constitutes a sort of side business entrance to the house.*

The walls are lined to the ceiling with bookshelves bearing calf-bound reports. There is a large desk at the right of center stage, a long library table between left door and folding doors, a revolving bookcase containing some encyclopedias of law, and a number of chairs scattered about.

When the curtain rises, BURROWS *and* RANDALL *are discovered.* RANDALL, *a boy hardly out of his teens, is seated at the table writing at* BURROWS' *dictation.* BURROWS, *a sensitive, slight, kindly-looking man of between thirty-five and*

forty, given to quick nervous gestures, is at the desk. Before
him is a heap of legal documents, and scattered over his desk
and on several chairs grouped around him, open volumes of
reports, marked with slips of paper for ready reference. The
table at which RANDALL *is writing is also littered with paper*
and books.

BURROWS. (*Dictating*) And, taking this view of the case,
even if it should be conceded that the homicide occurred
at a time when the defendant had no longer reason to
fear that his wife was in physical danger from the de-
ceased, it still must be admitted that the defendant was,
at the time of the shooting, still laboring under great
emotional stress occasioned by the threatened outrage,
and that his anger had not yet had reasonable time to
cool. (MARY *appears at the door at center left, open-*
ing it cautiously. BURROWS, *not perceiving her, pro-*
ceeds) The courts have not, so far as counsel is in-
formed, ever laid down any definite rule as to what
period could be considered a reasonable lapse of time in
cases of this sort —— (*Noticing* MARY) Well, Mary.
(MARY *enters. She is a slight girl of about fourteen*
and wears a pretty school dress of some dark woolen
material.)

MARY. I don't want anything, Bru'er Zeke. I just wanted to
come in. Go on with the brief. I won't bother you.
(*As she speaks, she seats herself, taking up a book out*
of the chair, and turning its leaves idly.)

BURROWS. I thought you had started off to Alice Bullock
by now.

MARY. (*Laughing nervously, apologetically*) I had a bad
dream, and don't want to go. I told Aunt Calline to
stop in as she went by and tell Alice I wasn't coming.
(*Impatiently*) If you're working on that Ragan brief

I'll go upstairs.   Only, it's lonesome up there; Cousin
Clara's gone down town.   You needn't be afraid to dic-
tate before me.   I know all about the case anyway.
(BURROWS *and* RANDALL *exchange significant glances.*)

MARY. (*Flaring up*) You two seem to think I'm foolish.
(*Recklessly*) I know enough about it to know that Mr.
Ragan didn't shoot Mr. Humphreys to defend his wife.

RANDALL. (*Patronizingly*) You don't know anything about
it, Mary.

MARY. Yes, I do!   I know that he shot because he was
drunk and felt like shooting!

BURROWS. (*Who has been hunting ineffectually through his
books for some reference*) Rand, you'll have to go over
to Adamson's and have him send me the report of that
recent Massachusetts case he was telling me about.   I
can't do much more until I've seen it.   (*Exit* RANDALL)
Well, Mary, what's the trouble?

MARY. (*Approaching his chair*) Bru'er Zeke, what did
Aunt Calline mean by saying somebody ought to kill
Bob Ragan?

BURROWS. I don't know.   Did she say that?

MARY. Yes.   She said that if white men wanted to be so
careful of women-folks they ought to keep out of nigger cabins.

BURROWS. Did she say that to you?

MARY. No.   She was talking to Josie Carson, and I was at
the swing and heard them.   Josie said that Dovey Rice,
that little yellow girl of Martha Rice's, looked more
like Rob Ragan than any of Mrs. Ragan's children,
and then Aunt Calline said, (*Imitating a Negro*) "Yes,
they's always talkin' about shootin' to defen' de wim-
men.   Dat's a mighty nice excuse when you ain't got no
other.   He says now he shot to defen' his wife, and he'd

shoot to defen' his mother or his sister or his little gal, but who's go'n' to defen' his yellow gal Dovey? She's just a nigger. Dat's just it! She's a little yellow nigger, an' we-all know what's coming to her, but we don't know how she's go'n' to feel about it!"

BURROWS. You mustn't stay around the quarters when the niggers are talking. I'll speak to Clara about Calline. I can't have this.

MARY. Bru'er Zeke, if Dovey is Mr. Ragan's daughter, wouldn't she be Mildred Ragan's sister?

BURROWS. (*Testily*) No! Dovey is a little nigger; that's all! Just a little nigger!

MARY. (*Looking at him wonderingly*) Oh!

BURROWS. Go on over to Alice's, Mary. I can't have you here. I've work to do. (MARY *shakes her head with a sort of calm obstinance.*)

BURROWS. (*Beginning to be impatient*) Why don't you go?

MARY. (*Pleadingly*) I'll be quiet. I won't say a word to you or Randall. I'll read; I won't listen.

BURROWS. You can't stay here. I won't be bothered. Why don't you go?

MARY. I'm afraid.

BURROWS. What are you afraid of?

MARY. Something bad is going to happen, Bru'er Zeke.

BURROWS. (*Puzzled, smiling*) Something bad going to happen!

MARY. (*Trying to overcome some embarrassment*) Yes, I think so—that dream——

BURROWS. (*Humoring her*) Well, what about the dream? Come and tell it to me, Mary.

MARY. It was so mixed up and foolish, and yet so real that I had to get up out of bed, and go take down mamma's picture and think back to be right sure she was really

dead, and couldn't be alive and in that awful fix—like
she was in the dream. (RANDALL *enters at left with
volume under his arm.*)

RANDALL. (*Good-humoredly*) Mrs. Silvy Wilkins, colored,
wants to see Mr. Burrows.

BURROWS. Let her wait! (RANDALL *closes door at left.*
BURROWS *looks about for some means of getting rid of*
RANDALL) And, Rand, I want a copy of the entire
opinion in this New York case, Rogers *versus* Thomson.
(*Hands* RANDALL *volume from his desk.* RANDALL
starts toward right door) And, Rand! Make three
carbons! (*Exit* RANDALL) (*Turning to* MARY) Go
on!

MARY. You see I thought I had just come into the library
this morning—looking just like it does now—and found
mamma sitting here by the fire—only, it was mixed up
and part of the time I seem to be you and part of the
time myself. I thought that we had all been mistaken;
she had never been dead at all; but somebody had taken
her from her grave—and I thought she wanted to stay
in her grave—I knew that!—but they had taken her and
made her live down in some awful place in Crowtown.
I thought she was dirty, and tired and hungry looking;
and I felt somehow that she was vile, and yet I couldn't
blame her. (*Breaking out*) Oh, Bru'er Zeke, it was
the most dreadful dream I have ever had. It was so
real! It was mamma—but her eyes! I can see them
now! Do you remember that woman I saw them taking
into the courthouse that day last summer, and you said
she was bad, and I mustn't look at her? I thought her
eyes looked like that woman's did—dull and sad, and I
thought she said she'd come to stay with us always, and
we went about wondering what we could do to make her

and ourselves less miserable. (*Begins crying*) I don't
understand it myself. Something dreadful must be
going to happen.

BURROWS. (*Soothingly*) Don't you know that nothing like
that can happen? You are awake now. The dead never
come back. You must remember what a woman your
mother was. It was just a bad dream, Mary; you were
sick or nervous. Mother would never come back that
way; don't you know that? (MARY *nods*) Run away
and have a fine time with Alice, and forget all about
your dream and everything else that's ugly. Run along,
now! (MARY *starts toward door, stops and comes
back.*)

MARY. But it must mean something, Bru'er Zeke, I know
it means something!

BURROWS. What could it mean?

MARY. I feel somehow it's something we've done wrong. Do
you suppose the dead suffer for the sins of others?

BURROWS. (*Tenderly, playfully*) Have you committed some
awful sin, Mary?

MARY. No; not I. But——

BURROWS. Run away, Mary, and be quiet. Your mother is
at peace if ever a soul was; and you're awake. Don't
be silly over a dream. (MARY *goes slowly to door*)
And Mary, tell Mrs. Wilkins to come in. (*Exit* MARY
and, after a few seconds, enter SILVY WILKINS, *a mulatto woman of about thirty. She is dressed poorly,
with a show of neatness but with no effort at coquetry.
She wears a short woolen jacket, the worse for wear
over her faded calico dress, and has a crocheted woolen
shawl over her head. She advances halfway across the
room and pauses uncertainly.*)

SILVY. You don' know me, Mistah Zeke.

BURROWS. No; I don't know you.

SILVY. I ust to be Silvy Wes'. (*A shadow of annoyance crosses* BURROWS' *face.*)

BURROWS. Sit down, Silvy. (SILVY *sits down. They both seem ill at ease*) Well, what's the trouble?

SILVY. I don' like to come heah botherin' you, but I'se had a lot of bad luck lately. You see, Jim—that's ma husban', Jim Wilkins—got a job down in Arkansaw in de sawmill, an' got his leg hurt, an' my oldes' gal Hallie, she been sick, an' de baby died, and I'se had a touch of croup myse'f dis winter ——

BURROWS. Do you want to borrow some money, Silvy?

SILVY. Dat's what I'se tellin' you. We come up heah las' summer 'cause de lumber camp shut down, an' I wanted to see de ol' place, but Jim, he's back thar now an' sick, an' if I could get to 'im ——

BURROWS. Where's this place in Arkansas?

SILVY. It's called Janesville. Mistah Ross, de railroad lawyer—I been washin' for his wife—he say he can get me a ticket thar, an' I can ca'y the two younges' chillun without a ticket, but de furniture am garnisheed an' dat man say ——

BURROWS. How much money do you need?

SILVY. 'Tain't dat, Mistah Zeke. Jim sent me seven dollars an' a ha'f, an' Mis' Ross, she got six dollars what she owe me what she's keeping fuh me.

BURROWS. (*Laughing*) Why, you seem to be rich!

SILVY. Yessah. (*She looks at him, hesitates, then drops her eyes and goes on in a lower tone*) You see, Mistah Zeke, it's about my bigges' gal, Hallie. I thought maybe you might take her.

BURROWS. (*Smiling*) What would I do with her?

SILVY. Well, Jim don't like her no way. She ain't his chile, and it caused me a heap of trouble. I never did like to see no chile beat up, no way.

BURROWS. How old is she?

SILVY. She's ten.

BURROWS. (*Unconcerned, and talking simply not to seem unkind*) Old enough to be useful. Can't Mrs. Ross find her a place as nurse girl somewhere?

SILVY. (*With a calm tragic sort of persistence*) I think you'd better take her, Mistah Zeke.

BURROWS. (*Still unconcerned*) I'm afraid Cousin Clara Cobb —you remember her, Silvy—isn't fond of children, especially nigger children. She runs this house now, you know.

SILVY. (*As before*) Does you remember dat June you lef' heah on dat trip to Mexico about ten yeahs ago?

BURROWS. (*Annoyed and on guard*) Yes.

SILVY. (*Looking at him curiously, and emphasizing her words with a sort of singsong*) Hallie was bawn December th'ud, de night yo' ma died. Ol' A'nt Nancy ust to call her Mis' Burrus' bird chile.

BURROWS. (*Half-angrily*) Called her my mother's bird child?

SILVY. Yessah. You remember you left heah in June, an' dat nex' November, yo' ma took me in an' let me stay in one of dose back offices in the yahd heah. She was one good-heahted woman! She didn't know nothin' about why I was dat way. She jus' knowed I was he'pless an' took me in. (*She drops again into the singsong, as though she were repeating some magic rigmarole to herself*) Dey called her "de bird chile" 'cause ob dat gray bird. It come in Mis' Burrus' room dat mornin' an' dey knowed by dat she was go'n' to die. Dey tried to get it out de sick room, but it stayed dar. An' A'nt

Nancy say jus' as Mis' Burrus breathed her las' it flew
out de window, an' dey watched it, an' it flew right
across de back yahd, an' in through de window of dat
back office whar we was, an' lit right on my baby's head.
Josie had let de window up 'cause de fire was smoking
an' A'nt Cherry Bassinger had de chile up in her arms,
an' Josie was standin' right by; an' we all seen it. A'nt
Nancy called it Mis' Burrus' bird chile, an' she always
say Hallie look like Mis' Burrus an' ac' like Mis' Burrus, an' (*Dropping the singsong, raising her head and
facing him*) I always let dem think, Mistah Zeke, it was
de bird what caused it.

BURROWS. Silvy, you've never said a word of this to me
before.

SILVY. I knows I ain't, Mistah Zeke. I knows as much how
dis thing happened as you does. I ain't blamed you, an'
you ain't took no time to blame me. I always say it
ain't de question who's to blame an' who ain't. Maybe
thar ain't nobody to blame. But, Mistah Zeke, when a
thing's done, it's done;—ain't it?

BURROWS. Why do you come here now?

SILVY. (*Almost under her breath*) 'Cause Mis' Burrus, yo'
ma, don' gi' me no res'.

BURROWS. (*Impatiently*) My mother doesn't give you "no
rest"?

SILVY. (*Muttering*) She haints me out ov dem eyes!

BURROWS. What eyes?

SILVY. Dat chile's eyes!

BURROWS. (*Breaking out almost hysterically*) What child's
eyes? What are you talking about? What's my mother
got to do with this? If you expect anything from me,
you'd better leave her out of this, Silvy.

SILVY. (*Impressively*) Mistah Zeke, we cayn't leave her out now. It's too late. No, she didn't have nothin' to do with it. Dat was all me and you. But she's in it now—Dar she is; right dar! (*Pointing to doorway of hall*)

BURROWS. (*Startled*) Where? What do you mean?

SILVY. Right out dar in dat gal Hallie. Mistah Zeke, Mistah Zeke, you's got to listen to me now.

BURROWS. (*Controlling himself*) If Hallie—your girl—is there, send her in. (*As though he could not bear the thought*) Don't bring her; wait outside.

SILVY. You'll keep her, Mistah Zeke?

BURROWS. I'll look at her.

SILVY. Yes, and when you's looked, you'll keep her. I ain't lied, Mistah Zeke, I ain't lied!

BURROWS. Send her in; but stay outside.

SILVY. I'll send her in, an' I won't come in with her, but I'se go'n' out dat front do' an' away from heah. I'se leaving her heah wid you, an' you's go'n to keep her —— (*Lowering her voice*) and Mis' Burrus won't haint me out of her eyes no mo'. (*Exit* SILVY. BURROWS *turns to the fire and waits.* HALLIE *enters noiselessly at the door at which* SILVY *went out. She is a slight child, much lighter in color than* SILVY. *Her features are small, and pinched looking; her eyes large, brooding, somber. Her skin, where it should be cream, is gray—the ashy color of a Negroid's face when frightened or ill. She is dressed in a plain frock of cheapest blue calico, absolutely untrimmed. Her shoes are worn and too large for her. She is hatless. Her hair, unusually smooth and straight for a mulatto's, is divided and plaited in several little strands which cling to the curve of her head. She is close to* BURROWS *before he perceives her presence.* BURROWS *regards her intently as she stands with her head dropped.*)

BURROWS. (*With a trace of whimsicality*) So! You're here!

HALLIE. (*Frightened*) Yessah. I'se heah.

BURROWS. And you want a job here with me?

HALLIE. Yessah.

BURROWS. Think you'll get homesick?

HALLIE. Nossah. (*She begins to cry very quietly.*)

BURROWS. You don't know much about work, do you?

HALLIE. Nossah.

BURROWS. (*Not unkindly*) Can you say anything besides "nossah" and "yessah"?

HALLIE. Yessah.

BURROWS. Try it! (HALLIE *stands silent.*)

BURROWS. (*More softly*) Hallie, look up! Look at me! (HALLIE *raises her head and he gets a full view of her face. Startled*) Who taught you to—(*Breaks off, lowering his voice*) My God—your eyes! (HALLIE *crestfallen and puzzled passes her hand across her brow and looks at the palm as though she expected to find some trace of some misdeed of her own there.*)

HALLIE. (*So low she can scarcely be heard*) Nobody ain't taught me nothin'.

BURROWS. No. (*He pauses*) Does Jim ever beat you?

HALLIE. (*Rapidly, as though afraid she would never dare to begin again, were she to stop*) He whip me wid de hawse strap, an' las' time mammy say she kill him, an' Jim say he kill me, an' mammy say for me to run quick,—run quick—an' I run over to Mis' Sallie Hawn's and Mis' Sallie had company, so I sleep on a pallet under her bed.

BURROWS. (*After a pause*) Maybe I won't send you back, Hallie. (HALLIE *looks up and smiles. Her face and voice change; her voice becomes musical, her face plaintively gracious.*)

HALLIE. (*Looking around the room shyly*) Is I gwine to stay heah? Is you-all de folks?

BURROWS. (*Startled by the change in her, catching her by the arm, drawing her to him*) Who taught you—why do you talk like that—that look! Here, look at me, Hallie!

HALLIE. (*Terrified*) I ain't talkin'. I'se lookin' at yer, I'se lookin' at yer! (BURROWS *holds her arm and gazes into her face intently. She shrinks, her shoulders begin to shake. Finally she throws herself in an agony of sobbing on the floor at his feet.*)

BURROWS. (*Bending over her*) Hallie! Hallie!

HALLIE. (*Hysterical, pleadingly*) Don't! Don't send me back there! He done things I can't tell—Jim did! I won't go back. Dey c'n kill me first! You kill me! Kill me right here! (*Shrinking from his gaze*) Oh, don't—don't! (BURROWS *lifts her to a sitting posture, takes her face between his hands and turns it to his own, still staring in her eyes as though fascinated.* HALLIE *is terrified by the look on his face, which she does not understand*) I don't want to go back. I ain't going! You's good; you's a kind man! You'll lemme stay here somewhere! I won't say nothin'—I won't talk no way. I'se lookin' at yer—lookin' at yer all de time! Oh don't! Don't! (BURROWS *keeps his eyes on her face as though hypnotized, and does not seem to hear what she is saying. Finally he rises abruptly, turns, goes to his desk, and buries his face in his arms.*)

BURROWS. (*The words are muffled, and as though wrung from him against his will*) God—Have mercy!—God! (HALLIE *as though his grief reassures her in some way, rises from the floor, sniffs a few times, dries her eyes, and regards him with calm curiosity. The folding doors at back part slowly, and* MARY *walks into the room. She looks from* HALLIE *to* BURROWS, *from* BURROWS *to* HALLIE, *in a sort of daze.*)

MARY. (*Softly*) Bru'er Zeke!

BURROWS. (*Starting up, almost screaming, and turning his hands palm first before his face as though to hide himself and push the image of* MARY *from his vision*) Mary! Mary! (*Recovering himself*) Where have you been? Didn't you go?

MARY. (*Simply*) I saw them in the hall, and waited. (*In a calm voice, indicating* HALLIE) Who is she? (BURROWS *does not answer*) Is she to stay here?

BURROWS. Yes.

MARY. (*Her voice breaking*) For good?

BURROWS. Yes, Mary, I reckon so. (MARY *gives a little cry in which instinctive enlightenment, perplexity, pity and horror are mingled; and regarding* HALLIE *with a sort of fascinated revulsion, retreats slowly to the door by which she entered.*)

CURTAIN

BALO

A ONE ACT SKETCH OF NEGRO LIFE

By

JEAN TOOMER

Reprinted by special permission of the author

CHARACTERS

WILL LEE, a Negro farmer
SUSAN LEE, his wife
TOM, his elder son
BALO, another son
JENNINGS, a white neighbor
"COUSIN" BOB
"COUSIN" MAMIE, his wife   ⎫ visiting friends
"UNCLE" NED   ⎬
SAM, "UNCLE" NED's companion ⎭
Some Children of the visiting party

Scene: Present-day Georgia.
Time: Harvest time.

Photo by Francis Bruguiere

THE AUCTION BLOCK SCENE FROM "THE EMPEROR JONES"

BALO

AUTUMN DAWN. *Any week day. Outside, it is damp
and dewy, and the fog, resting upon the tops of pine trees,
looks like fantastic cotton bolls about to be picked by the early
morning fingers of the sun. As the curtain rises, the scene is
that of a Negro farmhouse interior. The single room, at all
times used for sleeping and sitting, on odd occasions serves
as a kitchen, this latter due to the fact that a great fireplace,
with hooks for pots and kettles, occupies, together with a
small family organ, the entire space of the left-hand wall.
This huge hearth suggests that perhaps the place might once
have been a plantation cookroom. This is indeed the case,
and those who now call it home (having added two rooms to
it) remember the grandmother—in her day* MARSA HARRIS'
*cook—telling how she contrived to serve the dishes hot
despite the fact that the big house was some hundred yards
away. The old frame mansion still stands, or rather, the
ghost of it, in the direct vision of the front door, its habitable
portion tenanted by a poor-white family who farm the land
to the south of it and who would, but for the tradition of
prejudice and the coercion of a rural public opinion, be on
terms of a frank friendship with their colored neighbors, a
friendship growing out of a similarity of occupations and
consequent problems. As it is, there is an understanding and
bond between them little known or suspected by northern*

*people. The colored family farms the land to the north.
The dividing line, halfway between the two homes, has no
other mark save one solid stake of oak. Both farmers did
well last year, resisted the temptation to invest in automobiles and player-pianos, saved their money, and so, this
season, though their cotton crop failed with the rest, they
have a nest egg laid away, and naturally are more conscious
of their comparative thrift and prosperity than if the times
were good. As was said, the curtain rises upon the general
room of the Negro farmhouse. The man himself, in rough
gray baggy trousers and suspenders showing white against a
gray flannel shirt, is seen whittling a board for shavings and
small kindling sticks to start a fire with. As he faces the
audience, the half light shades his features, giving but the
faint suggestion that they are of a pleasing African sym-
metry. Having enough kindling, he arranges it in the
hearth, strikes a match, and, as the wood catches, tends and
coaxes it, squatting on his hams. The flames soon throw his
profile into relief. It is surprisingly like that of an Indian.
And his hair (lack of hair, really), having been shaved close,
completes the illusion. A quick glance around the room will
now reveal a closed door (to the left) in the back wall, under-
neath which a narrow strip of light shows. To the right of
the door, against the wall, is a heavy oak bed which has been
perfectly made even at this early hour. In the right wall, by
the bed, a curtained window lets in at first the gray, and then,
as the mist lifts, the yellow light of morning. This side of
the curtain is a magnificent oak dresser, a match for the bed,
but otherwise out of place and proportion in the room.
Both of these are gifts to the family (and have become heir-
looms) from old* MARSA. *A window may be understood to
be in the wall facing the audience. Likewise, in this wall,
to the left, a door opens on the outside. The walls are plas-*

*tered and whitewashed. They are sprinkled with calendars,
one or two cheap pictures of fruit (such as are supposed to
befit a dining room), and one or two inevitable deathlike
family portraits. Chairs are here and there about a central
table, in the middle of which, resting on a white covering, is
a wooden tray for nut picks and crackers. The floor is covered with a good quality carpet. The fire in the hearth now
burns brightly, but fails to fill all but a small portion of it,
and so, gives one the impression of insufficiency. While*
WILL LEE *is still crouching down, the rear door swings open
as his wife comes in. Her complexion is a none too healthy
yellow, and her large, deep-set, sad and weary eyes are
strangely pathetic, haunted, and almost unearthly in the
flamelight. With such a slim and fragile body it is sur-
prising how she manages to carry on her part of the contract.*

SUSAN LEE. (*Her voice is high and somewhat cracked*)
Come on in. (*She turns about, and re-enters the
kitchen.* WILL, *satisfied with his fire, rises and, as he
follows her, speaks.*)

WILL. Whar's Bob an' Bettie Kate?

SUSAN. (*Through the half-open door*) Sent them for to
catch an' milk th' cows.

WILL. Whar's th' boys?

SUSAN. You-all know they was up all night a-grindin' an'
a-boilin' cane. Come on in. (WILL *passes out, and
soon his voice is heard in blessing.*)

WILL. We thanks thee, Heavenly Father, fo' yo' blessin's
of th' night. Once more thou hast kept yo' children
thru' th' time of Satan an' of sin. Bless us, O Lord.
Thou hast brought us like th' dew thru' temptations of
th' evil darkness inter th' glory of th' mornin' light.
Have mercy, Lord. Keep us, an' give us strength t' do
yo' will terday. An' every day. An' we asks you t'

bless this yere food prepared in His dear name.   Amen.
Amen.   (*Just as* WILL *begins his prayer, two young
fellows enter through the front door, but on hearing the
blessing in progress, stop, and wait with bowed heads
until it is over.   Whereupon they advance, and are
heard by* WILL.)

WILL.   That you, Tom?

TOM.   (*The larger of the two boys.   A Negro farm hand
with a smiling face and easy gait, distinguished at first
from* BALO *only by his taller figure and the fact of a
seedy black coat which he wears over his patched blue
faded overalls*)   Yassur.

WILL.   How much you git?

TOM.   Mighty nigh eighty gallons.

WILL.   That's right.   Had yo' breakfast?

TOM.   Yassur.

WILL.   That you thar, Balo?

BALO.   Yassur, dat's me.

WILL.   Reckon you had yo' breakfast too?

BOTH.   Yassur we done et.

WILL.   Slept any?

BOTH.   Nasur, dat we ain't.

WILL.   Well, git yo' Bibles down an' read fo' fifteen minutes,
then you-all jes' stretch yo'selfs befo' th' fire an' I'll
wake you up by an' by.

BOTH.   Yassur.   (*They get their Bibles from the organ,
stretch out in front the hearth, and begin to read.
BALO is nearer the audience.   As he reads he mumbles
his words aloud, and, by the twitching of his face and
the movements of his hands, is seen to be of a curious
nervous texture beneath his surface placidity.   TOM
soon falls asleep, and begins to breathe deeply and
rhythmically.   The monotony of this respiration, to-*

gether with the sound of his own voice seems to excite
BALO *peculiarly. His strange, half-closed eyes burn
with a dancing light, and his entire body becomes animated and alive. At this juncture, young voices and
Young feet enter the room to the rear.* SUSAN *has
trouble in getting them seated, and* WILL *in blessing the
food. Laughs, shouts, and admonitions, in reality,
continue all during the following scene, but, as* BALO
does not hear them, and as the audience is absorbed in
BALO, *all sound from the kitchen ceases on the stage.*
BALO *by this time has risen to his feet. Facing the
audience, he continues to read, and his words become
audible. He is reading St. Matthew VII, 24.*)

BALO. "Therefore whosoever heareth these sayings of mine,
and doeth them, I will liken him unto a wise man, which
built his house upon a rock: And the rain descended,
and the floods came, and the winds blew, and beat upon
that house; and it fell not; for it was founded upon a
rock. And everyone that heareth these sayings of mine,
and doeth them not, shall be likened unto a foolish man,
which built his house upon the sand: And the rain descended, and the floods came, and the winds blew, and
beat upon that house; and it fell: and great was the fall
of it." (*Here* BALO'S *excitement is so considerable that
he leaves off the Bible and chants, with additions, certain passages of it from memory*)

An' th' floods came, an' th' winds blew,
An' th' floods came, an' th' winds blew,
An' th' floods came, an' th' winds blew,
O Lord, have mercy, Lord, O Lord
Have mercy on a soul what sins,
O Lord, on a darky sinner's soul.

(*He repeats this two or three times and is almost beside himself when the tumult from the rear room breaks in on him. He is at first entirely bewildered, but then, with an instinctive rapidity, and before the children enter, stretches himself beside* TOM *on the hearth, and pretends to be asleep. Before so very long, this pretended sleep passes into the real thing.* BOB *and* BETTIE KATE *run through, take a whack at both of them, and go out the front door.* WILL *and* SUSAN *follow them into the front room, and, after they have gone, seat themselves before the fire.*)

WILL. (*In substance, this is repeated each morning, so that* SUSAN *almost knows it now by heart*) Ain't much t' do this mornin', Susan. Farmin's gittin' p'oly down this way when a man what's used t' work can set afo' th' fire handlin' han's, an' it's yet a month t' Christmas. Money ain't t' be made when syrup can be bought fer what it takes t' haul th' cane, an' git it ground an' biled. An' corn at fifty cents a bushel. Cotton's th' crop fer Georgia. Weevils or no weevils. An' God will took them away when people ain't so sinful (*He indicates the boys*) when folks goes t' sleep with Bibles in their han's. Susan, whar is that there theology book? Mus' be studyin'. Can't afford t' waste no time when I's in th' service of th' Lord. Sho' can't.

SUSAN. It's around somewheres, Will. You-all still studyin' seriously t' be a preacher? Thought I changed you back a week ago.

WILL. That I is, sho', an' there's lots worse a-heap. Sin is stompin' up an' down th' world an' Satan's drivin' with loose reins. Needs a righteous man t' grab them from him 'round this way. Wouldn't let you had that frolic here t'night but what I thought 'twould be as good a

chance as any t' turn th' people t' His ways.   An' that
I wouldn't. . . . Cousin Bob an' Mamie comin' early.
(*Outside, a voice is heard calling* WILL.)

WILL. That you, Mr. Jennings?   Come in, sir.

JENNINGS. (*Coming in.   He is their white neighbor—a
well-built man with ruddy cheeks and pointed nose,
dressed like* WILL *but for his shirt which is of khaki*)
Nothin' ter do, eh, Will, but hold yer hands afore th'
fire?   Lucky last year put a few dollars in th' bank.

WILL. Yassur, lucky sho'.   (*Both remain standing, a little
awkwardly despite the friendly greeting.*   SUSAN *has
kept her seat, and says nothing until directly spoken to.*)

JENNINGS. (*Pointing to the sleeping boys*) Nothin' fer
them ter do, eh, sleepin' away th' days an' it ain't yet
Christmas.

WILL. Nasur.   Them's been up all night tho', grindin' cane.

JENNINGS. Saw Balo there a while back actin' like he was
crazy.   An' what do yer think he said?   An' kept on
repeatin' it, "White folks ain't no more'n niggers when
they gets ter heaven, white folks ain't no more'n niggers
when they gets ter heaven."   (*Laughs*) How much you
get?

WILL. 'Bout eighty gallons.

JENNINGS. Not bad from that little biddie piece of land, eh?

WILL. Nasur, not bad 'tall.   But us has more'n we can use,
an' 'twouldn't pay t' ship it at th' present price they pays
fer it.

JENNINGS. Trade?

WILL. Fer what?

JENNINGS. Corn; turnips.

WILL. Nasur, got too many of them myself.   Too much syrup,
too.   Take some along with you; don't want nothin', sir.

JENNINGS. All right, Will.   Noticed yer ax handle was

busted. I'll send th' boy over with a new one fer yer.
An' anything else you want, just ask. Heard someone
sayin' somethin' 'bout you goin' north ter live. I told
'em, na,—preachin' an' farmin' is th' line fer you. An'
there's only one place fer them an' that's in Georgia,
eh, Will?

WILL. Yassur, that's right, sho'.

JENNINGS. What you got ter say 'bout it, Susan?

SUSAN. I don't want him t' preach, Mr. Jennings. Preachin' means neglect th' farm. Up north they say there's
lots of things you don't get here. An' I don't know,
Mr. Jennings, but I'd like t' get somethin'.

JENNINGS. Wall, what do yer call somethin' if money in th'
bank ain't somethin' when th' times are hard?

SUSAN. Yassur, money, but there's somethin' more'n life besides all th' money in th' world. I want that somethin'
else; an' folks say I might could get it if I went up north.

JENNINGS. How 'bout that, Will?

WILL. Dunno, sir. Maybe so, but I knows this place, an' I
don't know that. 'Specks Georgia's big enuf t' hold me
till I dies.

JENNINGS. Me, too, Will. Wall, mus' be goin'. I'll send a
can here fer that there syrup. An' th' handle.

WILL. Don't mind th' can, Mr. Jennings, sir, jest roll a
barrel over, an' roll it back when you is thru'.

JENNINGS. All right. Thanks, Will—return th' same some
day. So long.

WILL. (*Seeing him to the door*) Yassur, good evenin', Mr.
Jennings. (*He closes the door and returns to* SUSAN.
The boys are still sleeping soundly.)

WILL. Wish you'd root me out that book, Susan. (SUSAN
gets up, rummages around, and finds the book. WILL
immediately drops into his chair, and is at once ab-

sorbed. Like BALO, *though in not quite so pronounced
a manner, he too mumbles as he reads.* SUSAN *enters
the rear room. At this point the curtain descends for a
moment to indicate the passing of the morning, and of
the first five hours of the afternoon. When it ascends,*
WILL *is seated as before, in front of the fire which now
burns briskly and with a sizzling sound in thankful contrast to the dull gray light that filters through the windows. It has clouded up outside, and threatens rain.
The boys have left the hearth.* WILL *has exchanged
his theology book for the Bible. His eyes seem to be
in a concentrated daze, focused on the glowing ashes.
A voice coming from the outside arouses him.*

VOICE. Whoo thar, you, Will?

WILL. (*Collecting himself*) That you, Cousin Bob? Come
on in. Don't need no ceremonies t' enter this yer house.
Come in. Come in. (COUSIN BOB *and his wife,
Negro country folks, and six small children from twelve
to two and a half years old enter through the rear door
by way of the kitchen.* COUSIN MAMIE *carries a large
basket covered with a spotless white napkin.*)

WILL. What's that fer on yo' arm, Cousin Mamie?

MAMIE. Supper, Cousin Will. Know'd you'd hab enuf t'
share with us-all, but reckoned I'd jes' tote it wid me,
'kase dese hungry mouths don't nebber git enuf t' eat,
does you, honey? (*Addressing the oldest, who shakes
his head bashfully in negation*) I'll jes warm 'tup over
yo' fire dar when you-all goes in t' eat. (*The family all
group themselves in a semicircle around the hearth, the
older folks on chairs, the younger ones on the floor or
standing, shifting ill at ease from foot to foot, uncom-
fortable in their Sunday shoes.*)

COUSIN BOB. Cotton po' wid you dis year I 'specks, Will.

WILL. P'oly, Cousin Bob, p'oly. Three bales at th' outset, an' doin' good at that.

BOB. Any corn?

WILL. More'n I know what t' do with.

BOB. Pigs?

WILL. Doin' well on hogs, Cousin Bob, doin' well. (*The conversation dies out. They sit in perfect silence. Then* SUSAN *and the children come in from somewhere.* SUSAN *greets the new arrivals, kissing each child.* BOB *and* BETTIE KATE *are boisterous and demonstrative, and take delight in their more backward playmates. By the time* SUSAN'S *ritual is through with, the front door opens and a middle-aged Negro comes in, assisting an old, (no one knows how old he is) gray-haired, bearded fellow who is blind. This old man has a dignity and a far-away, other-worldly expression such as might have characterized a saint of old. Indeed one immediately thinks of him as some hoary Negro prophet, who, having delivered his message, waits humbly and in darkness for his day to come. He is called* UNCLE NED, *and is so greeted by all as he enters. He returns the greeting.*)

UNCLE NED. (*Deep and low, and remarkably clear for one of his infirmities*) Chillun, chillun. Blind eyes ain't supposed t' see an' ain't supposed t' cry, but, chilluns, voices allus seem t' be so sad, an' I had reckoned as if th' Lord had minded Him t' make sech reservations fer th' old. An' Uncle Ned has had his chillun since th' days befo' th' war. 'Tain't now like it used t' be—he could see 'em with his two eyes then, an' now he has t' see 'em with his heart. An' 'tain't easy any more. Hearts ain't all a-shinin' as they used t' be. (*Abruptly*) God bless an' keep you all.

WILL. Th' kind Lord bless an' preserve you, Uncle Ned.

SAM. (UNCLE NED'S *companion*) Amen. Amen. (UNCLE NED *is seated in the center, before the fire.* SUSAN *goes out, and presently calls to* WILL. WILL *beckons to* BOB *and* BETTIE KATE, *and then asks all to have a bite with him.*)

WILL. Some supper, folks?

ALL. No, Will, no. Thank y' jest th' same.

MAMIE. I'll take t' feed all those that wants t' eat in here.

WILL. Reckon you will at that. (*He and the children go out.* TOM *comes in with an armful of wood, then follows* WILL. WILL *is heard blessing the food. Everyone in the front room bows his head.*)

WILL. Give us this day, our daily bread, O Lord, an' hearts filled up with thanks for Him in whose dear name all food an' goodness is prepared in. Amen. Amen.

SAM. (*After* WILL) Amen. Amen. (MAMIE *sets about warming up some sweet potatoes, meat, and corn bread. She gets a dish or two from the kitchen, and fixes one for* UNCLE NED. *The children eat from one large pan. The grown-ups talk in undertones.*)

SAM. What's got inter Will he lettin' Susan have a frolic?

BOB. Dunno.

MAMIE. 'Deed I dunno neither. Queer goin's on fer him sho'.

SAM. Ef I was a bettin' man I'd lay a dollar t' a cotton stalk Will'll turn this yer frolic inter a preacher's meetin' afo' he's thru'.

UNCLE NED. That's right; that's true. Will has got t' fear o' God in 'im as sho's you're born.

MAMIE. Ain't many comin' on a night like this.

SAM. That's right; niggers is sho' funny 'bout gettin' theyself wet. (BALO *comes in, but finding no seat around the fire, installs himself before the organ. His feet be-gin to pump, and his fingers to touch a key here and there. The sequence of notes finally arranges itself into a Negro melody. It is the one called "Steal Away." As his ear catches the tune, he begins to play in earnest. The folks all join in, at first by humming, and then they sing the words.* UNCLE NED'S *gray head swings slowly, and with his right hand he seems to be conducting.* TOM *enters from the kitchen. Like-wise* WILL *and* SUSAN *and the children. They all sing. As most everyone knows, the words are:*

Chorus:

Steal away, steal away, steal away to Jesus,
Steal away, steal away home,
I ain't got long to stay here.

Verse:

My Lord calls me, He calls me by the thunder,
I ain't got long to stay here.

My Lord calls me, He calls me by the lightning,
The trumpet sounds within my soul,
The trumpet sounds within my soul,
I ain't got long to stay here.

This is repeated several times. At each repetition the emotional excitation becomes greater. At about the third round, the ordered sequence of words is inter-rupted at will with such phrases as, "O Lord," "Have Mercy," yet the rhythm and the tune are maintained. Thus is achieved one of the striking, soul-stirring effects of Negro melody. The song reaches its climax, and then gradually sinks and fades away. After the singers once get well under way, BALO *stops playing, except that now and then he emphasizes a passage by a full chord. He sings, and his own emotion grows greater than the rest. As the song dies out, this seems to diminsh also. And when all is still, he seems more quiet than the others. But then, after a pause of some seconds, and utterly without warning, he bursts forth.*)

BALO. (*Rising from his seat and going to the center of the room as if in a somnambulistic trance*)

    An' th' floods came, an' th' winds blew,
    An' th' floods came, an' th' winds blew,
    An' th' floods came, an' th' winds blew,
    Have mercy, Lord, have mercy, Lord,
    On me, O yes, on me, on me,
    Have mercy, Lord, on me, on me.

(*The folks do not seem at all surprised at this outburst. A head or two are slowly nodded while it lasts.*)

SAM. (*As* BALO *finishes*)—Amen. Amen.

UNCLE NED. Have mercy, Lord, have mercy.

WILL. Amen. Amen. (*And now voices and raps on the door announce new arrivals. Two couples. They are strikingly similar both in looks and in dress. Black faces that in repose are sad and heavy, but when they break in smiles become light-hearted and gay. The men have on white shirts and collars, loose black coats, pressed dark trousers, and polished black shoes. The two women are in white shirt waists and plain dark skirts. The room, of course, is now quite crowded. The group around the fire breaks up to greet them.* BALO *is again left to compose himself. "Good evenin's" and "hellos" are exchanged, and by the time the wraps are disposed*

of on the bed, SAM *has proposed a game of "kyards."
They all look suspiciously, as if undecided, at* WILL.
*He, however, turns his gaze into the fire, and by his
silence gives consent. Two tables are arranged.
Seated around them are the two recent couples,* SAM
and SUSAN, BOB *and* MAMIE. *They begin to play, and,
as they forget* WILL'S *presence, become quite lively.
Some of the children watch the games. Some are still
around the fire.* WILL, *with* BALO, TOM, *and* UNCLE
NED *hug the hearth. Their conversation is audible,
for the players on the stage reduce their jollity to gestures, etc., though of course in fact such is not the case.*)

UNCLE NED. Cotton drapped this year as wus' as I ever
seed it. An' in every weevil I see sho' th' fingers of th'
Lord. Reckon you farmers better drap down on your
knees an' pray, an' pray ter th' Lord fer ter free you
fom yo' sins. White folks hit th' same as black this
time.

WILL. They sho' is.

UNCLE NED. Boll weevils come ter tell us that it's time ter
change our ways. Ain't satisfied with sinnin', but gettin'
wus'. An' th' Lord looks down an' is angry, an' he says,
"Stop," says he, "ken you stop now? If you ken you
ken be saved. I'm a-warnin' yer. An' them what heeds
my warnin' has time befo' th' Judgment ter repent their
sins an' ter be born again. Ter be born again."

WILL. Amen, Uncle Ned, Amen. An' true, true. Like
Saul y'know, Saul of Tarsus, we is all on our way t'
Damascus, an' breathin' out threatnin's an' slaughter
'gainst th' Lord. But we can be born again. We can
be born again an' see th' light that Saul saw when he
fell down t' th' earth, an' hear th' voice that Saul heard
when he lay there kickin' on th' ground an' stirrin' up

th' dust on th' road that led inter Damascus. We can be born again, that's sho'. Brother, we can be born again an' go out like Saul an' preach th' gospel of th' Lord. O Lord. (*They all, that is, all around the hearth, slip immediately and easily into humming an indefinite air derived from a melody. As this increases in volume,* BALO *is seen to tilt back in his chair, and his eyes roll ecstatically upward. Even more suddenly than before he jumps to his feet.*)

BALO. Jesus, Jesus, I've found Jesus,
> Th' light that came t' Saul when he was born again,
> Th' voice that spoke t' Saul when he was born again,
> Jesus, Jesus, I've found Jesus,
> One mo' sinner is a-comin' home.

(*Here he falls to his knees, face raised in pain and exaltation, hands clasped in supplication above his head*)
(*Continuing*)
> O Jesus, Jesus, savior of my soul,
> One mo' sinner is a-comin' home,
> One mo' sinner is a-comin' home.

> Th' light that came t' Saul when he was born again,
> Th' voice that spoke t' Saul when he was born again,
> Th' light that came t' Saul when he was born again,
> O Jesus, Jesus, savior of my soul,
> Jesus, Jesus, I've found Jesus,
> One mo' sinner is a-comin' home.

(BALO *stops, and gives a desperate glance around the room. Seeing* UNCLE NED, *who has turned to face him, he throws himself into his arms, and breaks into a violent and spasmodic sobbing.* UNCLE NED *raises one arm in blessing, while with the other he encircles him in love. The card players, having become uneasy when* UNCLE NED *first began to talk, stopped their game en-*

tirely at BALO'S *outburst, and now file out, heads lowered, in sheepishness and guilt. And as the curtain descends, the others, with the exception of* UNCLE NED *and* BALO, *are seen leaving.*)

CURTAIN

PLUMES

A FOLK TRAGEDY

By

GEORGIA DOUGLAS JOHNSON

OPPORTUNITY PRIZE PLAY, FIRST DRAMA PRIZE,
1927

*Reprinted by special permission of the author
and Opportunity, Journal of Negro Life*

CHARACTERS

CHARITY BROWN, the mother
EMMERLINE BROWN, the daughter
TILDY, the friend
DOCTOR SCOTT, physician

Scene: A poor cottage in the South.
Time: Contemporary.

PLUMES

SCENE: THE KITCHEN *of a two-room cottage. A window overlooking the street. A door leading to street, one leading to the back yard and one to the inner room. A stove, a table with shelf over it, a washtub. A rocking-chair, a cane-bottom chair. Needle, thread, scissors, etc. on table.*

Scene opens with CHARITY BROWN *heating a poultice over the stove. A groaning is heard from the inner room.*

CHARITY. Yes, honey, mamma is fixing somethin' to do you good. Yes, my baby, jus' you wait—I'm a-coming. (*Knock is heard at door. It is gently pushed open and* TILDY *comes in cautiously.*)

TILDY. (*Whispering*) How is she?

CHARITY. Poorly, poorly. Didn't rest last night none hardly. Move that dress and set in th' rocker. I been trying to snatch a minute to finish it but don't seem like I can. She won't have nothing to wear if she—she ——

TILDY. I understands. How near done is it?

CHARITY. Ain't so much more to do.

TILDY. (*Takes up dress from chair; looks at it*) I'll do some on it.

CHARITY. Thank you, sister Tildy. Whip that torshon on and turn down the hem in the skirt.

TILDY. (*Measuring dress against herself*) How deep?

CHARITY. Let me see, now (*Studies a minute with finger*

289

against lip) I tell you—jus' baste it, 'cause you see—
she wears 'em short, but—it might be —— (*Stops.*)

TILDY. (*Bowing her head comprehendingly*) Huh-uh, I see
exzackly. (*Sighs*) You'd want it long—over her feet—
then.

CHARITY. That's it, sister Tildy. (*Listening*) She's some
easy now! (*Stirring poultice*) Jest can't get this poltis'
hot enough somehow this morning.

TILDY. Put some red pepper in it. Got any?

CHARITY. Yes. There ought to be some in one of them
boxes on the shelf there. (*Points.*)

TILDY. (*Goes to shelf, looks about and gets the pepper*)
Here, put a-plenty of this in.

CHARITY. (*Groans are heard from the next room*) Good
Lord, them pains got her again. She suffers so, when
she's 'wake.

TILDY. Poor little thing. How old is she now, sister Charity?

CHARITY. Turning fourteen this coming July.

TILDY. (*Shaking her head dubiously*) I sho' hope she'll be
mended by then.

CHARITY. It don't look much like it, but I trusts so ——
(*Looking worried*) That doctor's mighty late this
morning.

TILDY. I expects he'll be 'long in no time. Doctors is mighty
onconcerned here lately.

CHARITY. (*Going toward inner room with poultice*) They
surely is and I don't have too much confidence in none of
'em. (*You can hear her soothing the child.*)

TILDY. (*Listening*) Want me to help you put it on, sister
Charity?

CHARITY. (*From inner room*) No, I can fix it. (*Coming
back from sick room shaking her head rather dejectedly.*)

TILDY. How is she, sister Charity?

CHARITY. Mighty feeble. Gone back to sleep now. My poor little baby. (*Bracing herself*) I'm going to put on some coffee now.

TILDY. I'm sho' glad. I feel kinder low-spirited.

CHARITY. It's me that low-sperited. The doctor said last time he was here he might have to oparate—said, she mought have a chance then. But I tell you the truth, I've got no faith a-tall in 'em. They takes all your money for nothing.

TILDY. They sho' do and don't leave a cent for putting you away decent.

CHARITY. That's jest it. They takes all you got and then you dies jest the same. It ain't like they was sure.

TILDY. No, they ain't sure. That's it exzactly. But they takes your money jest the same, and leaves you flat.

CHARITY. I been thinking 'bout Zeke these last few days— how he was put away——

TILDY. I wouldn't worry 'bout him now. He's out of his troubles.

CHARITY. I know. But it worries me when I think about how he was put away . . . that ugly pine coffin, jest one shabby old hack and nothing else to show—to show —what we thought about him.

TILDY. Hush, sister! Don't you worry over him. He's happy now, anyhow.

CHARITY. I can't help it! Then little Bessie. We all jest scrooged in one hack and took her little coffin in our lap all the way out to the graveyard. (*Breaks out crying.*)

TILDY. Do hush, sister Charity. You done the best you could. Poor folks got to make the best of it. The Lord understands——

CHARITY. I know that—but I made up my mind the time Bessie went that the next one of us what died would have a shore nuff funeral, everything grand,—with plumes!—I saved and saved and now—this yah doctor——

TILDY. All they think about is cuttin' and killing and taking your money. I got nothin' to put 'em doing.

CHARITY. (*Goes over to washtub and rubs on clothes*) Me neither. These clothes got to get out somehow, I needs every cent.

TILDY. How much that washing bring you?

CHARITY. Dollar and a half. It's worth a whole lot more. But what can you do?

TILDY. You can't do nothing—Look there, sister Charity, ain't that coffee boiling?

CHARITY. (*Wipes hands on apron and goes to stove*) Yes it's boiling good fashioned. Come on, drink some.

TILDY. There ain't nothing I'd rather have than a good strong cup of coffee. (CHARITY *pours* TILDY'S *cup.*) (*Sweetening and stirring hers*) Pour you some. (CHARITY *pours her own cup*) I'd been dead, too, long ago if it hadn't a been for my coffee.

CHARITY. I love it, but it don't love me—gives me the shortness of breath.

TILDY. (*Finishing her cup, taking up sugar with spoon*) Don't hurt me. I could drink a barrel.

CHARITY. (*Drinking more slowly—reaching for coffeepot*) Here, drink another cup.

TILDY. I shore will, that cup done me a lot of good.

CHARITY. (*Looking into her empty cup thoughtfully*) I wish Dinah Morris would drop in now. I'd ask her what these grounds mean.

TILDY. I can read 'em a little myself.

CHARITY. You can? Well, for the Lord's sake, look here and tell me what this cup says! (*Offers cup to* TILDY. TILDY *wards it off.*)

TILDY. You got to turn it 'round in your saucer three times first.

CHARITY. Yes, that's right, I forgot. (*Turns cup 'round, counting*) One, two, three. (*Starts to pick it up.*)

TILDY. Huhudh. (*Meaning no*) Let it set a minute. It might be watery. (*After a minute, while she finishes her own cup*) Now let me see. (*Takes cup and examines it very scrutinizingly.*)

CHARITY. What you see?

TILDY. (*Hesitatingly*) I ain't seen a cup like this one for many a year. Not since—not since——

CHARITY. When?

TILDY. Not since jest before ma died. I looked in the cup then and saw things and—I stopped looking . . .

CHARITY. Tell me what you see, I want to know.

TILDY. I don't like to tell no bad news——

CHARITY. Go on. I can stan' anything after all I been thru'.

TILDY. Since you're bound to know I'll tell you. (CHARITY *draws nearer*) I sees a big gethering!

CHARITY. Gethering, you say?

TILDY. Yes, a big gethering. People all crowded together. Then I see 'em going one by one and two by two. Long line stretching out and out and out!

CHARITY. (*In a whisper*) What you think it is?

TILDY. (*Awed like*) Looks like (*Hesitates*) a possession!

CHARITY. (*Shouting*) You sure!

TILDY. I know it is. (*Just then the toll of a church bell is heard and then the steady and slow tramp, tramp, of horses' hoofs. Both women look at each other.*)

TILDY. (*In a hushed voice*) That must be Bell Gibson's funeral coming 'way from Mt. Zion. (*Gets up and goes to window*) Yes, it sho' is.

CHARITY. (*Looking out of the window also*) Poor Bell suffered many a year; she's out of her pain now.

TILDY. Look, here comes the hearse now!

CHARITY. My Lord! ain't it grand! Look at them horses—look at their heads—plumes—how they shake 'em! Land o' mighty! It's a fine sight, sister Tildy.

TILDY. That must be Jer'miah in that first carriage, bending over like; he shorely is putting her away grand.

CHARITY. No mistake about it. That's Pickett's best funeral turnout he's got.

TILDY. I'll bet it cost a lot.

CHARITY. Fifty dollars, so Matilda Jenkins told me. She had it for Bud. The plumes is what cost.

TILDY. Look at the hacks—— (*Counts*) I believe to my soul there's eight.

CHARITY. Got somebody in all of 'em too—and flowers—She shore got a lot of 'em. (*Both women's eyes follow the tail end of the procession, horses' hoofs die away as they turn away from window. The two women look at each other significantly.*)

TILDY. (*Significantly*) Well!—— (*They look at each other without speaking for a minute.* CHARITY *goes to the washtub*) Want these cups washed up?

CHARITY. No don't mind 'em. I'd rather you get that dress done. I got to get these clothes out.

TILDY. (*Picking up dress*) Shore, there ain't so much more to do on it now. (*Knock is heard on the door.* CHARITY *answers knock and admits* Dr. Scott.)

DR. SCOTT. Good morning. How's the patient today?

CHARITY. Not so good, doctor. When she ain't 'sleep she suffers so; but she sleeps mostly.

DR. SCOTT. Well, let's see, let's see. Just hand me a pan of warm water and I'll soon find out just what's what.

CHARITY. All right, doctor. I'll bring it to you right away. (*Bustles about fixing water—looking toward dress* TILDY *is working on*) Poor little Emmerline's been wanting a white dress trimmed with torshon a long time—now she's got it and it looks like—well —— (*Hesitates*) t'warn't made to wear.

TILDY. Don't take on so, sister Charity—The Lord giveth and the Lord taketh.

CHARITY. I know—but it's hard—hard —— (*Goes into inner room with water. You can hear her talking with the doctor after a minute and the doctor expostulating with her—in a minute she appears at the door, being led from the room by the doctor.*)

DR. SCOTT. No, my dear Mrs. Brown. It will be much better for you to remain outside.

CHARITY. But, doctor ——

DR. SCOTT. NO. You stay outside and get your mind on something else. You can't possibly be of any service. Now be calm, will you?

CHARITY. I'll try, doctor.

TILDY. The doctor's right. You can't do no good in there.

CHARITY. I knows, but I thought I could hold the pan or somethin'. (*Lowering her voice*) Says he got to see if her heart is all right or somethin'. I tell you—nowadays ——

TILDY. I know.

CHARITY. (*Softly to* TILDY) Hope he won't come out here saying he got to operate. (*Goes to washtub.*)

TILDY. I hope so, too. Won't it cost a lot?

CHARITY. That's jest it. It would take all I got saved up.

TILDY. Of course, if he's goin' to get her up—but I don't believe in 'em. I don't believe in 'em.

CHARITY. He didn't promise tho'—even if he did, he said maybe it wouldn't do no good.

TILDY. I'd think a long time before I'd let him operate on my chile. Taking all yuh money, promising nothing and ten to one killing her to boot.

CHARITY. This is a hard world.

TILDY. Don't you trus' him. Coffee grounds don't lie!

CHARITY. I don't trust him. I jest want to do what's right by her. I ought to put these clothes on the line while you're settin' in here, but I jes hate to go outdoors while he's in there.

TILDY. (*Getting up*) I'll hang 'em out. You stay here. Where your clothespins at?

CHARITY. Hanging right there by the back door in the bag. They ought to dry before dark and then I can iron to-night.

TILDY. (*Picking up tub*) They ought to blow dry in no time. (*Goes toward back door.*)

CHARITY. Then I can shore rub 'em over to-night. Say, sister Tildy, hist 'em up with that long saplin' prop leaning in the fence corner.

TILDY. (*Going out*) All right.

CHARITY. (*Standing by the table beating nervously on it with her fingers—listens—and then starts to bustling about the kitchen*) (*Enter* DOCTOR *from inner room.*)

DR. SCOTT. Well, Mrs. Brown, I've decided I'll have to operate.

CHARITY. MY Lord! Doctor—don't say that!

DR. SCOTT. It's the only chance.

CHARITY. You mean she'll get well if you do?

Dr. Scott. No, I can't say that —— It's just a chance ——
a last chance. And I'll do just what I said, cut the
price of the operation down to fifty dollars. I'm will-
ing to do that for you. (Charity *throws up her hands
in dismay.*)

Charity. Doctor, I was so in hopes you wouldn't operate—
I—I—— And yo' say you ain't a bit sure she'll get
well—even then?

Dr. Scott. No. I can't be sure. We'll just have to take
the chance. But I'm sure you want to do everything——

Charity. Sure, doctor, I do want to—do—everything I can
do to—to—— Doctor, look at this cup. (*Picks up
fortune cup and shows the doctor*) My fortune 's jes'
been told this very morning—look at these grounds—
they says—— (*Softly*) it ain't no use, no use a-tall.

Dr. Scott. Why, my good woman, don't you believe in such
senseless things! That cup of grounds can't show you
anything. Wash them out and forget it.

Charity. I can't forget it. I feel like it ain't no use; I'd
just be spendin' the money that I needs—for nothing—
nothing.

Dr. Scott. But you won't though —— You'll have a clear
conscience. You'd know that you did everything you
could.

Charity. I know that, doctor. But there's things you don't
know 'bout—there's other things I got to think about.
If she goes—if she must go . . . I had plans—I been
getting ready—now —— Oh, doctor, I jest can't see
how I can have this operation—you say you can't promise—nothing?

Dr. Scott. I didn't think you'd hesitate about it—I imagined your love for your child ——

CHARITY. (*Breaking in*) I do love my child. My God, I do love my child. You don't understand . . . but . . . but—can't I have a little time to think about it, doctor? It means so much—to her—and—me!

DR. SCOTT. I tell you. I'll go on over to the office. I'd have to get my— (*Hesitates*) my things, anyhow. And as soon as you make up your mind, get one of the neighbors to run over and tell me. I'll come right back. But don't waste any time now, Mrs. Brown, every minute counts.

CHARITY. Thank you, doctor, thank you. I'll shore send you word as soon as I can. I'm so upset and worried I'm half crazy.

DR. SCOTT. I know you are . . . but don't take too long to make up your mind. . . . It ought to be done to-day. Remember—it may save her. (*Exits.*)

CHARITY. (*Goes to door of sick room—looks inside for a few minutes, then starts walking up and down the little kitchen, first holding a hand up to her head and then wringing them. Enter* TILDY *from yard with tub under her arm.*)

TILDY. Well, they're all out, sister Charity—— (*Stops*) Why, what's the matter?

CHARITY. The doctor wants to operate.

TILDY. (*Softly*) Where he—gone?

CHARITY. Yes—he's gone, but he's coming back—if I send for him.

TILDY. You going to? (*Puts down tub and picks up white dress and begins sewing.*)

CHARITY. I dunno—I got to think.

TILDY. I can't see what's the use myself. He can't save her with no operation—— Coffee grounds don't lie.

CHARITY. It would take all the money I got for the opera-

tion and then what about puttin' her away? He can't
save her—don't even promise ter. I know he can't—I
feel it . . . I feel it . . .

TILDY. It's in the air. . . . (*Both women sit tense in the
silence.* TILDY *has commenced sewing again. Just then
a strange, strangling noise comes from the inner room.*)

TILDY. What's that?

CHARITY. (*Running toward and into inner room*) Oh, my
God! (*From inside*) Sister Tildy—Come here—No,—
Some water, quick. (TILDY *with dress in hand starts
toward inner room. Stops at door, sighs and then goes
hurriedly back for the water pitcher.* CHARITY *is heard
moaning softly in the next room, then she appears at
doorway and leans against jamb of door*) Rip the hem
out, sister Tildy.

CURTAIN

THE BROKEN BANJO

A FOLK TRAGEDY

By

WILLIS RICHARDSON

KRIGWA PRIZE PLAY, FIRST PRIZE, 1925
*Reprinted by special permission of the author
and the Crisis Magazine*

CHARACTERS

MATT TURNER
EMMA, his wife
SAM, her brother
ADAM, her cousin
A POLICEMAN

Scene: A tenement room in the Negro district.
Time: Contemporary.

First performance by The Krigwa Players, New York,
August 1, 1925

THE BROKEN BANJO

THE DINING ROOM *of* MATT *and* EMMA TURNER *is dull and dark looking, with a door at the right leading to the outside and a door at the left leading through the kitchen. There is a square table in the center of the room with two chairs, the only ones in the room, near it. A cupboard is at the rear, and at the right of this is a window. At the left side below the door is a small closet concealed by curtains. When the play begins* MATT, *a short, strongly-built man of thirty, is sitting at the left of the table picking his banjo. He is not by any means a good player, but his desire to play well is his religion. He plays on for a few moments until his wife,* EMMA, *a woman of twenty-seven, appears at the kitchen door.*

EMMA. (*In disagreeable tones*) Matt, for God's sake stop that noise!

MATT. (*Looking up and stopping for a moment*) What the devil's the matter with you?

EMMA. Ah got a headache and Ah'm tired o' hearin' that bum music. It's a wonder you wouldn't find somethin' else to do. You can come out in the back yard and split me some wood if you want to.

MATT. Didn't Ah work all night? You think Ah'm goin' to work all night, then come home and split wood in the daytime? If you don't like this music put your head in a bag, then you won't hear it.

EMMA. You ain't got no feelin's for nobody but yourself. You just got that old job, and before you got it Ah had to work my hands almost off to keep things goin'; this is the thanks Ah get for what Ah done.

MATT. You needn't throw that in ma face; you didn't have to work if you didn't want to.

EMMA. If Ah hadn't worked, we'd 'a' gone to the poorhouse.

MATT. Maybe we would 'a' been better off.

EMMA. If you wasn't so selfish you'd get along better; but you don't care a thing about nobody or nothin' but that old banjo.

MATT. Have Ah got any cause to care about anything else?

EMMA. How about me?

MATT. Well, that's different. If Ah didn't care nothin' about you Ah'd 'a' been gone long ago. But what about me? Don't everybody in town hate me? Don't your whole family despise the very ground Ah walk on?

EMMA. It ain't their fault.

MATT. It is their fault. Didn't they all try to stop me from comin' to see you? Didn't Ah have to beat the devil out o' that black brother and cousin o' yours before they'd let me alone? And don't they hate me?

EMMA. (*Defending her family*) Now don't start to callin' nobody black, 'cause you ain't got no room to call nobody black. Sam and Adam is just as light as you.

MATT. Maybe they is, but they ain't as honest; and they ain't nothin' but loafin' jailbirds.

EMMA. Ah don't see where you get nothin' by throwin' that at me.

MATT. You know it's the truth; and you know Ah ain't never been to jail.

EMMA. It ain't too late, don't be braggin'.

MATT. You talk like you'd like to see me go to jail.

EMMA. You ought to have better sense than that.

MATT. Well, here's somethin' Ah want to tell you about Sam and Adam before Ah forget it.

EMMA. What?

MATT. Ah want you to keep 'em out o' here. They don't do nothin' but loaf around all the time and come here to eat everything they c'n get.

EMMA. Sam and Adam ain't doin' nobody no harm.

MATT. Yes, they is; they're doin' me harm.

EMMA. How's they doin' you harm?

MATT. They come here and eat up ma grub, then go around and talk about me. Ah wouldn't mind you givin' 'em a bite now and then if they was friends o' mine.

EMMA. Is you got any friends at all?

MATT. No, Ah ain't got no friends. Ain't nobody likes me but you, and you ain't crazy about me.

EMMA. Well, you oughtn't to be so disagreeable, then you'd have some friends.

MATT. Ah don't know, Ah reckons Ah get along just as well without 'em.

EMMA. No, you don't. Ain't nobody that gets along just as well without friends.

MATT. When you ain't got so many friends you ain't got so many people to come around and eat you up.

EMMA. Ain't nothin' in bein' so stingy.

MATT. Ah ain't givin' nobody nothin'; that's why Ah'm tellin' you to tell them two fools to keep out o' here.

EMMA. Ah ain't goin' to insult nobody.

MATT. If you don't tell 'em, Ah will; cause Ah don't want 'em in here. That settles it.

EMMA. Ah ain't after makin' no more enemies. We got enemies enough.

MATT. You don't look out for ma interest much.

EMMA. Yes, Ah do; Ah'm thinkin' for you every minute o'
ma life, but you don't know it. You never will know it
till you get in a big pinch.

MATT. There ain't no use o' us quarrellin'. We quarrel too
much anyhow, Ah reckon.

EMMA. Ah reckon we do. (*He begins to pick the banjo
again, and after looking at him for a moment half
fondly, she goes back to the kitchen. There are a few
moments of silence save the picking of the banjo. Presently* EMMA *reappears at the door and addresses* MATT
in kinder tones) Matt?

MATT. Huh?

EMMA. Is you got any money?

MATT. No.

EMMA. That's mighty funny.

MATT. Funny how?

EMMA. You workin' every night makin' good wages, and you
don't give me nothin' but the money to run the house.
What does you do with the rest of it? (MATT *is silent*)
You mean you ain't got a cent, Matt?

MATT. Ah ain't got no spare money.

EMMA. No spare money?

MATT. No.

EMMA. Well, what is you got?

MATT. Ah got five dollars Ah been savin' to buy some music
with.

EMMA. You wouldn't buy music when Ah need the money for
somethin' else, would you, Matt?

MATT. What you need money for?

EMMA. Ah needs shoes, for one thing.

MATT. Ah need shoes too.

EMMA. (*Coming forward and showing her worn shoes*) Look at mine.

MATT. (*Looking at them*) They is pretty bad.

EMMA. There ain't nothin' to 'em but uppers.

MATT. How much your shoes goin' to cost?

EMMA. Ah don't know. You can get 'em secondhanded if you want to. You ought to get a good secondhanded pair for two or three dollars.

MATT. Ah tell you what Ah'll do.

EMMA. What?

MATT. Ah'll get you them shoes if you'll tell Sam and Adam to keep out o' here.

EMMA. Why don't you tell 'em, Matt?

MATT. Ah'll tell you the truth, Emma; Ah don't want to tell 'em 'cause Ah don't want to have no trouble. Time Ah tell 'em to stay out Ah know they'll start a' argument, then Ah'll have to beat 'em up like Ah done once before. And Ah get tired o' fightin' some time, 'deed Ah do.

EMMA. Ah'll tell 'em, then.

MATT. (*Rising*) All right, Ah'll get the shoes.

EMMA. Go out the alley through the back way to that Jew store. Ah seen some secondhanded ones in the window.

MATT. What size you want?

EMMA. Sevens.

MATT. What kind?

EMMA. Black. That's the only kind Ah ever wear.

MATT. A pair o' black sevens. All right, if Ah can't get 'em there, Ah'll get 'em somewhere else. (*He goes out through the kitchen leaving his banjo on the table. EMMA picks up the banjo, looks at it and shakes her head. As she puts it down and starts back to the kitchen SAM and ADAM enter from the other door.*

SAM *is thirty-three, taller than* MATT, *but not so sturd-ily built.* ADAM *is thirty, about* MATT'S *height, but not so stout as* MATT. *Both are careless loafers; the former is gruff, with a mean temper; the latter is lively and playful.*)

ADAM. (*As they enter*) Hi, Emma.

EMMA. (*Stopping in the doorway and speaking in unwel-come tones*) Hi.

SAM. (*Roughly*) What's the matter with you?

EMMA. Nothin'.

SAM. Got anything to eat?

EMMA. No.

ADAM. That's mighty funny. You used to always have somethin' to eat around here.

EMMA. Don't you-all never think about nothin' but eatin'? (SAM *and* ADAM *look at each other puzzled.*)

SAM. (*Sitting at the left of the table*) Is you and Matt been fussin' this mornin'?

EMMA. No.

ADAM. (*Sitting on the table*) Somethin' must be wrong; you never did act like this before.

EMMA. Ain't nothin' wrong with me.

SAM. (*Looking towards the kitchen*) Seems like Ah smell cabbage. Ain't you cookin' cabbage?

EMMA. Yes.

SAM. Thought you didn't have nothin' to eat?

EMMA. Them cabbage is for Matt's dinner.

SAM. Can't we have some?

EMMA. No, Ah ain't goin' to let you all eat up his dinner.

ADAM. Ah know what's the matter now, Sam.

SAM. (*Turning to him*) What?

ADAM. Matt's been spoonin' with huh and turned huh against us.

THE BROKEN BANJO

EMMA. (*Angrily*) You go to the devil! (*She goes quickly to the kitchen.*)

SAM. Ah'll bet that damn bully's been talkin' about us.

ADAM. Ah'll bet so too. Lend me your knife.

SAM. (*Handing* ADAM *the knife*) Ah'd like to run this between his ribs.

ADAM. (*Taking the knife and a match from his pocket*) Don't let him see you first.

SAM. He ain't as bad as you think he is.

ADAM. (*Making a toothpick with the match*) Ah'll always remember how he beat us up once.

SAM. He won't never beat us up again. Ah got him in the palm o' ma hand.

ADAM. (*Putting the knife into his pocket*) How you goin' to stop him from beatin' us up?

SAM. (*Holding out his hand*) Wait a minute. Gimme that knife.

ADAM. Lemme keep it a day or two.

SAM. No, give it right back here now.

ADAM. Ah'll give it back to you tomorrow.

SAM. (*Catching him by the pocket*) No, give it right here now.

ADAM. What's the use o' bein' so mean?

SAM. (*Looking him in the eye and speaking more firmly*) Gimme that knife here!

ADAM. (*Putting the knife on the table*) Don't be such a sorehead.

SAM. You better stop kidding with me. Ah don't feel like kiddin' today. Ah feel like runnin' this knife in a certain feller's ribs.

ADAM. Don't cut at him and miss him, 'cause if you do you know what'll happen.

SAM. Ain't nothin' goin' to happen. Didn't Ah say Ah had him in the palm o' ma hand?

ADAM. (*Laughing*) You tryin' to kid me?

SAM. No, Ah ain't kiddin'. Ah don't kid when Ah talk about him. Ah could tell you a thing or two if Ah wanted to. You know they ain't caught the one that killed old man Shelton yet.

ADAM. (*Interested*) You talk like you know somethin'.

SAM. You bet your life Ah know somethin'.

ADAM. What is it?

SAM. That's all right, Ah'll talk at the right time. Watch me call huh in here and bawl huh out. (*Calling*) Emma! Emma!

EMMA. (*From the kitchen*) What?

SAM. Come here. (*Emma comes to the kitchen door.*)

EMMA. What you want?

SAM. Is Matt been talkin' about me?

EMMA. What would Matt be talkin' about you for?

SAM. Ain't no use o' lyin', Ah know somethin's been goin' on. Now what is it?

EMMA. If you want to get told Ah'll tell you, all right. Matt don't want you and Adam hangin' around here eatin' up his grub.

SAM. Oh, he don't, don't he?

EMMA. No.

SAM. Ah reckon you don't, neither.

EMMA. That ain't for me to say; Matt rents the house and buys the grub, and it's up to him to say who he wants 'round and who he don't.

ADAM. Ah told you Matt had been lovin' with huh.

SAM. Well, Matt better be careful: Ah know a thing or two about him.

"THE BROKEN BANJO"

EMMA. Now there ain't no use o' you goin' makin' up nothin' on Matt.

SAM. Ah ain't makin' up nothin'; this is the truth. Ah seen it with ma own eyes.

EMMA. (*Interested*) You seen what?

SAM. Ah know it's goin' to knock you bald-headed when Ah tell you.

EMMA. You better be careful how you talk about Matt; that's all Ah got to say.

SAM. Careful or not careful, Matt killed old man Shelton and Ah seen him do it.

EMMA. It's a lie! You know it's a lie!

SAM. No, it ain't no lie. Ah seen him do it, and if he ain't careful how he acts with me Ah'll get him strung up by his neck.

EMMA. Don't everybody know the one that killed old man Shelton got away and ain't never been caught?

SAM. Matt's the one that got away and ain't never been caught.

EMMA. You can't make nobody believe that. If you had 'a' knowed that about Matt you'd 'a' told it long ago much as you hate him.

SAM. Ah didn't tell it cause he's your husband and Ah didn't want to put you in a hole; but now you turned against me and Ah don't care.

EMMA. Ah ain't turned against you.

SAM. Yes, you is. You don't even believe what Ah'm sayin' now.

EMMA. Ain't no way for you to make me believe that.

SAM. It ain't, ain't it? Well, Ah'll tell you just how it happened.

EMMA. You gettin' ready to make up somethin' now.

SAM. Ah was standin' right in the bushes when Ah seen

Matt comin' along pickin' his banjo and not watchin'
where he was walkin'. He walked right in old man
Shelton's potato patch. Then old man Shelton ran
out and started to beatin' Matt over the head with his
stick. He hit Matt once or twice, but the next time
Matt put up his banjo to knock off the lick, and the
lick broke the banjo. That made Matt so mad that
before he knowed it he had picked up a rock and hit
old man Shelton right in the head, and the old feller
fell like a log. Matt grabbed his banjo and beat it
and they ain't caught him yet.

EMMA. Ah know you don't think Ah'm believin' that.

SAM. That's all right, Ah'll prove it when he comes in here.

EMMA. You sure got to prove it to me. Ah don't believe
a word you say. You all let me alone anyhow, and let
me cook ma husband's dinner. (*She goes into the
kitchen.*)

ADAM. It's mighty funny you ain't said nothin' to me about
that before now.

SAM. Didn't Ah tell you Ah was holdin' ma tongue cause Ah
didn't want to get Emma in bad? You wouldn't want
me to hurt ma own sister, would you?

ADAM. Seems like you might 'a' told me anyhow, long as we
been runnin' together. You didn't think Ah'd pimp, did
you?

SAM. (*Closing the whole matter*) Ain't no use to argue
about it now. (*He takes the banjo up and looks at it.*)
This old thing's give that guy a lot o' trouble. (*He
tries to pick the banjo, but is not successful.*)

ADAM. (*Taking hold of the banjo*) Lemme show you how
to pick it.

SAM. (*Still holding on to it*) No, you can't pick it.

EMMA. (*Appearing at the kitchen door*) You-all better put that banjo down before you break it.

SAM. Let go the thing, Adam; and quit your playin'! (*He pulls the banjo suddenly from* ADAM'S *hand and it accidentally strikes the table and is broken.*)

EMMA. (*Coming forward*) Now look what you done! You broke that banjo and Matt's goin' to raise the devil!

SAM. (*To* ADAM) Ah told you to quit your kiddin'!

ADAM. If you had 'a' let me have the thing ——

EMMA. (*Snatching the banjo from* SAM) Ain't no use o' makin' excuses now! The thing's broke! What you goin' to do about it?

SAM. Ah ain't goin' to do nothin' about it.

EMMA. Both of you better get out o' here before Matt comes back.

SAM. We ain't scared o' Matt long as we know what we know.

EMMA. Ah'm goin' to hide this thing 'cause Ah don't want to see nobody hurt. (*She puts the banjo into the closet.*)

SAM. Don't worry, ain't nobody goin' to get hurt.

EMMA. (*Listening*) Ah believe Ah hear him comin' now.

SAM. Let him come. (*They are silent until* MATT *enters from the kitchen with a package under his arm.*)

ADAM. Hi, Matt.

MATT. (*Shortly*) Hi. (*To* EMMA *in a different tone*) Here's the shoes, Emma. (*He takes the shoes to the table and as he puts them down notices that the banjo is not there.*)

MATT. Where's ma banjo?

EMMA. You don't want no banjo now. Lemme see the shoes.

MATT. No, Ah want ma banjo. Who moved it?

EMMA. Ah moved it. Wait till you get your dinner, then get it.

MATT. (*Striking the table with his open hand*) Ah want it right now, right now!

EMMA. Matt, for God's sake, don't be thinkin' about that old banjo all the time.

MATT. (*Beginning to look around*) Ah'll find it myself. (*He goes to the cupboard, and in his eagerness pulls the drawer and all its contents out on the floor.*)

EMMA. (*Beginning to untie the package*) Ah'm goin' to look at these shoes.

MATT. (*Turning to her*) Don't touch them shoes till Ah find ma banjo! Now, where is it?

EMMA. (*After a pause pointing to the curtains*) In there. (*MATT reaches behind the curtains and brings out the banjo.*)

MATT. (*In consternation*) Broke! Who the devil broke this banjo? (*All are silent*) Emma, who broke ma banjo?

EMMA. (*Pleading with him*) Don't make no trouble, Matt; please don't make no trouble.

MATT. (*Taking the shoes from the table*) If you don't tell me who broke ma banjo Ah'm goin' to take these shoes right back! (*EMMA is silent*) All right, back they go!

EMMA. (*As he starts out*) Don't take 'em back, Matt! Don't take 'em back!

MATT. Who broke it, then?

EMMA. Sam broke it! Sam and Adam!

MATT. (*Throwing the shoes on the table and starting for* SAM) Ah'll fix you, you black dog! (*SAM leaves the chair quickly and jumps behind the table.* MATT *takes the chair up to throw it at him.*)

SAM. Don't you hit me with that chair! Ah know who killed old man Shelton! (MATT *holds the chair in the air as if he is fastened in that position and stares at* SAM *in wonder*) Ain't no use o' looking at me like that. Ah seen you when you hit him with that rock. (MATT *lets the chair come slowly to the floor.* SAM *coming around the table and snapping his fingers in* MATT'S *face*) You ain't so smart now, is you? You ain't so anxious to smash that chair over ma head, is you? Ah got you where Ah want you now! Ah got you in the palm o' ma hand! (MATT *does not speak, but goes quietly over to the hall door and locks it, putting the key into his pocket. He comes back to the table.*) Who the devil you think you're scarin' by lockin' that door? (MATT *goes over and locks the kitchen door before he speaks.*)

MATT. (*Coming to the table again*) You might have me in the palm o' your hand, but you won't have me there long.

EMMA. For God's sake, Matt! What you goin' to do?

MATT. You keep out o' this!

SAM. You can't scare me now.

ADAM. (*At last finding his voice*) No, you can't scare us now with what we know on you.

MATT. What you-all know on me ain't goin' to do you no good, 'cause ain't neither one of you goin' out o' this house till you swear by the God that made you you won't never say no more about me and old man Shelton.

SAM. How you goin' to make us swear?

MATT. (*More determined and angry*) Ah'm goin' to beat you till you do, or keep you right here and starve you to

death! (*To* EMMA) Bring that Bible out here,
Emma! (EMMA *gets the Bible from behind the curtains and puts it on the table.*)

MATT. Ah know both of you believe in God and the devil
and heaven and hell, 'cause you ain't got the guts not to;
and you goin' to raise your right hands and swear on
this book!

SAM. (*Taking the knife from his pocket*) If you lay your
hands on me Ah'll stick this knife in you!

MATT. (*Reaching behind the curtains and bringing out an
ax handle*) Ain't no use for you to start that 'cause Ah
can settle you with one lick on the head!

ADAM. Aw, we'll swear; what's the use o' fightin' about it?

MATT. Come on, then; and be quick about it!

SAM. Don't you do it, Adam!

ADAM. Ah ain't goin' to stay in here all day. (ADAM *comes
around and puts his left hand on the Bible.*)

MATT. Lift up your right hand! (ADAM *raises his right
hand.*)

MATT. Do you swear by the God that made you you won't
never say nothin' about me and old man Shelton?

ADAM. Yes.

MATT. Don't say that! Say "Ah do"!

ADAM. Ah do.

MATT. (*To* SAM *who turns away*) Now it's your turn!

SAM. You'll have a nice time makin' me swear!

MATT. If you don't swear Ah'm goin' to keep you right
here and beat the devil out o' you till you change your
mind!

ADAM. (*Winking at* SAM *while* MATT *is glaring at him*)
Come on and do it, Sam; Ah want to get out o' here.

MATT. If he don't come on he'll be sorry for it!

SAM. (*After looking steadily at* ADAM *for a moment*)   All right, Ah'll swear not to tell.

MATT. No, you don't! You can't play that with me! Come on around here to this Bible! (SAM *goes to the table, puts his left hand on the Bible and raises his right hand.*)

MATT. Do you swear by the God that made you you won't never say nothin' about me and old man Shelton?

SAM. Ah do.

MATT. Now both of you can go; and don't never put your foot in here no more. (*He throws the key over on the floor.*)

ADAM. (*As he picks up the key*) We'll go, all right.

SAM. (*After the door is unlocked*) We'll go, but Ah'll get even with you one way or the other!

MATT. (*Starting towards them angrily*) Get out o' here! (*They hasten out closing the door behind them.*)

MATT. (*Coming back to the table after unlocking the kitchen door*) Ah didn't think that would ever get out about old man Shelton; but you never can tell.

EMMA. Ah didn't know you had done that, Matt.

MATT. Ah didn't think nobody did. Ah didn't mean to kill him. When he broke ma banjo, Ah hit him harder than Ah thought.

EMMA. What you goin' to do now?

MATT. Nothin' but keep quiet about it.

EMMA. Yes, you is goin' to do somethin', too. You goin' to make your get-away.

MATT. Get-away for what? Didn't they swear not to tell?

EMMA. And when they was swearin' Ah seen Adam winkin' at Sam. Swearin' don't amount to a row o' pins with them.

MATT. They'd be scared to tell after swearin' on the Bible.

EMMA. Don't you believe it. Soon as Sam gets full o' moonshine whiskey he'll tell everything he knows and that he don't know, too. He'll forget he ever seen a Bible.

MATT. Ah don't feel like runnin' from nobody.

EMMA. Sam's mad now; and Sam mad is just like Sam drunk, he'll do anything. (*There is a pause while* EMMA *awaits* MATT'S *decision*) Well, if you won't get ready, Ah'll get you ready. (*She hurries out through the hall door.* MATT *sits resting his head on his hands. Presently* EMMA *returns with a bundle of clothes which she puts on the table as she hurries to the kitchen. In a few moments she returns, wrapping some bread in a paper. She puts the bread in with the clothes.*)

MATT. Ah reckon you're right about goin', Emma.

EMMA. Ah know Ah'm right. They're gettin' ready to play some trick on you. Ah seen it in their eyes.

MATT. Where must Ah go? Ah ain't got a cent.

EMMA. That's all right, you go out the back way across the fields to Uncle Silas and get him to row you across the river. When you get over, beat it to Aunt Linda's and tell huh to hide you till Ah come.

MATT. You reckon Uncle Silas'll take me over? He don't like me. Nobody never did like me.

EMMA. Tell him Ah said so. He'll do it for me.

MATT. When you comin'?

EMMA. Ah'll start out in the mornin'.

MATT. But how about the money? We'll need money if we're goin' anywhere.

EMMA. That's all right about the money. Ah got a hund'ed and forty dollars sewed up in ma mattress. Ah been denyin' maself things that Ah wanted and needed and savin' a little at a time, cause Ah knowed with that temper o' yours you'd get in trouble one time or the other.

MATT. (*Taking the bundle in one hand and the banjo in the other and going to the kitchen door*) Ah reckon Ah been a mighty poor husband to you, but you been a mighty good wife to me, Emma; and if we ever get out o' this trouble, Ah'm goin' to turn over a new leaf. Ah'm goin' now and don't you be long comin'.

EMMA. Ah'll be there first thing in the mornin'.

MATT. All right, so long.

EMMA. (*Starting towards him as if to kiss him*) So long, Matt. (*While* MATT *is hesitating at the kitchen door* SAM *and* ADAM *enter hurriedly through the other door followed by an officer.*)

SAM. (*Pointing to* MATT) There he is!

OFFICER. Wait a minute, Matt; Ah want you.

MATT. (*Still standing in the doorway*) What you want with me?

OFFICER. Sam told me all about old man Shelton.

SAM. Ah told you Ah'd fix you, you bully!

MATT. (*Dropping his banjo and bundle and quickly getting his club*) All right, if you want me, take me!

OFFICER. (*Pointing a warning finger at* MATT) There ain't no use for you to try that, you can't get away with it.

EMMA. (*Catching* MATT's *arm and holding him*) Don't do that, Matt! Don't do it! You'll just get in more trouble!

MATT. Ah'm in all the trouble Ah can get in! It can't be no worse!

EMMA. Yes, it can be worse! They won't give you but ten or fifteen years for old man Shelton 'cause you didn't mean to do that, but if you kill this man they'll hang you!

MATT. (*Surrendering*)   Ah reckon you're right, Emma; you always been right and Ah always been wrong. If Ah ever get out o' this Ah'll have sense enough to mind what you say. (*Allowing her to take the club from him, he goes to the officer*)   Ah'm ready.

SAM. Better put the irons on him.

OFFICER. That's all right, he'll go.

MATT. (*Turning to* EMMA *as they are about to go*)   Goodbye, Emma.

EMMA. (*Standing at the left of the table, her whole body trembling*)   Goodbye, Matt. (*As they close the door* EMMA *raises her hands to her eyes as if to hold back the tears.*)

CURTAIN

THE DEATH DANCE

AN AFRICAN PLAY

By

THELMA DUNCAN

*Reprinted by special permission of The
Howard Players, Washington, D. C.*

CHARACTERS

ASUMANA, an African maiden
KAMO, the accused
THE MEDICINE MAN
ALIHU, the Medicine Man's attendant
A NUMBER OF NATIVES—counsellors, warriors, tribesmen,
   townsfolk of a Vai village, West Coast Africa

Scene: A village stockade, near the Medicine Man's hut, near
   an African jungle.

Time: Present. Just on the eve of a Court palaver.

First performance by The Howard Players, Howard
University, Washington, D. C., April 7, 1923.

THE DEATH DANCE

DOWN RIGHT, *a log; in front of log a low-burning camp fire. Upper left is the grass hut of the* MEDICINE MAN, *with the usual small rounded-doorway opening. Lying on the stage, just in front of the doorway is the warrior's shield, upon which is a spear. A rather gruesomely decorated staff leans up against the hut, by the doorway. Some earthen water jugs, and pots are lying about the hut. A gourd cup hangs just beside doorway of the hut.*

Along sides and across back is the usual barricaded, fence-like protection, with a narrow opening at center stage (thus giving exits to right and left through rear center). Exit into hut for MEDICINE MAN, *alone.*

Discovered: Crowd of natives and warriors standing about, all restless, and apparently in quite angry mood. KAMO, *the accused, stands with his hands tied behind him, up center. In distance is faintly heard the rhythmic beat of the tribal drums—noise of dissatisfaction grows loud and louder, and natives begin to work up to point of frenzied anger.* ASUMANA *is standing in the crowd down lower right, but takes no part in the angry demonstrations of the warriors or natives. Drums sound more loudly. Warriors enter.*

FIRST NATIVE.   Kamo is the guilty one.

SECOND NATIVE. Yes, yes, he is guilty. I saw him. I saw him.

THIRD NATIVE. He has the gold. I saw him take it.

FIRST NATIVE. Speak thief, what can you say for yourself?

CHORUS. Yes, speak, speak.

KAMO. Dear friends, will you not hear me when I tell you that I am not guilty! I did not take the gold.

SECOND NATIVE. (*Interrupting him*) Hear him—listen—it is not so. He did take the gold, and from one of his own. That is taboo.

CHORUS. He must be punished. He is guilty. He must be punished.

FIRST NATIVE. Send for the Medicine Man. We will see if he is guilty or not.

CHORUS. Yes, yes, send for the Medicine Man. We will see. (*Exit a native.*)

FIRST NATIVE. (*Mockingly*) Kamo, the mighty one, the fearless one—now a thief! (*He laughs.*)

SECOND NATIVE. He steals from the helpless, he steals from his own!

CHORUS. Kamo, the mighty one, the fearless—now a thief. (*They laugh mockingly*) (*Enter the native with the* MEDICINE MAN. *He carries a bag of medicine.*)

MEDICINE MAN. What have you here?

CHORUS. A thief, a thief.

SECOND NATIVE. A guilty thief. He says he is not, but it is so. I saw him steal, I saw him.

THIRD NATIVE. He stole from old Nanda, and mocked his elders.

MEDICINE MAN. Mocked his elders,—eh; then greater will be the punishment. You shall drink the red water.

CHORUS. Give him the red water to drink.

FIRST NATIVE. It will find him guilty.

SECOND NATIVE. It will not make him sick, for he is the

guilty one. Someone stole from Nanda—and it is he.
I know, I know.

THIRD NATIVE. The Medicine Man will find him out. His
medicine never fails.

MEDICINE MAN. Bring in the pot. (*He opens his bag.
ALIHU exits into hut—returns with an earthen bowl.
MEDICINE MAN reaches in his skin belt for his vials,
scrutinizes them, and begins pouring into bowl. ASU-
MANA has been in the crowd all the time, but does not
take part in the condemnation of KAMO. She comes forward now, pulls the MEDICINE MAN by the arm. He
looks up and faces her.*)

ASUMANA. I would have a word with you. (*She glances
around at the natives*) Tell them to go until you send
for them.

MEDICINE MAN. My beautiful girl, can you not wait until
I give this thief the ordeal?

ASUMANA. No, no, I must see you now—before you give
him the ordeal.

MEDICINE MAN. Very well, I will dismiss them. (*To the
natives*) Go until I come for you. It will not be long.
(*Shakes his staff.*)

CHORUS. But the thief, what shall we do with him?

MEDICINE MAN. Take him along, too. I will call for you
soon. (*Exit all but ALIHU, a servant of the MEDICINE
MAN, ASUMANA and the MEDICINE MAN. ASUMANA,
a comely dancer, begins to coquette to win the MEDI-
CINE MAN'S favor. She begins to dance slowly, with
feigned indifference, but watching the effect of her
charms. The MEDICINE MAN relaxes ecstatically. She
pauses finally*) Now what will you have of me, pretty
maid?

ASUMANA. Are you not the Medicine Man who saved the poor widow?

MEDICINE MAN. (*Proudly*) Yes, I am he. It was my medicine that saved her.

ASUMANA. And you saved the cripple boy, and found the thief who stole from the farmer. Ah, you see I know all about you. You are wonderful, and so is your medicine.

MEDICINE *Man*. (*Proudly*) There is no one yet that has medicine like mine. It is the best. It cures the sick and points out the guilty. I am the mighty Medicine Man of Vai.

ASUMANA. You *are* the mighty Medicine Man of Vai, and for your mightiness, I will dance for you. I am Asumana the dancer.

MEDICINE MAN. Asumana, you are a beautiful creature. How like a wild flower you are; and your eyes, they sparkle like dew glistens in the morning sun. Dance. Let me see you dance!

ASUMANA. Only for your mightiness do I dance—remember.

MEDICINE MAN. For my mightiness you will dance. (ASUMANA *dances. The* MEDICINE MAN *is much enthused over her dancing. Suddenly she stops.*)

MEDICINE MAN. Do not stop, pretty creature. Dance again—dance again for the mighty Medicine Man of Vai!

ASUMANA. (*Distressed*) I dance, mighty one, but I am not happy. You could make me happy, very, very happy.

MEDICINE MAN. (*Pleased*) Gladly will I make you happy, if it is in my power to do so. What would you have me do?

ASUMANA. Promise me something.

MEDICINE MAN. I would promise you anything, beautiful

one. Speak. What shall it be? And remember, when
I promise, it is because you have danced for me.

ASUMANA. Promise me that you will save Kamo, the youth
whom you call a thief. Promise me, please.

MEDICINE MAN. (*Startled*) What? You would not have
me save a thief! He must take the ordeal and it will
decide.

ASUMANA. He is not a thief, though. He did not steal. It
would not be just for him to die. It is your mighty
medicine that alone can save him. (MEDICINE MAN
frowns) Oh, can't you save him, won't you save him?
(*A pause. She dances a few steps*) Would you have
me dance again,—the dance only the bridegrooms see?

MEDICINE MAN. (*Smiling*) Dance, Asumana, dance. Go
on with your dance.

ASUMANA. Not until you promise. Will you promise?

MEDICINE MAN. (*Reluctantly*) I promise.

ASUMANA. Good. Now Asumana, the dancer, will dance
for you. (*She dances.*)

MEDICINE MAN. (*Half aloud to himself, but is overheard
by his servant* ALIHU, *who has stealthily entered and is
standing near*) It is my mighty medicine that can save
him, and it is mighty medicine that can kill him, for I
will give him too much, and then Asumana will be mine.
(*He smiles*) (ASUMANA *finishes dancing. The* MEDI-
CINE MAN *is greatly pleased with her.*)

MEDICINE MAN. You are a priceless gem, Asumana. You
dance as beautifully as you look, and all for the mighty
Medicine Man of Vai. Now I must prepare the ordeal.
Hear the natives! They are becoming impatient. Come,
Asumana, let us go for them. (*They go out, and the
medicine bag is left in charge of* ALIHU, *his servant.*)

ALIHU. (*Opening the bag*) She loves Kamo, and I am a

fool to love her! But she would be unhappy without him. (*He rearranges the bottles in the case. The medicine which is used on this occasion he takes out and puts in his bosom. He puts another bottle in its place*) This will affect him but it will not kill him, because it is weak. He will get well, and then she will be happy. I only want her to be happy. It would grieve me to let my master kill him, and take the girl. He has done enough already. This he must not do. (*Looking back, he hastens*) I hear voices. They are coming. (*He leaves the bag where it was and resumes his former position.* KAMO, *surrounded by warriors, enters. When they return they form a circle around the pot, which is in the center of the floor. The* MEDICINE MAN *kneels and chants over his potions.* KAMO *stands center. He is still tied with his hands behind him. He is calm and rather stolid during the entire trial scene, accepting the test with stoical indifference—the only emotion shown being when he is drinking the "Red Water"—when he looks at* ASUMANA, *as if questioning the right to undergo the ordeal. She turns towards him, but does not permit too great a show of emotion. Natives and warriors are eagerly expectant of the ordeal. The* MEDICINE MAN *is gloating over the expected result.* ALIHU *is most watchful of the effect, half afraid that it might prove more powerful than the liquid he intended to mix.* MEDICINE MAN *crosses down by the camp fire. He stands there rather arrogantly.* ALIHU *brings the bowl containing the fatal medicine, and then stands up stage from him.* ASUMANA *is down lower left. Warriors and natives grouped about back stage.*)

MEDICINE MAN. Kamo! My people accuse you of stealing.

They say you took gold from the poor and old.—Enter
now the circle,—and *drink* of the *red water. If it makes
you sick* —— Then you are guiltless and are free to
go your way —— BUT if there be no effect—then
guilty you must be—and—and *you must meet death at
the hands of your brothers. Drink, Kamo. Drink of
the red water!* (KAMO *slowly enters the circle. The
natives begin the "Death Dance,"* ASUMANA *leading
the dance. They dance around and around the circle.
Presently the medicine takes effect, and* KAMO *falls to
the floor. The dance continues.* KAMO *lies motionless
as if dead. The* MEDICINE MAN *smiles, believing him
dead. Suddenly* ASUMANA *stops the dancing.*)

ASUMANA. The Death Dance, oh, the Death Dance! Have
I danced Kamo to his death? (*She rushes to* KAMO's
side) Wake, Kamo! You are not guilty. Wake, Kamo!
Open your eyes—let me see you smile—I am Asumana,
your dancing Asumana—Oh, he is so still, so motionless! He is not—surely he is not dead. (*She looks at
the natives, and then her eyes rest upon the* MEDICINE
MAN) You—you have killed him. And you promised.
I believed you, too.

MEDICINE MAN. You asked me to save him from being
guilty. Have I not done so? See, the medicine took
effect. Surely he will waken soon.

ASUMANA. You gave him too much. I fear—I fear he is
dead. He is so still—so quiet. (*She weeps.*)

ALIHU. (*Coming forth to* ASUMANA) Weep not, Asumana.
Kamo is not dead. He is only asleep. He will waken
soon. But look friends, look upon the mighty Medicine Man of Vai. Look upon my master (*They look
upon him*) He is the guilty one— I, Alihu, know

his secrets.   He promised to save Kamo—promised Asumana—(*whereupon the* MEDICINE MAN *threatens* ALIHU,—*the natives cower before his outstretched wand.* ALIHU, *in desperation, seizes the wand, holding it high over his head, he snaps it in two: the natives howl and cower, expecting a catastrophe.* ALIHU, *triumphantly holding up the broken staff, as the* MEDICINE MAN *threatens in speechless wrath and fear*)—You think my master the mighty Medicine Man.   Look! He is not good, neither is he mighty.   He is a cheater, a robber, and a murderer.   He boasts of his cures, but he never boasts of how he kills the innocent.   For years I have been his servant, and I know his evil doings.   Now you know him.   I, Alihu, have spoken the truth.   (*As the* MEDICINE MAN *cowers, the natives suddenly turn upon him.*)

FIRST NATIVE. Murderer, coward!   You wanted to kill Kamo.   Shango has left you—for look—Alihu lives.

SECOND NATIVE. You shall be punished.   You are no longer the mighty Medicine Man of Vai.   Shango has left you.

ASUMANA. He has looked on the Dance of the Bridegroom. (*The crowd shudders with horror and rage.*)

CHORUS. (*Crowding the* MEDICINE MAN *off stage*)   Murderer!   Coward!   You shall be punished!

ASUMANA. (*Turning to* ALIHU, *who is leaving behind the natives*)   You are wonderful.   You have saved Kamo. Here, (*She slips one of her bracelets from her arm and gives it to him*) take it.   I give it to you because you are so good, so noble.

ALIHU. I will always remember Asumana, the beautiful dancer.   But I must go away now.   I have no master.   (*He crosses and looks at* KAMO *and nods reassuringly, then leaves*) Good-bye, Asumana. He will awaken soon. Good-bye.

ASUMANA. Alihu was kind. Why was Alihu so kind? (*She stands in a trance.*)

KAMO. (*Faintly, waking*) Asumana. . . . Asumana.

ASUMANA. (*Rushing to his side*) Yes, Kamo. I am here.

CURTAIN

THE EMPEROR JONES

By

EUGENE G. O'NEILL

Reprinted by special permission of the author and the American Play Company, New York City

CHARACTERS

BRUTUS JONES, Emperor
HENRY SMITHERS, a Cockney trader
AN OLD NATIVE WOMAN
LEM, a native chief
SOLDIERS, adherents of Lem
The Little Formless Fears; Jeff; The Negro Convicts; The
  Prison Guard; The Planters; The Auctioneer; The
  Slaves; The Congo Witch Doctor; The Crocodile God.

Scene: The action of the play takes place on an island in
  the West Indies as yet not self-determined by White
  Marines. The form of native government is, for the
  time being, an Empire.
Time: Contemporary.

Scene I: In the palace of the Emperor Jones. After-
  noon.
Scene II: The edge of the Great Forest. Dusk.
Scene III: In the forest. Night.
Scene IV: The same—later.
Scene V: The same—later.
Scene VI: The same—later.
Scene VII: The same—later.
Scene VIII: Same as *Scene* Two—the edge of the Great
  Forest. Dawn.

First performance at The Provincetown Playhouse,
November 3, 1920

THE EMPEROR JONES

SCENE I

THE AUDIENCE CHAMBER *in the palace of the* EMPEROR—
*a spacious, high-ceilinged room with bare, whitewashed walls.
The floor is of white tiles. In the rear, to the left of center,
a wide archway giving out on a portico with white pillars.
The palace is evidently situated on high ground, for beyond
the portico nothing can be seen but a vista of distant hills,
their summits crowned with thick groves of palm trees. In
the right wall, center, a smaller arched doorway leading to
the living quarters of the palace. The room is bare of furniture with the exception of one huge chair made of uncut wood
which stands at center, its back to rear. This is very apparently the* EMPEROR'S *throne. It is painted a dazzling, eye-
smiting scarlet. There is a brilliant orange cushion on the
seat and another smaller one is placed on the floor to serve
as a footstool. Strips of matting, dyed scarlet, lead from
the foot of the throne to the two entrances.*

*It is late afternoon but the sunlight still blazes yellowly
beyond the portico and there is an oppressive burden of ex-
hausting heat in the air.*

*As the curtain rises, a native Negro woman sneaks in cau-
tiously from the entrance on the right. She is very old,
dressed in cheap calico, barefooted, a red bandana handker-*

chief covering all but a few stray wisps of white hair. A bundle bound in colored cloth is carried over her shoulder on the end of a stick. She hesitates beside the doorway, peering back as if in extreme dread of being discovered. Then she begins to glide noiselessly, a step at a time, toward the doorway in the rear. At this moment, SMITHERS *appears beneath the portico.*

SMITHERS *is a tall, stoop-shouldered man about forty. His bald head, perched on a long neck with an enormous Adam's apple, looks like an egg. The tropics have tanned his naturally pasty face with its small, sharp features to a sickly yellow, and native rum has painted his pointed nose to a startling red. His little, washy-blue eyes are red rimmed and dart about him like a ferret's. His expression is one of unscrupulous meanness, cowardly and dangerous. His attitude toward* JONES *is that of one who will give vent to a nourished grudge against all superiority—as far as he dares. He is dressed in a worn riding suit of dirty white drill, puttees, spurs, and wears a white cork helmet. A cartridge belt with an automatic revolver is around his waist. He carries a riding whip in his hand. He sees the woman and stops to watch her suspiciously. Then, making up his mind, he steps quickly on tiptoe into the room. The woman, looking back over her shoulder continually, does not see him until it is too late. When she does,* SMITHERS *springs forward and grabs her firmly by the shoulder. She struggles to get away, fiercely but silently.*

SMITHERS. (*Tightening his grasp—roughly*) Easy! None o' that, me birdie. You can't wriggle out now. I got me 'ooks on yer.

WOMAN. (*Seeing the uselessness of struggling, gives away to frantic terror, and sinks to the ground, embracing his knees supplicatingly*) No tell him! No tell him, Mister!

SMITHERS. (*With great curiosity*) Tell 'im? (*Then scornfully*) Oh, you mean 'is bloomin Majesty. What's the gaime, any'ow? What are you sneakin' away for? Been stealin' a bit, I s'pose. (*He taps her bundle with his riding whip significantly.*)

WOMAN. (*Shaking her head vehemently*) No, me no steal.

SMITHERS. Bloody liar! But tell me what's up. There's somethin' funny goin' on. I smelled it in the air first thing I got up this mornin'. You blacks are up to some devilment. This palace of 'is is like a bleedin' tomb. Where's all the 'ands? (*The woman keeps sullenly silent.* SMITHERS *raises his whip threateningly*) Ow, yer won't, won't yer? I'll show yer what's what.

WOMAN. (*Coweringly*) I tell, Mister. You no hit. They go—all go. (*She makes a sweeping gesture toward the hills in the distance.*)

SMITHERS. Run away—to the 'ills?

WOMAN. Yes, Mister. Him Emperor—Great Father—— (*She touches her forehead to the floor with a quick mechanical jerk*) Him sleep after eat. Then they go— all go. Me old woman. Me left only. Now me go, too.

SMITHERS. (*His astonishment giving way to an immense mean satisfaction*) Ow! So that's the ticket! Well, I know bloody well wot's in the air—when they runs orf to the 'ills. The tom-tom 'll be thumping out there bloomin' soon. (*With extreme vindictiveness*) And I'm bloody glad of it, for one! Serve 'im right! Puttin' on airs, the stinkin' nigger! 'Is Majesty! Gawd blimey! I only 'opes I'm there when they takes 'im out to shoot 'im. (*Suddenly*) 'E's still 'ere all right, ain't 'e?

WOMAN. Him sleep.

SMITHERS. 'E's bound to find out soon as 'e wakes up. 'E's cunnin' enough to know when 'is time's come. (*He goes to the doorway on right and whistles shrilly with his fingers in his mouth. The old woman springs to her feet and runs out of the doorway, rear.* SMITHERS *goes after her, reaching for his revolver*) Stop or I'll shoot! (*Then stopping—indifferently*) Pop orf then, if yer like, yer black cow! (*He stands in the doorway, looking after her.* JONES *enters from the right. He is a tall, powerfully-built, full-blooded Negro of middle age. His features are typically Negroid, yet there is something decidedly distinctive about his face—an underlying strength of will, a hardy, self-reliant confidence in himself that inspires respect. His eyes are alive with a keen, cunning intelligence. In manner, he is shrewd, suspicious, evasive. He wears a light-blue uniform coat, sprayed with brass buttons, heavy gold chevrons on his shoulders, gold braid on the collar, cuffs, etc. His pants are bright red with a light-blue stripe down the side. Patent leather laced boots with brass spurs, and a belt with a long-barreled, pearl-handled revolver in a holster complete his make-up. Yet there is something not altogether ridiculous about his grandeur. He has a way of carrying it off.*)

JONES. (*Not seeing anyone—greatly irritated and blinking sleepily—shouts*) Who dare whistle dat way in my palace? Who dare wake up de Emperor? I'll git de hide frayled off some o' you niggers sho'!

SMITHERS. (*Showing himself—in a manner half-afraid and*

half-defiant) It was me whistled to yer. (*As* JONES *frowns angrily*) I got news for yer.

JONES. (*Putting on his suavest manner which fails to cover up his contempt for the white man*) Oh, it's you, Mister Smithers. (*He sits down on his throne with easy dignity*) What news you got to tell me?

SMITHERS. (*Coming close to enjoy his discomfiture*) Don't you notice nothin' funny today?

JONES. (*Coldly*) Funny? No, I ain't perceived nothin' of de kind!

SMITHERS. Then you ain't so foxy as I thought you was. Where's all your court— (*Sarcastically*) the Generals and the Cabinet Ministers and all?

JONES. (*Imperturbably*) Where dey mostly runs to, minute I closes my eyes—drinkin' rum and talkin' big down in de town. (*Sarcastically*) How come you don't know dat? Ain't you sousin' with 'em most every day?

SMITHERS. (*Stung but pretending indifference—with a wink*) That's part of the day's work. I got ter—ain't I—in my business?

JONES. (*Contemptuously*) Yo' business!

SMITHERS. (*Imprudently enraged*) Gawd blimey, you was glad enough for me ter take you in on it when you landed here first. You didn' 'ave no 'igh and mighty airs in them days!

JONES. (*His hand going to his revolver like a flash—menacingly*) Talk polite, white man! Talk polite, you heah me! I'm boss heah now, is you fergettin'? (*The Cockney seems about to challenge this last statement with the facts, but something in the other's eyes holds and cows him.*)

SMITHERS. (*In a cowardly whine*) No 'arm meant, old top.

JONES. (*Condescendingly*) I accepts yo' apology. (*Lets*

his hand fall from his revolver) No use'n you rakin'
up ole times. What I was den is one thing. What I
is now 's another. You didn't let me in on yo' crooked
work out o' no kind feelin's dat time. I done de dirty
work fo' you—and most o' de brain work, too, fo' dat
matter—and I was wu'th money to you, dat's de reason.

SMITHERS. Well, blimey, I give yer a start, didn't I?—when
no one else would. I wasn't afraid to hire yer like the
rest was—'count of the story about your breakin' jail
back in the States.

JONES. No, you didn't have no s'cuse to look down on me
fo' dat. You been in jail yo'self more'n once.

SMITHERS. (*Furiously*) It's a lie! (*Then trying to pass it
off by an attempt at scorn*) Garn! Who told yer that
fairy tale?

JONES. Dey's some things I ain't got to be tole. I kin see
'em in folks' eyes. (*Then after a pause—meditatively*)
Yes, you sho' give me a start. And it didn't take long
from dat time to git dese fool woods' niggers right
where I wanted dem. (*With pride*) From stowaway
to Emperor in two years! Dat's goin' some!

SMITHERS. (*With curiosity*) And I bet you got yer pile o'
money 'id safe some place.

JONES. (*With satisfaction*) I sho' has! And it's in a for-
eign bank where no pusson don't ever get it out but me
no matter what come. You don't s'pose I was holdin'
down dis Emperor job for de glory in it, did you? Sho!
De fuss and glory part of it, dat's only to turn de heads
o' de low-flung, bush niggers dat's here. Dey wants
de big circus show for deir money. I gives it to 'em
an' I gits de money. (*With a grin*) De long green,
dat's me every time! (*Then rebukingly*) But you ain't
got no kick agin me, Smithers. I'se paid you back all

THE EMPEROR

you done for me many times. Ain't I pertected you
and winked at all de crooked tradin' you been doin'
right out in de broad day. Sho' I has—and me makin'
laws to stop it at de same time! (*He chuckles*)

SMITHERS. (*Grinning*) But, meanin' no 'arm, you been
grabbin' right and left yourself ain't you? Look at the
taxes you've put on 'em! Blimey! You've squeezed
'em dry!

JONES. (*Chuckling*) No dey ain't *all* dry yet. I'se still heah,
ain't I?

SMITHERS. (*Smiling at his secret thought*) They're dry right
now, you'll find out. (*Changing the subject abruptly*)
And as for me breaking laws, you've broke 'em all yer-
self just as fast as yer made 'em.

JONES. Ain't I de Emperor? De laws don't go for him.
(*Judicially*) You heah what I tells you, Smithers.
Dere's little stealin' like you does, and dere's big stealin'
like I does. For de little stealin' dey gits you in jail
soon or late. For de big stealin' dey makes you Emperor and puts you in de Hall o' Fame when you croaks.
(*Reminiscently*) If dey's one thing I learns in ten years
on de Pullman ca's listenin' to de white quality talk,
it's dat same fact. And when I gits a chance to use it
I winds up Emperor in two years.

SMITHERS. (*Unable to repress the genuine admiration of
the small fry for the large*) Yes, you turned the bleedin'
trick, all right. Blimey, I never seen a bloke 'as 'ad the
bloomin' luck you 'as.

JONES. (*Severely*) Luck? What you mean—luck?

SMITHERS. I suppose you'll say as that swank about the silver bullet ain't luck—and that was what first got the
fool blacks on yer side the time of the revolution,
wasn't it?

JONES. (*With a laugh*) Oh, dat silver bullet! Sho' was luck! But I makes dat luck, you heah? I loads de dice! Yessuh! When dat murderin' nigger old Lem hired to kill me takes aim ten feet away and his gun misses fire and I shoots him dead, what you heah me say?

SMITHERS. You said yer'd got a charm so's no lead bullet'd kill yer. You was so strong only a silver bullet could kill yer, you told 'em. Blimey, wasn't that swank for yer—and plain, fat-'eaded luck?

JONES. (*Proudly*) I got brains and uses 'em quick. Dat ain't luck.

SMITHERS. Yer knew they wasn't 'ardly liable to get no silver bullets. And it was luck 'e didn't 'it you that time.

JONES. (*Laughing*) And dere all dem fool bush niggers was kneelin' down and bumpin' deir heads on de ground like I was a miracle out o' de Bible. Oh, Lawd, from dat time on I has dem all eatin' out of my hand. I cracks de whip and dey jumps through.

SMITHERS. (*With a sniff*) Yankee bluff done it.

JONES. Ain't a man's talkin' big what makes him big— long as he makes folks believe it. Sho', I talks large when I ain't got nothin' to back it up, but I ain't talkin' wild just de same. I knows I kin fool 'em—I *knows* it—and dat's backin' enough fo' my game. And ain't I got to learn deir lingo and teach some of dem English befo' I kin talk to 'em? Ain't dat work? You ain't never learned ary word er it, Smithers, in de ten years you been heah, dough yo' knows it's money in yo' pocket tradin' wid 'em if you does. But you'se too shiftless to take de trouble.

SMITHERS. (*Flushing*) Never mind about me. What's this

I've 'eard about yer really 'avin' a silver bullet moulded for yourself?

JONES. It's playin' out my bluff. I has de silver bullet moulded and I tells 'em when de time comes I kills myself wid it. I tells 'em dat's 'cause I'm de on'y man in de world big enuff to git me. No use'n deir tryin'. And dey falls down and bumps deir heads. (*He laughs*) I does dat so's I kin take a walk in peace widout no jealous nigger gunnin' at me from behind de trees.

SMITHERS. (*Astonished*) Then you 'ad it made—'onest?

JONES. Sho' did. Heah she be. (*He takes out his revolver, breaks it, and takes the silver bullet out of one chamber*) Five lead an' dis silver baby at de last. Don't she shine pretty? (*He holds it in his hand, looking at it admiringly, as if strangely fascinated.*)

SMITHERS. Let me see. (*Reaches out his hand for it*)

JONES. (*Harshly*) Keep yo' hands whar de b'long, white man. (*He replaces it in the chamber and puts the revolver back on his hip.*)

SMITHERS. (*Snarling*) Gawd blimey! Think I'm a bleedin' thief, you would.

JONES. No. 'Tain't dat. I knows you'se scared to steal from me. On'y I ain't 'lowing nary body to touch dis baby. She's my rabbit's foot.

SMITHERS. (*Sneering*) A bloomin' charm, wot? (*Venomously*) Well, you'll need all the bloody charms you 'as before long, s' 'elp me!

JONES. (*Judicially*) Oh, I'se good for six months yit 'fore dey gits sick o' my game. Den, when I sees trouble comin', I makes my get-away.

SMITHERS. Ho! You got it all planned, ain't yer?

JONES. I ain't no fool. I knows dis Emperor's time is sho't. Dat why I make hay when de sun shine. Was you thinkin' I'se aimin' to hold down dis job for life? No, suh! What good is gittin' money if you stays back in dis raggedy country? I wants action when I spends. And when I sees dese niggers gittin' up deir nerve to tu'n me out, and I'se got all de money in sight, I resigns on de spot and beats it quick.

SMITHERS. Where to?

JONES. None o' yo' business.

SMITHERS. Not back to the bloody States, I'll lay my oath.

JONES. (*Suspiciously*) Why don't I? (*Then with an easy laugh*) You mean 'count of dat story 'bout me breakin' from jail back dere? Dat's all talk.

SMITHERS. (*Skeptically*) Ho, yes!

JONES. (*Sharply*) You ain't 'sinuatin' I'se a liar, is you?

SMITHERS. (*Hastily*) No, Gawd strike me! I was only thinkin' o' the bloody lies you told the blacks 'ere about killin' white men in the States.

JONES. (*Angered*) How come dey're lies?

SMITHERS. You'd 'ave been in jail if you 'ad, wouldn't yer then? (*With venom*) And from what I've 'eard, it ain't 'ealthy for a black to kill a white man in the States. They burn 'em in oil, don't they?

JONES. (*With cool deadliness*) You mean lynchin' 'd scare me? Well, I tells you, Smithers, maybe I does kill one white man back dere. Maybe I does. And maybe I kills another right heah 'fore long if he don't look out.

SMITHERS. (*Trying to force a laugh*) I was on'y spoofin' yer. Can't yer take a joke? And you was just sayin' you'd never been in jail.

JONES. (*In the same tone—slightly boastful*) Maybe I goes to jail dere for gettin' in an argument wid razors ovah a crap game. Maybe I gits twenty years when dat colored man die. Maybe I gits in 'nother argument wid de prison guard was overseer ovah us when we're wukin' de roads. Maybe he hits me wid a whip an' I splits his head wid a shovel an' runs away an' files de chain off my leg an' gits away safe. Maybe I does all dat an maybe I don't. It's a story I tells you so's you knows I'se de kind of man dat if you evah repeats one word of it, I ends yo' stealin' on dis yearth mighty damn quick!

SMITHERS. (*Terrified*) Think I'd peach on yer? Not me! Ain't I always been yer friend?

JONES. (*Suddenly relaxing*) Sho' you has—and you better be.

SMITHERS. (*Recovering his composure—and with it his malice*) And just to show yer I'm yer friend, I'll tell yer that bit o' news I was goin' to.

JONES. Go ahead! Shoot de piece. Must be bad news from de happy way you look.

SMITHERS. (*Warningly*) Maybe it's gettin' time for you to resign—with that bloomin' silver bullet, wot? (*He finishes with a mocking grin*)

JONES. (*Puzzled*) What's dat you say? Talk plain.

SMITHERS. Ain't noticed any of the guards or servants about the place today, I 'aven't.

JONES. (*Carelessly*) Dey're all out in de garden sleepin' under de trees. When I sleeps, dey sneaks a sleep, too, and I pretends I never suspicions it. All I got to do is to ring de bell an' dey come flyin', makin' a bluff dey was wukin' all de time.

SMITHERS. (*In the same mocking tone*) Ring the bell now an' you'll bloody well see what I means.

JONES. (*Startled to alertness, but preserving the same careless tone*) Sho' I rings. (*He reaches below the throne and pulls out a big common dinner bell which is painted*

the same vivid scarlet as the throne. He rings this
vigorously—then stops to listen. Then he goes to both
doors, rings again, and looks out.)

SMITHERS. (*Watching him with malicious satisfaction—*
after a pause—mockingly) The bloody ship is sinkin'
an' the bleedin' rats 'as slung their 'ooks.

JONES. (*In a sudden fit of anger flings the bells clattering*
into a corner) Low-flung, woods' niggers! (*Then*
catching SMITHERS'S *eye on him, he controls himself*
and suddenly bursts into a low chuckling laugh.) Reckon
I overplays my hand dis once! A man can't take de
pot on a bobtailed flush all de time. Was I sayin' I'd
sit in six months mo'? Well, I'se changed my mind den.
I cashes in and resigns de job of Emperor right dis
minute.

SMITHERS. (*With real admiration*) Blimey, but you're a
cool bird, and no mistake.

JONES. No use'n fussin'. When I knows de game's up I
kisses it goodbye widout no long waits. Dey've all run
off to de hills, ain't dey?

SMITHERS. Yes—every bleedin' man jack of 'em.

JONES. Den de revolution is at de post. And de Emperor
better get his feet smokin' up de trail. (*He starts for*
the door in rear.)

SMITHERS. Goin' out to look for your 'orse? Yer won't
find any. They steals the 'orses first thing. Mine was
gone when I went for 'im this mornin'. That's wot first
give me a suspicion of wot was up.

JONES. (*Alarmed for a second, scratches his head, then*
philosophically) Well, den I hoofs it. Feet, do yo'
duty! (*He pulls out a gold watch and looks at it*)
Three-thuty. Sundown's at six-thuty or dereabouts.

(*Puts his watch back—with cool confidence*) I got plenty o' time to make it easy.

SMITHERS. Don't be so bloomin' sure of it. They'll be after you 'ot and 'eavy. Ole Lem is at the bottom o' this business an' 'e 'ates you like 'ell. 'E'd rather do for you than eat 'is dinner, 'e would!

JONES. (*Scornfully*) Dat fool no-'count nigger! Does you think I'se scared o' him? I stands him on his thick head more'n once befo' dis, and I does it again if he comes in my way— (*Fiercely*) And dis time I leave him a dead nigger fo' sho'!

SMITHERS. You'll 'ave to cut through the big forest—an' these blacks 'ere can sniff and follow a trail in the dark like 'ounds. You'd 'ave to 'ustle to get through that forest in twelve hours even if you knew all the bloomin' trails like a native.

JONES. (*With indignant scorn*) Look-a heah, white man! Does you think I'se a natural bo'n fool? Give me credit fo' havin' some sense, fo' Lawd's sake! Don't you s'pose I'se looked ahead and made sho' of all de chances? I'se gone out in dat big forest, pretendin' to hunt, so many times dat I knows it high an' low like a book. I could go through on dem trails wid my eyes shut. (*With great contempt*) Think dese ignerent bush niggers, dat don't got brains enuff to know deir own names even, can catch Brutus Jones? Huh, I s'pects not! Not on yo' life! Why, man, de white men went after me wid bloodhounds where I come from an' I jes' laughs at 'em. It's a shame to fool dese black trash around heah, dey're so easy. You watch me, man. I'll make dem look sick. I will. I'll be 'cross de plain to de edge of de forest by time dark comes. Once in de woods in de night, dey got a swell chance o' findin'

dis baby! Dawn tomorrow I'll be out at de oder side
and on de coast whar dat French gunboat is stayin'.
She picks me up, take me to the Martinique when she
go dar, and dere I is safe wid a mighty big bank roll
in my jeans. It's easy as rollin' off a log.

SMITHERS. (*Maliciously*) But s'posin' somethin' 'appens
wrong an' they do nab yer?

JONES. (*Decisively*) Dey don't.—Dat's de answer.

SMITHERS. But, just for argyment's sake,—what'd you do?

JONES. (*Frowning*) I'se got five lead bullets in dis gun good
enuff fo' common bush niggers—an' after dat I got de
silver bullet left to cheat 'em out o' gittin' me.

SMITHERS. (*Jeeringly*) Ho, I was fergettin' that silver bullet. You'll bump yourself orf in style, won't yer?
Blimey!

JONES. (*Gloomily*) Yo' kin bet yo' whole roll on one thing,
white man. Dis baby plays out his string to de end and
when he quits, he quits wid a bang de way he ought.
Silver bullet ain't none too good for him when he go,
dat's a fac'! (*Then shaking off his nervousness—with
a confident laugh*) Sho'! What is I talkin' about?
Ain't come to dat yit an' I never will—not wid trash
niggers like dese yere. (*Boastfully*) Silver bullet bring
me luck anyway. I kin outguess, outrun, outfight, an'
outplay de whole lot o' dem all ovah de board any time
o' de day er night! You watch me!

(*From the distant hills comes the faint, steady thump of
a tom-tom, low and vibrating. It starts at a rate exactly
corresponding to normal pulse beat—seventy-two to the minute—and continues at a gradually accelerating rate from this
point uninterruptedly to the very end of the play.*)

(JONES *starts at the sound; a strange look of apprehension*

creeps into his face for a moment as he listens. Then he
asks, with an attempt to retain his most casual manner—)
What's dat drum beatin' fo'?

SMITHERS. (*With a mean grin*) For you. That means the
bleedin' ceremony 'as started. I've 'eard it before and I
knows.

JONES. Cer'mony? What cer'mony?

SMITHERS. The blacks is 'oldin' a bloody meetin', 'avin' a
war dance, gettin' their courage worked up b'fore they
starts after you.

JONES. Let dem! Dey'll sho' need it!

SMITHERS. And they're there 'oldin' their 'eathen religious
service—makin' no end of devil spells and charms to
'elp 'em against your silver bullet.) (*He guffaws loudly*)
Blimey, but they're balmy as 'ell.

JONES. (*A tiny bit awed and shaken in spite of himself*)
Huh! Takes more'n dat to scare dis chicken!

SMITHERS. (*Scenting the other's feeling—maliciously*) Ter-
night when it's pitch black in the forest, they'll 'ave their
pet devils and ghosts 'oundin' after you. You'll find
yer bloody 'air 'll be standin' on end before tomorrow
mornin'. (*Seriously*) It's a bleedin' queer place, that
stinkin' forest, even in daylight. Yer don't know what
might 'appen in there, it's that rotten still. Always
sends the cold shivers down my back minute I gets
in it.

JONES. (*With a contemptuous sniff*) I ain't no chicken liver
like you is. Trees an' me, we'se friends, an' dar's a
full moon comin' to bring me light. And let dem po'
niggers make all de fool spells dey'se a min' to. Does
yo' s'pect I'se silly enuff to b'lieve in ghosts an' ha'nts
an' all dat ole woman's talk? G'long, white man! You
ain't talkin' to me. (*With a chuckle*) Doesn't you

knows dey's got to do wid a man was member in good
standin' o' de Baptist Church? Sho' I was dat when
I was porter on de Pullman, an' befo' I gits into my little trouble. Let dem try deir heathen tricks. De Baptist Church done pertect me an' land dem all in hell.
(*Then with more confident satisfaction*) And I'se got
little silver bullet o' my own, don't forgit.

SMITHERS. Ho! You 'aven't give much 'eed to your Baptist
Church since you been down 'ere. I've heard myself you
'ad turned yer coat an' was takin' up with their blarsted
witch-doctors, or whatever the 'ell yer calls the swine.

JONES. (*Vehemently*) I pretends to! Sho' I pretends!
Dat's part o' my game from de fust. If I finds out dem
niggers believes dat black is white, den I yells it out
louder 'n some deir loudest. It don't git me nothin'
to do missionary work for de Baptist Church. I'se after
de coin, an' I lays my Jesus on de shelf for de time bein'.
(*Stops abruptly to look at his watch—alertly*) But I
ain't got de time to waste no more fool talk wid you.
I'se gwine away from heah dis secon'. (*He reaches
in under the throne and pulls out an expensive Panama
hat with a bright multicolored band and sets it jauntily
on his head.*) So long, white man! (*With a grin*)
See you in jail sometime, maybe!

SMITHERS. Not me, you won't. Well, I wouldn't be in yer
bloody boots for no bloomin' money, but 'ere's wishin'
yer luck just the same.

JONES. (*Contemptuously*) You're de frightenedest man
evah I see! I tells you I'se safe 's'f I was in New York
City. It take dem niggers from now to dark to git up
de nerve to start somethin'. By dat time, I'se got a
head start dey never ketch up wid.

THE FUGITIVE

SMITHERS. (*Maliciously*) Give my regards to any ghosts yer meets up with.

JONES. (*Grinning*) If dat ghost got money, I'll tell him never ha'nt you less'n he wants to lose it.

SMITHERS. (*Flattered*) Garn! (*Then curiously*) Ain't yer takin' no luggage with yer?

JONES. I travels light when I wants to move fast. And I got tinned grub buried on de edge o' de forest. (*Boastfully*) Now say dat I don't look ahead an' use my brains! (*With a wide, liberal gesture*) I will all dat's left in de palace to you—an' you better grab all you kin sneak away wid befo' dey gits here.

SMITHERS. (*Gratefully*) Righto—and thanks ter yer. (*As* JONES *walks toward the door in rear—cautioningly*) Say! Look 'ere, you ain't goin' out that way, are yer?

JONES. Does you think I'd slink out de back door like a common nigger? I'se Emperor yit, ain't I? And de Emperor Jones leaves de way he comes, and dat black trash don't dare stop him—not yit, leastways. (*He stops for a moment in the doorway, listening to the far-off but insistent beat of the tom-tom.*) Listen to dat roll call, will yo'? Must be mighty big drum carry dat far. (*Then with a laugh*) Well, if dey ain't no whole brass band to see me off, I sho' got de drum part of it. So long, white man. (*He puts his hands in his pockets and with studied carelessness, whistling a tune, he saunters out of the doorway and off to the left.*)

SMITHERS. (*Looks after him with a puzzled admiration*) 'E's got 'is bloomin' nerve with 'im, s'elp me! (*Then angrily*) Ho—the bleedin' nigger—puttin' on 'is bloody airs! I 'opes they nabs 'im an' gives 'im what's what!

CURTAIN

SCENE II

NIGHTFALL. *The end of the plain where the Great Forest begins. The foreground is sandy, level ground dotted by a few stones and clumps of stunted bushes cowering close against the earth to escape the buffeting of the trade wind. In the rear the forest is a wall of darkness dividing the world. Only when the eye becomes accustomed to the gloom can the outlines of separate trunks of the nearest trees be made out, enormous pillars of deeper blackness. A somber monotone of wind lost in the leaves moans in the air. Yet this sound serves but to intensify the impression of the forest's relentless immobility, to form a background throwing into relief, its brooding, implacable silence.*

JONES *enters from the left, walking rapidly. He stops as he nears the edge of the forest, looks around him quickly, peering into the dark as if searching for some familiar landmark. Then, apparently satisfied that he is where he ought to be, he throws himself on the ground, dog-tired.*

JONES. Well, heah I is. In de nick o' time, too! Little mo' an' it'd be blacker'n de ace of spades heahabouts. (*He pulls a bandana handerchief from his hip pocket and mops off his perspiring face.*) Sho'! Gimme air! I'se tuckered out sho' 'nuff. Dat soft Emperor job ain't no trainin' fo' a long hike ovah dat plain in de brilin' sun. (*Then with a chuckle*) Cheer up, nigger, de worst is yet to come. (*He lifts his head and stares at the forest. His chuckle peters out abruptly. In a tone of awe*) My goodness, look at dem woods, will you? Dat no-'count Smithers said dey'd be black an' he sho' called de turn. (*Turning away from them quickly and looking down at his feet, he snatches at a chance to change the subject—solicitously*) Feet, yo' is holdin' up yo' end fine an' I sutinly hopes you ain't blisterin' none. It's time you git a rest. (*He takes off his shoes, his eyes studiously avoiding the forest. He feels of the soles of his feet gingerly.*) You is still in de pink—only a little mite feverish. Cool you'selfs. Remember yo' done got a long journey yit befo' yo'. (*He sits in a weary attitude, listening to the rhythmic beating of the tom-tom. He grumbles in a loud tone to cover up a growing uneasiness.*) Bush niggers! Wonder dey wouldn't git sick o' beatin' dat drum. Sound louder, seem like. I wonder if dey's startin' after me? (*He scrambles to his feet, looking back across the plain.*) Couldn't see dem now, nohow, if dey was hundred feet away. (*Then shaking himself like a wet dog to get rid of these depressing thoughts*) Sho', dey's miles an' miles behind. What yo' gittin' fidgety about? (*But he sits down and begins to lace up his shoes in great haste, all the time muttering reassuringly*) You know what? Yo' belly is empty, dat's what's de matter wid you. Come time to eat! Wid nothin' but wind on yo' stumach, o' course yo' feels jiggedy. Well, we eats right heah an' now soon's I gits dese pesky shoes laced up. (*He finishes lacing up his shoes.*) Dere! Now le's see! (*Gets on his hands and knees and searches the ground around him with his eyes*) White stone, white stone, where is you? (*He sees the first white stone and crawls to it—with satisfaction.*) Heah you is! I knowed dis was de right place. Box of grub, come to me. (*He turns over the stone and feels in under it —in a tone of dismay.*) Ain't heah! Gorry, is I in de right place or isn't I? Dere's 'nother stone. Guess dat's it. (*He scrambles to the next stone and turns it over.*) Ain't heah, neither! Grub, what is you? Ain't heah. Gorry, has I got to go hungry into dem woods— all de night? (*While he is talking he scrambles from one stone to another, turning them over in frantic haste. Finally he jumps to his feet excitedly.*) Is I lost de place? Must have! But how dat happen when I was followin' de trail across de plain in broad daylight? (*Almost plaintively*) I'se hungry, I is! I gotta git my food. Whar's my strength gonna come from if I doesn't? Gorry, I gotta find dat grub high an' low somehow! Why it come dark so quick like dat? Can't see nothin'. (*He scratches a match on his trousers and peers about him. The rate of the beat of the far-off tom-tom increases perceptibly as he does so. He mutters in a bewildered voice.*) How come all dese white stones come heah when I only remembers one? (*Suddenly, with a frightened gasp, he flings the match on the ground and stamps on it.*) Nigger, is yo' gone crazy mad? Is you lightin' matches to show dem whar you is? Fo' Lawd's sake, use yo' haid. Gorry, I'se got to be careful! (*He stares at the plain behind him apprehensively, his hand on his revolver.*) But how come all dese white stones? And whar's dat tin box o' grub I hid all wrapped up in oilcloth? (*While his back is turned, the Little Formless Fears creep out from the deeper blackness of the forest. They are black, shapeless; only their glittering little eyes can be seen. If they have any describable form at all it is that of a grubworm about the size of a creeping child. They move noiselessly, but with deliberate, painful effort, striving to raise themselves on end, failing and sinking prone again.* JONES *turns about to face the forest. He stares up at the*

*tops of the trees, seeking vainly to discover his where-
abouts by their conformation.*) Can't tell nothin' from
dem trees! Gorry, nothin' 'round heah look like I evah
seed it befo'. I'se done lost de place sho' 'nuff! (*With
mournful foreboding*) It's mighty queer! It's mighty
queer! (*With sudden forced defiance—in an angry
tone*) Woods, is yo' tryin' to put somethin' ovah on
me? (*From the formless creatures on the ground in
front of him comes a tiny gale of low mocking laughter
like a rustling of leaves. They squirm upward toward
him in twisted attitudes.* JONES *looks down, leaps backward with a yell of terror, yanking out his revolver as
he does so—in a quavering voice*) What's dat? Who's
dar? What 's you? Git away from me befo' I shoots
yo' up! You don't?—(*He fires. There is a flash, a
loud report, then silence broken only by the far-off,
quickened throb of the tom-tom. The formless creatures have scurried back into the forest.* JONES *remains
fixed in his position, listening intently. The sound of
the shot, the reassuring feel of the revolver in his hand
have somewhat restored his shaken nerve. He addresses
himself with renewed confidence.*) Dey're gone. Dat
shot fix 'em. Dey was only little animals—little wild
pigs, I reckon. Dey've maybe rooted out yo' grub an'
eat it. Sho', yo' fool nigger, what yo' think dey is—
ha'nts? (*Excitedly*) Gorry, you give de game away
when yo' fire dat shot. Dem niggers heah dat fo' su'tin!
Time yo' beat it in de woods widout no long waits.
(*He starts for the forest—hesitates before the plunge
—then urging himself in with manful resolution*) Git in,
nigger! What yo' skeered at? Ain't nothin' dere but
de trees! Git in! (*He plunges boldly into the forest.*)

SCENE III

NINE O'CLOCK. *In the forest. The moon has just risen. Its beams drifting through the canopy of leaves, make a barely perceptible, suffused eerie glow. A dense low wall of underbrush and creepers is in the nearer foreground forming a small triangular clearing. Beyond this is the massed blackness of the forest like an encompassing barrier. A path is dimly discerned leading down to the clearing from left, rear, and winding away from it again toward the right. As the scene opens nothing can be distinctly made out. Except for the beating of the tom-tom, which is a trifle louder and quicker than in the previous scene, there is silence broken every few seconds by a queer, clicking sound. Then gradually the figure of the Negro, JEFF, can be discerned crouching on his haunches at the rear of the triangle. He is middle-aged, thin, brown in color, is dressed in a Pullman porter's uniform, cap, etc. He is throwing a pair of dice on the ground before him, picking them up, shaking them, casting them out with the regular, rigid, mechanical movements of an automaton. The heavy, plodding footsteps of someone approaching along the trail from the left are heard and* JONES'S *voice, pitched in a slightly higher key and strained in a cheering effort to overcome its own tremors.*

JONES. De moon's rizen. Does yo' heah dat, nigger? Yo' gits more light from dis out. No mo' buttin' yo' fool head agin' de trunks an' scratchin' de hide off yo' legs in de bushes. Now yo' sees whar yo'se gwine. So cheer up! From now on yo' has a snap. (*He steps just to the rear of the triangular clearing and mops off his face on his sleeve. He has lost his Panama hat. His face is scratched, his brilliant uniform shows several large rents.*) What time's it gittin' to be, I wonder? I das-

sent light no match to find out. Phoo'. It's wa'm an'
dat's a fac'! (*Wearily*) How long I been makin' tracks
in dese woods? Must be hours an' hours. Seems like
fo'evah! Yit can't be, when de moon's jes' riz. Dis
am a long night fo' yo', yo' Majesty! (*With a mournful chuckle*) Majesty! Der ain't much majesty 'bout
dis baby now. (*With attempted cheerfulness*) Never
min'. It's all part o' de game. Dis night come to an
end like everythin' else. An' when yo' gits dar safe an'
has dat bank roll in yo' hands, yo' laughs at all dis.
(*He starts to whistle but checks himself abruptly.*)
What yo' whistlin' for, you po' dope! Want all de
worl' to heah you? (*He stops talking to listen.*) Heah
dat ole drum! Sho' gits nearer from de sound. Dey're
packin' it along wid 'em. Time fo' me to move. (*He
takes a step forward, then stops—worriedly.*) What's
dat odder queer clickety sound I heah? Der it is! Sound
close! Sound like—fo' God sake, sound like some nigger was shootin' crap! (*Frightenedly*) I better beat it
quick when I gits dem notions. (*He walks quickly into
the clear space—then stands transfixed as he sees* JEFF
—*in a terrified gasp*) Who dar? Who dat? Is dat
you, Jeff? (*Starting toward the other, forgetful for a
moment of his surroundings and really believing it is a
living man that he sees—in a tone of happy relief.*)
Jeff! I'se sho' mighty glad to see yo'! Dey tol' me
yo' done died from dat razor cut I gives you. (*Stopping suddenly, bewilderedly*) But how you come to be
heah, nigger? (*He stares fascinatedly at the other
who continues his mechanical play with the dice.
JONES's eyes begin to roll wildly. He stutters.*) Ain't
you gwine—look up—can't you speak to me? Is you—
is yo'—a ha'nt? (*He jerks out his revolver in a frenzy*

of terrified rage.) Nigger, I kills yo' dead once. Has I got to kill yo' agin? You take it den. (*He fires. When the smoke clears away* JEFF *has disappeared.* JONES *stands trembling—then with a certain reassurance*) He's gone, anyway. Ha'nt or no ha'nt, dat shot fix him. (*The beat of the far-off tom-tom is perceptibly louder and more rapid.* JONES *becomes conscious of it —with a start, looking back over his shoulder*) Dey's gittin' near! Dey'se comin' fast! An' heah I is shootin' shots to let 'em know jes' whar I is. Oh, gorry, I'se got to run. (*Forgetting the path he plunges wildly into the underbrush in the rear and disappears in the shadow.*)

SCENE IV

ELEVEN O'CLOCK. *In the forest. A wide dirt road runs diagonally from right, front, to left, rear. Rising sheer on both sides the forest walls it in. The moon is now up. Under its light the road glimmers ghostly and unreal. It is as if the forest had stood aside momentarily to let the road pass through and accomplish its veiled purpose. This done, the forest will fold in upon itself again and the road will be no more.* JONES *stumbles in from the forest on the right. His uniform is ragged and torn. He looks about him with numbed surprise when he sees the road, his eyes blinking in the bright moonlight. He flops down exhaustedly and pants heavily for a while. Then with sudden anger.*

JONES. I'm meltin' wid heat! Runnin' and runnin' an' runnin'! Damn dis heah coat! Like a strait jacket! (*He tears off his coat and flings it away from him, revealing himself stripped to the waist.*) Dere! Dat's better! Now I kin breathe! (*Looking down at his feet, the spurs catch his eyes.*) An' to hell wid dese high-fangled spurs. Dey're what's been a-trippin' me up an' breakin' my neck. (*He unstraps and flings them away disgustedly.*) Dere! I gits rid o' dem frippety Emperor trappin's an' I travels lighter. Lawd! I'se tired! (*After a pause, listening to the insistent beat of the tom-tom in the distance*) I must 'a' put some distance between myself an' dem—runnin' like dat—an' yet—dat damn drum sound jes' de same—nearer, even. Well, I guess I a'most holds my lead anyhow. Dey won't never cotch up. (*With a sigh*) If on'y my fool legs stands up. Oh, I'se sorry I evah went in for dis. Dat Emperor job is sho' hard to shake. (*He looks around him suspiciously.*) How'd dis road evah git heah? Good level road, too. I never remembers seein' it befo'. (*Shaking his head apprehensively*) Dese woods is sho' full o' de queerest things at night. (*With sudden terror*) Lawd God, don't let me see no more o' dem ha'nts! Dey gits my goat! (*Then trying to talk himself into confidence*) Ha'nts! Yo' fool nigger, dey ain't no such things! Don't de Baptist parson tell you dat many time? Is yo' civilized, or is yo' like dese ign'rent black niggers heah? Sho'! Dat was all in yo' own head. Wasn't nothin' there! Wasn't no Jeff! Know what? Yo' jus' get seein' dem thing 'cause yo' belly's empty an' you's sick wid hunger inside. Hunger 'fects yo' head an' yo' eyes. Any fool know dat. (*Then pleading fervently*) But, Bless' God, I don't come across no more o' dem, whatever dey is! (*Then cautiously*) Rest! Don't talk! Rest! You needs it. Den yo' gits on yo' way again. (*Looking at the moon*) Night's half gone a' most. Yo' hits de coast in de mawning! Den you'se all safe. (*From the right forward a small gang of*

*Negroes enter. They are dressed in striped convicts'
suits, their heads are shaven, one leg drags limpingly,
shackled to a heavy ball and chain. Some carry picks,
the others shovels. They are followed by a white man
dressed in the uniform of a prison guard. A Winchester
rifle is slung across his shoulders and he carries a heavy
whip. At a signal from the guard they stop on the road
opposite where* JONES *is sitting.* JONES, *who has been
staring up at the sky, unmindful of their noiseless approach, suddenly looks down and sees them. His eyes
pop out, he tries to get to his feet and fly, but sinks
back, too numbed by fright to move. His voice catches
in a choking prayer.) Lawd Jesus!* (The PRISON
GUARD *cracks his whip—noiselessly—and at that
signal all the convicts start to work on the road. They
swing their picks, they shovel, but not a sound comes
from their labor. Their movements, like those of* JEFF
*in the preceding scene, are those of automatons,—rigid,
slow and mechanical. The prison guard points sternly
at* JONES *with his whip, motions him to take his place
among the other shovellers.* JONES *gets to his feet in a
hypnotized stupor. He mumbles subserviently.) Yes,
suh! Yes, suh! I'se comin'!* (As he shuffles, dragging one foot, over to his place, he curses under his
breath with rage and hatred.) God damn yo' soul, I
gits even wid yo' yit, sometime.* (As if there was a
shovel in his hands he goes through weary, mechanical
gestures of digging up dirt, and throwing it to the road-
side. Suddenly the guard approaches him angrily,
threateningly. He raises his whip and lashes* JONES
viciously across the shoulders with it. JONES *winces
with pain and cowers abjectly. The guard turns his
back on him and walks away contemptuously. Instantly*

FOREST FEAR

JONES *straightens up. With arms upraised as if his shovel were a club in his hands he springs murderously at the unsuspecting guard. In the act of crashing down his shovel on the white man's skull,* JONES *suddenly becomes aware that his hands are empty. He cries despairingly.*) Whar's my shovel? Gimme my shovel 'till I splits his damn head! (*Appealing to his fellow convicts*) Gimme a shovel, one o' yo' fo' God's sake! (*They stand fixed in motionless attitudes, their eyes on the ground. The guard seems to wait expectantly, his back turned to the attacker.* JONES *bellows with baffled, terrified rage, tugging frantically at his revolver.*) I kills you, you white debil, if it's de last thing I evah does! Ghost or debil, I kill you agin! (*He frees the revolver and fires pointblank at the guard's back. Instantly the walls of the forest close in from both sides, the road and the figures of the convict gang are blotted out in an enshrouding darkness. The only sounds are a crashing in the underbrush as* JONES *leaps away in mad flight and the throbbing boom of the tom-tom, still far distant, but increased in volume of sound and rapidity of beat.*)

SCENE V

ONE O'CLOCK. *A large circular clearing, enclosed by the serried ranks of lofty, gigantic trunks of tall trees whose tops are lost to view. In the center is a big dead stump worn by time into a curious resemblance to auction block. The moon floods the clearing with a clear light.* JONES *forces his way in through the forest on the left. He looks wildly about the clearing with hunted, fearful glances. His pants are in tatters, his shoes cut and misshapen, flapping about his feet.*

*He slinks cautiously to the stump in the center and sits down
in a tense position, ready for instant flight. Then he holds
his head in his hands and rocks back and forth moaning to
himself miserably.*

JONES. Oh, Lawd, Lawd! Oh, Lawd, Lawd! (*Suddenly
he throws himself on his knees and raises his clasped
hands to the sky—in a voice of agonized pleading.*)
Lawd Jesus, heah my prayer! I'se a poor sinner, a poor
sinner! I knows I done wrong, I knows it! When I
cotches Jeff cheatin' wid loaded dice my anger over-
comes me an' I kills him dead! Lawd, I done wrong!
When dat guard hits me wid de whip, my anger over-
comes me, and I kills him dead. Lawd, I done wrong!
An' down heah whar dese fool bush niggers raises me
up to the seat o' de mighty, I steals all I could grab.
Lawd, I done wrong! I knows it! I'se sorry! Forgive me, Lawd! Forgive dis po' sinner! (*Then be-
seeching terrifiedly*) An' keep dem away, Lawd! Keep
dem away from me! An' stop dat drum soundin' in my
ears! Dat begin to sound ha'nted, too. (*He gets to
his feet, evidently slightly reassured by his prayer—with
attempted confidence*) De Lawd'll preserve me from
dem ha'nts after dis. (*Sits down on the stump again*)
I ain't skeered o' real men. Let dem come. But dem
odders— (*He shudders—then looks down at his feet,
working his toes inside the shoes—with a groan.*) Oh,
my po' feet! Dem shoes ain't no use no more 'ceptin'
to hurt. I'se better off widout dem. (*He unlaces them
and pulls them off—holds the wrecks of the shoes in
his hand and regards them mournfully.*) You was real,
A-one patin' leather, too. Look at yo' now. Emperor,
you'se gittin' mighty low! (*He sighs dejectedly and
remains with bowed shoulders staring down at the shoes*

in his hands as if reluctant to throw them away. While his attention is thus occupied, a crowd of figures silently enter the clearing from all sides. All are dressed in Southern costumes of the period of the fifties of the last century. There are middle-aged men who are evidently well-to-do planters. There is one spruce, authoritative individual—the AUCTIONEER. *There is a crowd of curious spectators, chiefly young belles and dandies who have come to the slave market for diversion. All exchange courtly greetings in dumb show and chat silently together. There is something stiff, rigid, unreal, marionettish about their movements. They group themselves about the stump. Finally a batch of slaves are led in from the left by an attendant—three men of different ages, two women, one with a baby in her arms, nursing. They are placed to the left of the stump, beside* JONES.

The white planters look them over appraisingly as if they were cattle, and exchange judgments on each. The dandies point with their fingers and make witty remarks. The belles titter bewitchingly. All this in silence save for the ominous throb of the tom-tom. The AUCTIONEER *holds up his hand, taking his place at the stump. The groups strain forward attentively. He touches* JONES *on the shoulder peremptorily, motioning for him to stand on the stump—the auction block.*

JONES *looks up, sees the figures on all sides,* looks *wildly for some opening to escape, sees none, screams and leaps madly to the top of the stump to get as far away from them as possible He stands there, cowering, paralyzed with horror. The auctioneer begins his silent spiel. He points to* JONES, *appeals to the planters to see for themselves. Here is a good field hand, sound in wind and limb as they can see. Very strong still in spite of his being middle-aged. Look at that back. Look at those shoulders. Look at the muscles in his arms and his sturdy legs. Capable of any amount of hard labor. Moreover, of a good disposition, intelligent and tractable. Will any gentleman start the bidding?* The PLANTERS *raise their fingers, make their bids. They are apparently all eager to possess* JONES. *The bidding is lively, the crowd interested. While this has been going on,* JONES *has been seized by the courage of desperation. He dares to look down and around him. Over his face abject terror gives way to mystification, to gradual realization—stutteringly*) What yo' all doin', white folks? What's all dis? What yo' all lookin' at me fo'? What yo' doing wid me, anyhow! (*Suddenly convulsed with raging hatred and fear*) Is dis a auction? Is yo' sellin' me like dey uster befo' de war? (*Jerking out his revolver just as the auctioneer knocks him down to one of the planters—glaring from him to the purchaser*) An' *you* sells me? An' *you* buys me? I shows you I'se a free nigger, damn yo' souls! (*He fires at the auctioneer and at the planter with such rapidity that the two shots are almost simultaneous. As if this were a signal the walls of the forest fold in.—Only blackness remains and silence broken by* JONES *as he rushes off, crying with fear—and by the quickened, ever louder beat of the tom-tom.*)

SCENE VI

THREE O'CLOCK. *A cleared space in the forest. The limbs of the trees meet over it forming a low ceiling about five feet from the ground. The interlocked ropes of creepers reaching upward to entwine the tree trunks give an arched appearance to the sides. The space this encloses is like the dark, noisome hold of some ancient vessel. The moonlight is almost completely shut out and only a vague, wan light filters through. The scene is in complete darkness at first. There is the noise of someone approaching from the left, stumbling and crawling through the undergrowth.* JONES'S *voice is heard, between chattering moans.*

JONES. Oh, Lawd, what I gwine do now? Ain't got no bullet left on'y de silver one. If mo' o' dem ha'nts come after me, how I gwine skeer dem away? Oh, Lawd, on'y de silver one left—an' I gotta save dat fo' luck. If I shoots dat one I'm a goner sho'! Lawd, it's black heah! Whar's de moon? Oh, Lawd, don't dis night evah come to an end? (*By the sounds, he is feeling his way cautiously forward.*) Dere! Dis feels like a clear space. I gotta lie down an' rest. I don't care if dem niggers does catch me. I gotta rest. (*He is well forward now where his figure can be dimly made out. His pants have been so torn away that what is left of them is no better than a breechcloth. He flings himself full length, face downward on the ground, panting with exhaustion. Gradually it seems to grow lighter in the enclosed space and two rows of seated figures can be seen behind* JONES. *They are sitting in crumpled, despairing attitudes, hunched facing one another with their backs touching the forest walls as if they were shackled to them. All are Negroes, naked save for loin cloths. At first they are silent and motionless. Then they begin to sway slowly forward toward each other and back again in unison, as if they were laxly letting themselves follow the long roll of a ship at sea. At the same time, a low, melancholy murmur rises among them, increasing gradually by rhythmic degrees which seems to be directed and controlled by the throb of the tom-tom in the distance, to a long, tremendous wail of despair that reaches a certain pitch, unbearably acute, then falls by slow gradations of tone into silence and is taken up again.* JONES *starts, looks up, sees the figures, and throws himself down again to shut off the sight. A shudder of terror shakes his whole body as the wail rises up about him again. But the next time, his voice, as if under some uncanny compulsion, starts with the others. As their chorus lifts he rises to a sitting posture similar to the others, swaying back and forth. His voice reaches the highest pitch of sorrow, of desolation. The light fades out, the other voices cease, and only darkness is left.* JONES *can be heard scrambling to his feet and running off, his voice sinking down the scale and receding as he moves farther and farther away in the forest. The tom-tom beats louder, quicker, with a more insistent, triumphant pulsation.)*

SCENE VII

FIVE O'CLOCK. *The foot of a gigantic tree by the edge of a great river. A rough structure of boulders, like an altar, is by the tree. The raised river bank is in the nearer background. Beyond this the surface of the river spreads out, brilliant and unruffled in the moonlight, blotted out and merged with a veil of bluish mist in the distance.* JONES'S *voice is heard from the left rising and falling in the long, despairing wail of the chained slaves, to the rhythmic beat of the tom-tom.—As his voice sinks into silence, he enters the open space.—The expression of his face is fixed and stony, his eyes have an obsessed glare, he moves with a strange deliberation like a sleepwalker or one in a trance. He looks*

around at the tree, the rough stone altar, the moonlit surface
of the river beyond and passes his hand over his head with
a vague gesture of puzzled bewilderment. Then, as if in
obedience to some obscure impulse, he goes into a kneeling,
devotional posture before the altar. Then he seems to come
to himself partly, to have an uncertain realization of what
he is doing, for he straightens up and stares about him hor-
rifiedly—in an incoherent mumble.

JONES. What—what is I doin'? What is—dis place?
Seems like—seems like I know dat tree—an' dem stones
—an' de river. I remember—seems like I been heah
befo'. (*Tremblingly*) Oh, gorry, I'se skeered in dis
place! I'se skeered! Oh, Lawd, pertect dis sinner!
(*Crawling away from the altar, he cowers close to the
ground, his face hidden, his shoulders heaving with sobs
of hysterical fright. From behind the trunk of the tree,
as if he had sprung out of it, the figure of the* CONGO
WITCH DOCTOR *appears. He is wizened and old,
naked except for the fur of some small animal tied about
his waist, its bushy tail hanging down in front like a
Highlander's. His body is stained all over a bright red.
Antelope horns are on each side of his head, branching
upward. In one hand he carries a bone rattle, in the
other a charm stick with a bunch of white cockatoo
feathers tied to the end. A great number of glass beads
and bone ornaments are about his neck, ears, wrists, and
ankles. He struts noiselessly with a queer prancing
step to a position in the clear ground between* JONES
*and the altar. Then with a preliminary, summoning
stamp of his foot on the earth, he begins to dance and
to chant. As if in response to his summons the beating
of the tom-tom grows to a fierce, exultant boom whose
throbs seem to fill the air with vibrating rhythm.* JONES

looks up, starts to spring to his feet, reaches a half-
kneeling, half-squatting position and remains rigidly
fixed there, paralyzed with awed fascination by this
new apparition. The WITCH DOCTOR sways,
stamping with his foot, his bone rattle clicking the time.
His voice rises and falls in a weird, monotonous croon,
without articulate word divisions. Gradually his dance
becomes clearly one of a narrative in pantomime, his
croon is an incantation, a charm to allay the fierceness
of some implacable deity demanding sacrifice. He flees,
he is pursued by devils, he hides, he flees again. Ever
wilder and wilder becomes his flight, nearer and nearer
draws the pursuing evil, more and more the spirit of
terror gains possession of him. His croon, rising to
intensity, is punctuated by shrill cries. JONES has become completely hypnotized. His voice joins in the incantation, in the cries, he beats time with his hands and
sways his body to and fro from the waist. The whole
spirit and meaning of the dance has entered into him,
has become his spirit. Finally the theme of the pantomime halts, on a howl of despair, and is taken up again
in a note of savage hope. There is a salvation. The
forces of evil demand sacrifice. They must be appeased.
The WITCH DOCTOR points with his wand to the
sacred tree, the river beyond, to the altar, and finally to
JONES with a ferocious command. JONES seems to sense
the meaning of this. It is he who must offer himself for
sacrifice. He beats his forehead abjectly to the ground,
moaning hysterically.) Mercy, oh, Lawd! Mercy!
Mercy on dis po' sinner! (The witch doctor springs
to the river bank. He stretches out his arms and calls
to some God within its depths. Then he starts back-

ward slowly, his arms remaining out. *A huge head of a crocodile appears over the bank and its eyes, glittering greenly, fasten upon* JONES. *He stares into them fascinatedly. The witch doctor prances up to him, touches him with his wand, motions with hideous command toward the waiting monster.* JONES *squirms on his belly nearer and nearer, moaning continually.*) Mercy, Lawd! Mercy! (*The crocodile heaves more of his enormous hulk on to the land.* JONES *squirms toward him. The witch doctor's voice shrills out in furious exultation, the tom-tom beats madly.* JONES *cries out in fierce, exhausted spasms of anguished pleading.*) Lawd, save me! Lawd Jesus, heah my prayer! (*Immediately, in answer to his prayer, comes the thought of the one bullet left him. He snatches at his hip, shouting defiantly.*) De silver bullet! Yo' don't git me yit! (*He fires at the green eyes in front of him. The head of the crocodile sinks back behind the river bank, the witch doctor springs behind the sacred tree and disappears.* JONES *lies with his face to the ground, his arms outstretched, whimpering with fear as the throb of the tom-tom fills the silence about him with a somber pulsation, a baffled but revengeful power.*)

SCENE VIII

DAWN. *Same as* SCENE TWO, *the dividing line of forest and plain. The nearest tree trunks are dimly revealed but the forest behind them is still a mass of glooming shadow. The tom-tom seems on the very spot, so loud and continuously vibrating are its beats.* LEM *enters from the left, followed by a small squad of his soldiers, and by the Cockney trader,* SMITHERS. LEM *is a heavy-set, ape-faced old savage of the extreme African type, dressed only in a loin cloth. A revolver and cartridge belt are about his waist. His soldiers are in different degrees of rag-concealed nakedness. All wear broad palm-leaf hats. Each one carries a rifle.* SMITHERS *is the same as in* SCENE ONE. *One of the soldiers, evidently a tracker, is peering about keenly on the ground. He grunts and points to the spot where* JONES *entered the forest.* LEM *and* SMITHERS *come to look.*)

SMITHERS. (*After a glance, turns away in disgust*) That's where 'e went in right enough. Much good it'll do yer. 'E's miles orf by this an' safe to the Coast, damn 'is 'ide! I tole yer yer'd lose 'im, didn't I——wastin' the 'ole bloomin' night beatin' yer bloody drum and castin' yer silly spells! Gawd blimey, wot a pack!

LEM. (*Gutturally*) We cotch him. You see. (*He makes a motion to his soldiers, who squat down on their haunches in a semicircle.*)

SMITHERS. (*Exasperatedly*) Well, ain't yer goin' in an' 'unt 'im in the woods? What the 'ell's the good of waitin'?

LEM. (*Imperturbably—squatting down himself*) We cotch him.

SMITHERS. (*Turning away from him contemptuously*) Aw! Garn! 'E's a better man than the lot o' you put together. I 'ates the sight o' 'im but I'll say that for 'im. (*A sound of snapping twigs comes from the forest. The soldiers jump to their feet, cocking their rifles alertly.* LEM *remains sitting with an imperturbable expression, but listening intently. He makes a quick signal with his hand. His followers creep quickly into the forest, scattering so that each enters at a different spot.*)

SURRENDER

SMITHERS. (*In the silence that follows—in a contemptuous whisper*) You ain't thinkin' that would be 'im, I 'ope?

LEM. (*Calmly*) We cotch him.

SMITHERS. Blarsted fat'eads. (*Then after a second's thought—wonderingly*) Still an' all, it might happen. If 'e lost 'is bloody way in these stinkin' woods 'e'd likely turn in a circle without 'is knowin' it. They all does.

LEM. (*Peremptorily*) Ssshh! (*The reports of several rifles sound from the forest, followed a second later by savage, exultant yells. The beating of the tom-tom abruptly ceases. LEM looks up at the white man with a grin of satisfaction.*) We cotch him. Him dead.

SMITHERS. (*With a snarl*) 'Ow d'yer know it's 'im an' 'ow d'yer know 'e's dead?

LEM. My men's dey got 'um silver bullets. Dey kill him shore.

SMITHERS. (*Astonished*) They got silver bullets?

LEM. Lead bullet no kill him. He got um strong charm. I cook um money, make um silver bullet, make um strong charm, too.

SMITHERS. (*Light breaking upon him*) So that's wot you was up to all night, wot? You was scared to put after 'im till you'd moulded silver bullets, eh?

LEM. (*Simply stating a fact*) Yes. Him got strong charm. Lead no good.

SMITHERS. (*Slapping his thigh and guffawing*) Haw-haw! If yer don't beat all 'ell! (*Then recovering himself—scornfully*) I'll bet you it ain't 'im they shot at all, yer bleedin' looney!

LEM. (*Calmly*) Dey come bring him now. (*The soldiers come out of the forest, carrying JONES' limp body. He is dead. They carry him to LEM, who examines his body with great satisfaction.* SMITHERS *leans over his shoulder—in a tone of frightened awe.*)

SMITHERS. Well, they did for yer right enough, Jonesy, me lad! Dead as a 'erring! (*Mockingly*) Where's yer 'igh an' mighty airs now, yer bloomin' Majesty? (*Then with a grin*) Silver bullets! Gawd blimey, but yer died in the 'eighth o' style, any'ow!

CURTAIN

THE DANSE CALINDA

A PANTOMIME WITH FOLK-MUSIC

By

RIDGLEY TORRENCE

CHARACTERS

LOUIS LAFON ⎫
ZIZI, his sister ⎰ Creoles Nègres
JUDGE PREVAL
DENISE PREVAL
DON LOPEZ O'REILLY
Many others.

Scene: New Orleans.
Time: Early part of the Nineteenth Century during Mardi
     Gras.

First performance by The Howard Players, June 8, 1922

DANSE CALINDA

Scene I

The Place Congo, New Orleans

AN OPEN SQUARE, faced by small houses in front of which are bazaar booths, bright with cheap decorations, mounds of fruit, cakes, colored syrups, gauds, etc. At back over the low roofs are seen the spires and prouder buildings of the city.

The rising curtain discloses the square empty except for the motionless figures of the bazaar vendors, who sit asleep in their pavilions.

There is the silence of expectancy.

Suddenly the door of a house at centre back, in front of which is the liveliest of all booths, opens.

Zizi, radiant, shines from the threshold.

She poises there listening intensely until, after a moment, unable to contain her vibrating eagerness, she whirls into a dance about the square, looking off with fiery anticipation. Then abruptly she pauses. She hears what she has listened for.

The faint far-off sound of drums can be heard.

Expressing great joy, she dances again until, reaching her house, she darts within it.

Presently Louis emerges, dancing backward, from the

375

same doorway. He is followed by Zizi, who gayly pursues him with the same dance step as she tries to make him accept his vendor's tray for the peddling of sweets. She catches him. He takes the tray with a kiss. She runs again into their house.

Louis listens to the sound of the drums approaching, mingled with faint cries and dancing joyfully about to all the booths he awakens the vendors and points off toward the nearing sounds. Each vendor, rousing, follows, with arms and head, the rhythm of Louis's dance.

Zizi reappears with a great pan of ginger cakes, called "estomac mulattre," smoking hot. Rhythmically she spreads them on the tables in her booth, Louis helping her. They laugh and dance with delight. She returns to the house and fetches a second pan of cakes. From this she fills the tray of Louis, who carries it by a bright ribbon 'round his neck. All is done in rhythm.

The drums and cries now approach rapidly, mingled with strains from other instruments, notably banjos and also reed pipes, bound together in the form the Creoles know as "the quills."

Suddenly a riotously gay company enters the square.

All have some tincture of African blood. Free for a few hours of the city's festival, they are making the most of their holiday, and dispose themselves about the scene with great agility.

In a great circle the instrument players form an orchestra, seated on the ground.

Two-thirds have drums, very primitive, mostly beaten by the hands. One-third have banjos, and two men play "the quills."

The Bamboula, from which the song takes its name, is a

drum made of a section of giant bamboo, with skin stretched over the ends. It is beaten very rapidly with the hands.

The largest drum, four feet long, is beaten with sticks by two men sitting astride of it.

Inside the circle all the dancing begins and ends.

Outside the circle the crowd amuses itself by watching, clapping, promenading, love-making and bartering with pedlars.

Occasionally the booth vendors momentarily accompany the orchestra by touching triangles, rattling bones or gourds filled with pebbles, playing on jew's-harps and other instruments that hang beside them for sale.

The orchestra begins to play the Bamboula.

The merrymakers, aflame with the rhythms of their blood and the joy of freedom, begin a dancing contest, singly, by couples and in groups. Six dances follow, three to Bamboula tunes and three to Counjaille tunes.

Between these dances another sound reaches faintly to the square from the city beyond the houses at back. It is music, but of another kind; of European origin. Marching and minuet tunes of the eighteenth-century French school are caught in brief phrases, played by brass bands.

It is the music of the Mardi Gras.

This music is seen to produce a profound impression upon Louis. At each recurrent strain of the distant melody he pauses in his gay course, and motionless, wistfully listening, he looks toward the city.

Zizi, earnestly watching him, interrupts each of his abstractions. She expresses joy when she is able to recall him to the scenes about them and anxiety whenever his attention is caught by the distant music.

As each dance ends, Louis is solicited by girls to enter the contest. He refuses all, continuing his peddling, but with growing enthusiasm for the dance until the six numbers have been executed, when his excitement becomes irrepressible, and tossing his empty tray in the booth, he enteres the circle to the whirling tumult of a Calinda tune, which he dances so well that the admiration of the others reaches frenzy.

With one impulse the whole company rushes to the booths to buy a prize for Louis.

An old woman vendor offers a man's court costume, formerly belonging to some master. It is sumptuous and complete, with ruffled linen, embroidered coat, smalls, silk stockings and pumps. The suit is settled upon as the prize. It is purchased, and all turn to present it to Louis.

Louis is discovered again absently listening and looking toward the city, for the strains of Mardi Gras music are now plainer than ever.

Zizi stands anxiously watching him. She perceives, before her brother does, the prize that the merrymakers intend for him, and, comprehending, she runs toward them to prevent the gift.

This she is not able to do, for Louis, when their intention dawns upon him and he sees the magnificence of the dress, receives it with joy. Then, as a louder call of the Mardi Gras music reaches him, he looks from the dress toward the city and back again. A thrilling idea breaks upon him.

He will put on the dress and go to the city.

Zizi, anxiously reading his purpose, seizes him, begging him not to go, but he shakes her off and dashes into the house, bearing the suit, while the orchestra begins a new Calinda measure, and the whole assembly begins to dance wildly.

At the height of their abandon the tolling of a great bell from the city beyond announces the end of the afternoon's freedom, and the throng instantly breaks up, and with great swiftness disperses, accompanied only by "the quills" and by a subdued marching measure on the drums.

As the bell ceases the square is empty with the exception of the booth-keepers, who have fallen asleep again, and Zizi, who looks with an anxious face toward her doorway.

Again the Mardi Gras tunes float to the square, and Louis suddenly bounds out of the house. He is arrayed in all the finery. He doesn't even observe that the others have left the square.

All his attention is fixed toward the city as he listens to the distant lure.

He starts toward it.

Zizi intercepts him desperately.

He halts a moment and, with a return of his gayety, makes her a low bow. She admires him, but fearfully. He examines his new clothes, searching the pockets. From one of these he draws a mask. He puts this on, dons the hat and stands completely disguised.

He turns again toward the city, and in spite of Zizi's tears he runs off as if called imperiously by the far music.

Zizi stands for a moment agonizedly watching. Then turning, she faces the booth of the old woman who sold the costume for Louis.

Zizi, seeing the crone, is seized by a new thought: to follow Louis. She runs to the old woman, wakens her and demands a costume for herself. The vendor produces a woman's court costume, the counterpart of Louis's. For this she demands all the money Zizi has. Zizi produces her store, receives the dress, and with it runs hastily into the house, looking back toward the direction in which Louis went.

Again the Mardi Gras music is heard and, as Zizi disappears, the curtain falls.

Scene II

The Place d' Armes in New Orleans, a few hours later

At back is a row of stately brick houses with wrought-iron gateways and balconies and brick-walled gardens. On each side the scene extends into the wings.

At the extreme left is a dais, upon which rest two flower-decked thrones. Over one of these is a placard, on which is chalked "Pour le Roi Comus." Over the other appears the words "Pour la Reine." Ermine-trimmed mantles are thrown over the backs of the thrones.

The balconies at back are filled with spectators of the carnival. On the balcony of the house at center back sits Judge Preval, his daughter Denise and her suitor, Don Lopez O'Reilly. The Judge is a pompous, portly old man. Denise is young, beautiful and a coquette. Don Lopez is scowling, redheaded, red-faced, with a forked beard and bristling moustaches. On a balcony next the Prevals sit the Judges of the Carnival, a number of old ladies and gentlemen in gorgeous finery of the pre-Napoleonic era.

The place is filled with maskers disporting themselves gayly and watching the competition for King and Queen. All present are, needless to say, whites. One by one the competitors, a man and women alternately, parade and present themselves before the Judges. The contestants step to light music, each to some different measure from old French dance tunes.

The Judges examine them keenly through lorgnons, converse apart about them, but withhold their decision. They are evidently still unsatisfied.

At last, all those among the throng who wished to contest, have done so. Is there no one else? All look about.

Suddenly there is a commotion among the maskers. Don Lopez rises and points to the beautiful Denise. She has not contested, and sits laughing and inscrutable among the shadows of her balcony. All beseech her to contest, and at last she consents and rises to withdraw from the balcony. Don Lopez wishes to accompany her, but she pushes him back into his chair.

While the attention of all is drawn toward the Preval doorway, waiting for Denise, a new figure appears at the extreme right, apart from the others.

It is Louis.

He has mingled for some time with the maskers, and has watched the contestants eagerly, but disdainfully, as they show their lack of grace. He now executes a few stately steps as though practising to enter the lists.

As he does so a woman masker enters the Place from the right. She sees Louis at once, and running swiftly to him she draws him aside, down front. He looks wonderingly at the graceful and beautifully-dressed stranger.

She raises her mask and discloses herself to be Zizi.

Louis starts back with delighted amazement. Zizi is dressed in the finery purchased from the old woman. She has come to entreat her brother to withdraw from this forbidden ground.

She begs Louis to fly with her.

He refuses, his whole soul subject to the enchantment of the Carnival. Seizing Zizi gayly, he forces her to dance a few steps. They are far more graceful than any of the whites.

The others, however, do not observe them, for at this moment Denise emerges from her house, and stands lovely and laughing upon her doorstep. All those assembled in the Place show great admiration and enthusiasm, those above lean far out of their balconies, striving to see her while she still stands beneath them in her doorway.

At last she steps forth. The music begins. Denise stands still, demanding a partner.

But who is worthy to dance with her? Someone must volunteer, for she will not dance alone. One by one then the men maskers, urged by their friends and by the Judges, present themselves, and essay a measure with her. But they only display their awkwardness, embarrassed as they are by Denise's satirical laughter. The Judges will have none of them, and make a great show of scorn and disgust.

At last there seems to be none left who could aspire to dance with her. The Judges urge her to present herself alone. She is unwilling, and still looks about for a partner.

Suddenly she breaks into wilder laughter. She has spied her suitor, Don Lopez, as he sits mooning and doting on the balcony. He, of course, has not competed. She beckons to him, convulsed with jeering merriment. Don Lopez can scarcely believe he is chosen, but she repeats her summons, and he descends, flattered to ecstasy.

The Judges settle themselves pompously. With a grandee in the lists the occasion rises in importance.

Profoundly bowing, the two figures begin their measure, he solemnly, she mockingly.

But Don Lopez quickly proves to be the awkwardest dancer that has yet appeared. He steps on his lady's toes, he bumps against her, almost knocking her down, while she, for her part, still further harasses him by fairly staggering with laughter. Again and again he attempts to withdraw, but she holds him to his task until at last, desperately entangled, he trips on his sword and falls flat. The spectators are overwhelmed by a wave of laughter. But Don Lopez, having risen painfully to his feet, glares about him with such a fierce and terrible face that their mirth is smitten as by a blow. The enraged grandee withdraws beneath the Judges' balcony.

Denise now becomes the single center of interest. Will she not now present herself alone before the Judges? But she delays, looking about the throng, still searching for a partner.

Suddenly her eyes, for the first time, rest upon Louis. He is looking at her through his mask. They stand motionless for a moment. She seems to beckon with her eyes. He takes a step toward her as though drawn by an unseen force.

Zizi vainly reaches out to stay him, but afterwards only follows him agonizedly with her eyes.

After his first step toward Denise, Louis halts. Again she lures him. One further step toward her and again he stands motionless.

In spite of the potency of her enchantment there seems to be some impassable barrier between them. What is it? Denise cannot understand. She stands wondering, but still compelling the masked figure of Louis to approach her. He does so by single steps and slight withdrawals until he has covered the entire distance between them.

When he finally reaches her they again stand motionless, gazing at each other as if under a spell.

Then the music begins. Denise reaches out her hands. Louis takes them. They begin to dance.

Both are adepts. Spectators and Judges are enthralled. Never has such dancing been seen at the Carnival.

Measure after measure they dance, lighter and swifter grow their steps, until at last the musicians pause. They plead that they know no further tunes. But Denise will not stop. She demands that they find some fresh music. But there is no response.

Suddenly from a distance sound the wild notes of the Calinda.

Denise and Louis are electrified. They step forth to the new air.

Wildly and more swiftly the music whirls them, until the throng itself is caught up into the spirit of it and follows the flying pair, who dance with a winged grace and charm unequaled, until at last, with a tremendous thunder of the drums and a soaring cry of "the quills" and banjos, the music stops and the dancers halt, drooping with fatigue but ecstatic.

The enthusiasm of the Judges is beyond measure. They eagerly descend from their balcony, lead Denise and Louis to the thrones, and bid them be seated. They then place the ermine upon the shoulders of the pair, and with ceremony crown them Comus and his Queen.

Louis submits wonderingly like one in a dream, Denise with laughing triumph. She turns on her throne and holds out her hand to Louis. He slowly takes it, and they gaze at each other earnestly.

Delight and admiration are called forth by the lovely Queen and the handsome figure of the King. The Carnival throng rushes forward to lift the thrones and carry them in procession. But before this can happen it is intercepted.

Don Lopez, since his discomfiture, has been glowering apart in the Preval doorway. From the moment that Louis began to dance he has not taken his eyes off the dancer. During the Calinda he took a single step toward the dancers as though smitten by a stinging thought. Now, as the crowd prepares to lift the thrones, Don Lopez rushes forward, and springing like an animal at Louis, he tears the mask from the dancer's face and the hat from his head.

The sight disclosed blasts the assembly as with a thunder-stroke.

A Negro! At the Carnival in the Place d'Armes! Dancing with the fairest of the city's daughters and crowned as King!

There is an instant's pause, as of a receding wave of life, and then, with a roar as from a jungle, rage is let loose.

Dozens rush forward and tear the King from his throne. They drag him before the balcony of Judge Preval. The Judge stands trembling, white with fury. He cannot yet recover his breath and pronounce sentence upon the criminal.

Denise meanwhile remains standing on the dias before her throne, looking at Louis somewhat regretfully, but yet with disdain.

At length the Judge is able to speak. He turns to the Judges of the Carnival. What have they decided? They yield to an outraged father.

He turns to the throng. They have all been witnesses of the crime. They agree that it remains for him to pronounce sentence.

He does so by signing that he gives over the prisoner to Don Lopez, who shall avenge the crime.

They lead Louis before Lopez. Lopez surveys his rival with cold malice for a moment, then suddenly whips out his sword. Louis folds his arms and stands before his executioner.

There is a scream, and Zizi, rushing forward, throws herself upon Don Lopez. The grandee seizes her and strips the mask from her face.

A Negress! Zizi! She is well known. The sister and the brother! Both criminals. She also shall be judged.

Don Lopez gives her to be guarded. Then, turning again to Louis, he looks into his unflinching victim's face for a moment and plunges his rapier through the dancer's breast. Louis falls lifeless.

A shudder passes through the crowd. Don Lopez coolly sheathes his blade. Then, turning to Judge Preval, he asks what sentence shall be imposed upon Zizi. The Judge, however, has enough of blood, and merely waves his hand, giving over ZIZI to be imprisoned in the Calaboza, which is at the right.

Don Lopez turns and observes Zizi. She is beautiful. He seizes her and drags her off to the left.

The maskers all disperse in shadow and dejection.

The Place d'Armes is left empty except for the body of Louis, the tinsel thrones, crowns, sceptres, ermine, strewn flowers, confetti and holiday débris.

Suddenly from a distance come the strains of the Marseillaise, which is one of the tunes that has been heard in brief snatches more than once during the pantomime. It comes brokenly and for a few bars only at a time—played on violins and flutes.

All at once another sound rises, also from a distance, and mingles with the French tune. It is a wild and melancholy air, played on "the quills." Higher and higher and more sorrowful it winds. The Marseillaise contests with it for a few moments, but finally hushes, and "the quills" cry alone.

CURTAIN

SAHDJI

AN AFRICAN BALLET

By

RICHARD BRUCE

CHARACTERS

KONOMBJU, an Azandé Chieftain
MRABO, heir of Konombju
SAHDJI, favorite wife of Konombju
The Seven Other Wives of Konombju
THE MEDICINE MAN
Dancing Women, attendants of the Medicine Man
Three Counsellors, aged attendants of Konombju
THE CHANTER, the Interpreter of the Ballet

Scene: Ancestral Central Africa; a hunting feast of the
    Azandé tribe.

SAHDJI

SCENE: AN OPEN CLEARING, *near the dense forest to the left, where trunks of trees and vines weave a dense pattern in scarlet, yellow, and green on the black of the shadowy depths of the jungle. At right centre is a chief's hut, with bamboo side curtains, its one doorway framed in lashed bamboo, and one bamboo latticed window. An elliptical shield leans against the doorpost,—a brilliantly decorated clay jug stands on the bare ground under the window. Early morning—just after dawn. The tribe is preparing for a hunt.*

Curtain rises on scene as described. The women are grouped before the chief's hut; the MEDICINE MAN *and attendants grouped at left centre, and at extreme left, completing the half-circle, is* KONOMBJU *with his* THREE COUNSELLORS. *The* CHANTER, *an enormous black man, is discernible at the extreme left, who stands stationary throughout the ballet. A ceremonial blanket falls from his left shoulder, in rippling folds to the ground. His right arm, free of the robe, is striped above and below the elbow with curious metal bands of white and gilt metal, and he grasps an enormous spear. A glistening bush of silver hair bristles all over his head. From time to time, making only gestures with his spear, he chants in a booming singsong voice, the African proverbial sayings which are indicated for his rôle. All other action is dance pantomime.*

The tom-toms have been beaten for several minutes, at a rapid pace, before the curtain rises, and are on the stage manipulated by three men, straddling their drums in back centre. As the curtain rises, the drumming slows down somewhat, and in the foreground six or eight bucks, dressed in warriors garb, some with spears and some with bows and arrows, are dancing—it being the time of the feast before the hunt. There is the thud-thud of bare feet on the bare ground, beating in a rhythm separate from that of the tom-toms and the accompanying gourd-rattles. Gradually as the dance slows down, and the circle of the dancers closes in in an ever contracting circle, a chant picks up from the male voices.

CHANT

God of the thousand-flamed fire,
God of the lights and shadows
Many-tongued fire,
In the heart of the jungle,
In the middle of the forest,
In the center of the hearth-fire,
Thou of many places,
Visit upon us the light of your shining,
Visit upon us your shadows to hide us
So that we see and be not seen
So that we conquer
And to you,—for your trouble
Your care for your children,
We feast on our first kill. To you, and you only.

At the end of the Hunting Chant, the women raise their arms in salute to the warriors, and SAHDJI *appears at the doorway of the chief's hut, standing motionless.*

THE CHANTER. Be silent, tree! Don't listen to the noise
    of hatchets!

SAHDJI *glances quickly in the direction of* KONOMBJU,
and re-enters the hut. The MEDICINE MAN *comes forward
to charm the King's spear, while the dancing attendants
bring his shield to him from the doorway. They prostrate
themselves as they deliver the shield to the* MEDICINE MAN,
*who gives it to the chief. The women attendants then begin
to dance in flattery to the chief a Victory Chant for the success of the hunt:*

CHANT

Sharper than spears
Are the eyes of the hunter,——
Stronger than shields
Is the strength of his sinews,——
And when he has killed,
He has slain in his bosom,
Fear and the gods of mischance.

Only the tiger conquers the tiger,
Only the lion's kin stalks down
The king of the forest.
Hail to the man possessed of the might
Of the jungle, the thousand-fold
Might of the jungle!

Hail to the man possessed of the might
Hail to the hunter of hunters!
Empty handed he goes to his forest,
Heavy with spoils he returns to his women;
Lean and sly are his early out-goings,
Fat are his feats at the home-coming.

As their chant nears its end, SAHDJI *appears again in the doorway, her robe laid aside, smeared in red ochre and clad only in a girdle. As she is noticed, a shudder of horror spreads over the crowd, the wives of* KONOMBJU *leave in dignified affront, the dancing women stare, and the* COUN-SELLORS *cloak their faces.*

THE CHANTER. There is blood in the dregs.

SAHDJI *moves undaunted toward the chief, and begins to hum the Victory Chant, slowly beginning to dance it. She dances the same figures as the dancing women, only more gracefully. The dancing attendants, recovering from their astonishment, weave her an accompaniment, and the tom-toms and the chant merge into a minor variant of the Victory Chant. Body bent forward from the waist, head thrown high and arms extended tautly behind her, she dances in unison with the tom-tom beat till the chant and the drumming abruptly stop and leave her in a suppliant posture before* KONOMBJU. *Flattered, he makes a gesture of defiant approval.*

THE CHANTER. The flames from the ground are already
          catching the branches.

KONOMBJU *rises before the* COUNSELLORS *have uncloaked their faces; his stir moves them to rise and begin preparations for the hunt. The dancing women grimace and shrug their shoulders discreetly. A warmer gold begins to appliqué the clearing, throwing into sharper relief the crescent of young bucks and the half-moon of the* MEDICINE MAN *and women. With an imperious gesture,* KONOMBJU, *ignoring the prostrate* SAHDJI, *commands the warriors to the hunt. Four bucks, with shields and spears, go off left, the* COUNSELLORS *salute,* KONOMBJU *exits followed by the remaining warriors.*

THE CHANTER. A man does not use one finger to take out
an arrow.

SAHDJI *slowly rises to her feet, and with her head high,
walks to the hut. The dancing women assume the familiar-
ity that they dared not show in the chief's presence and smirk
at her. She ignores them. They turn to the* MEDICINE
MAN *in chagrin. He motions them off back center, and
going up to the* COUNSELLORS, *for a minute they cluster in
conference; they yawn behind the flattened palms of their
hands, then make a gesture of warding off evil, and exit.*

THE CHANTER. Death is at the end of the cloak.

SAHDJI, *after a long pause peers furtively from the doorway, makes a gesture of impatience and re-enters the hut.
After a little, a lithe bronze figure, dressed for the hunt,
with shield and lance, comes from the left, stealthily scans
the scene, and crosses to the hut, resting his shield and spear
under the bamboo window. It is* MRABO, *nephew of*
KONOMBJU—*a royal leopard skin is about his shoulders.*
SAHDJI'S *form appears at the window and her hand waves
through the bamboo bars.* MRABO, *up to this time self-
possessed, starts and rather hastily rushes into the hut.
After a moment, he re-enters and starts to take his spear
and shield inside. He hesitates, beckons an attendant, gives
him his spear, and takes from him a short side-sword, which
he buckles on and re-enters.*

THE CHANTER. You can daub yourself with ochre, but not
with kingship.

NUMBO, MRABO'S *attendant, can be seen on skirmish
watch, first one side of the hut, then the other. His friend-
liness is indicated by his evident concern to screen the lovers
from intruders.*

THE CHANTER. The fig tree does not call the birds.

The curtain is lowered to indicate a passage of time, but

lifts on the same scene. As it lifts, the CHANTER *exclaims solemnly—*

THE CHANTER. Time is no longer than a rope.

It is now sunset. The lights have been shifted to cast a sunset pattern of mauve and orange. The shadows run in the opposite direction from the previous scene, and a glow is seen through the background of the forest.

MRABO *comes out of the hut, followed by* SAHDJI, *who hands him his shield. They linger a moment, and* MRABO *then suddenly makes off centre stage, behind the hut.* SAHDJI *gazes after him, and then enters the hut.*

THE CHANTER. The little fountain ahead makes one very
       thirsty.

SAHDJI *peeps furtively out of the doorway . . . then with light steps, skips into the clearing. With improvised dance steps she gathers twigs and fragments of wood, and builds a fire, fanning the embers with her hands and breath. In the midst of the ceremony—*

THE CHANTER. God's fire is never quenched.

SAHDJI *pays no attention but concentrates in hypnotic gaze on the glowing flames, which mount higher and higher and cast long graceful shadows. Then she begins the Fire Dance, in, around and behind the fire, leaping with graceful bounds over the blaze, as graceful and capricious as the tongues of the flames she dances about. Throughout, her dance keeps the rhythm of the fire, and as the flames die down, her movements become slower and slower, until as the fire flares, her dance becomes intermittent, and as the flames fail and flicker out in one last spurt,* SAHDJI *sinks to the ground.*

THE CHANTER. Darkness has eaten her own child.

The forest that was fantastically alive with red gleams and yellow flares and quivering shadows is now veiled in purple

*silence. Out of the sepulchral darkness, the booming voice
of the* CHANTER *is heard*—

THE CHANTER. Darkness gossips about no one. (*A pause*)
One link only sounds because of another! (*A longer
pause, and then in a voice of foreboding*—) Watcher
of the moon, beware of darkness!

*An evening breeze, after the short stillness, begins to stir
the foliage. Gradually, with intervals of silence as if varied
with the wind, distant but approaching drum-beats are heard,
and then wails in chorus.* SAHDJI *quickly rises and lights
a flare torch. She is in evident terror and alarm.*

THE CHANTER. It is nothing—we shall meet near the ox-
hide. *The tread and the dull chant come nearer and
nearer.*

> Goare go shinoa
> Go elui ruri
> Goare go shuioa
> Go elui ruri

THE CHANTER *makes his first decided movement as he hears
the Death Chant, clashes his spear against the metal boss of
his shield, and then drops the spear point to the ground.   In
a rumbling voice, he echoes the chant*—

> Go elui ruri—Go elui ruri—
> When a man dies, he departs forever.

*The other wives file in from behind the hut, extreme right,
and dishevel their hair as they enter, softly wailing, and in
evident alarm.* SAHDJI *startled by them, commences to
dishevel her hair, but then rearranges it, facing the forest
clearing.*

*With rhythmic funeral tread, black shadows are seen be-
tween the tree trunks, and a streaming file of natives slowly
comes through the underbrush, bearing a burden swung
between shoulder poles.* SAHDJI *waits swaying softly, and as*

*she recognizes the situation retreats backward to her door-
way. The body-bearers file in; already some of the men are
smeared with ash-colored ochre.* KONOMBJU'S *shield is
being carried behind the bearers.* SAHDJI *perceiving it,
stops her ears with her hands, while the wives break out in
loud, rhythmic wails. The bearers place the body at*
SAHDJI'S *feet, as the* MEDICINE MAN, *rushing on, prostrates
himself over the body. With grave hocus-pocus, he crawls
around the body, sniffs, listens, chafes the hands, which drop
with a thud on the ground as he releases them, beats on the
ground with his wand,—threatens the bearers, who flee to a
safe distance, and then as he realizes the situation smears his
face with white ochre from his pouch and snaps his wand
ceremonially in two. At the crackling sound, the whole assembly break out in hysterical wails, and in the first lull the*
CHANTER *speaks.*

THE CHANTER. It is not hunger, the chooser of servants,
but spears, the slayers of princes.

MRABO *comes forward, glances quickly at* SAHDJI, *who
casts her gaze to the ground, and approaches the* MEDICINE
MAN. *They glare at one another for a moment then*
MRABO *adjusts his leopard skin with an air of authority and
the* MEDICINE MAN *prostrates himself in obeisance.
Fumbling for the king's sceptre, he finds it in the girdle of
the corpse and hands it to* MRABO. SAHDJI *jangles her
bracelets.*

THE CHANTER. (*Lifting his spear, and in a fresh tone of
voice*) When a man dies, a man remains. Always
build a fence round the king's word.

*As if listening to some supernatural voice from another
direction,* MRABO *stretches his height, takes on full composure, and grips his scepter with an air of authority. He
orders the* MEDICINE MAN *to prepare the body for the*

funeral ceremonies. The elder wives of KONOMBJU *have smeared themselves with white ochre and put on mourning dress—they re-enter in pairs and singly from right and left of hut.* MRABO *takes his stand in the doorway of* KONOMBJU'S *hut. The women wail before the body and then, with obeisance before* MRABO, *file past him into the hut.*

THE CHANTER. We are wandering in the belly of a bullock.

SAHDJI *alone has not shown signs of grief, but gazes at* MRABO, *who avoids her gaze. Slowly the warrior-bucks, dressed for the funeral rites, file on stage and take up gradually the heavy sway and stomp of the Death Dance. It has the same arm movement of the homage of the women, but a leg movement stomp (beating the ground with the sole of the foot) that is more and more terrific as it mounts to a crescendo in the unison of the dancing.*

SAHDJI, *as if for the first time awake to the terror of the situation, flees, as the* CHANTER *says—*

THE CHANTER. Those who pick berries in the same wood do not love each other.

The Death Dance reaches an orgiastic climax around the grass-strewn couch which the MEDICINE MAN *and his attendants have made for* KONOMBJU, *and is subsiding as* SAHDJI *re-enters, dressed for bridal ceremony in red ochre instead of the white ochre of the funeral rites. Again there is astonishment on all sides, registered differently—but especially by the elders who cloak their faces.* MRABO *starts to cloak his face, but is restrained by curiosity.*

THE CHANTER. They say that an ant once made an errand boy of an elephant.

Swaying slowly to the boom of the off-stage funeral drums, SAHDJI, *with a dagger and a pot of ointment approaches the body of* KONOMBJU, *ignoring the outstretched wand of the*

MEDICINE MAN. *The crowd shiver at the sacrilege; turn their backs. The elders appeal to* MRABO *with gestures, but he stands hypnotically transfixed, his eyes on* SAHDJI. *She places the dagger in* KONOMBJU'S *hand, and anoints the body with the ointment. Over her and around her, warriors and attendants erect a four-cornered canopy of native cloth supported at the corners by four long spears, and lean* KONOMBJU'S *shields at the two corners and over the body. The* MEDICINE MAN *comes on with the Death Figure, which he installs at the head of the chief. Attendants bring the food vessels, which are placed beside the body, and then the death mask is erected on* KONOMBJU'S *spear point. This is the signal for* MRABO *to approach the bier—the drums beat a march rhythm in anticipation, but he approaches reluctantly and with evident dread. Seeing his dismay, the elders try to persuade* SAHDJI *to leave the bier, but she takes the dagger from* KONOMBJU'S *hand, and turns the point toward her own bosom. As they sense the import of the gesture, they shrink back, and* MRABO *turns his back on the scene in grief. The women are amazed and strain forward. The men recoil.*

THE CHANTER. A word can never turn back, only a finger can.

*The drum music becomes fainter—*MRABO, *with a sudden start, decides to leave the scene, and commands the wives, and then the warriors to leave. They exit slowly right and back centre. He then goes into the hut with his Counsellors, who glance furtively at the bier in passing it. Only the* MEDICINE MAN *hesitates.* MRABO *turns back with a threatening gesture, which he suddenly breaks off as the* MEDICINE MAN *in turn raises his wand. There is derision and triumph on the* MEDICINE MAN'S *face. Both exit sep-*

arately; the MEDICINE MAN *extreme left into the forest,*
MRABO *into the hut.* (*After a pause in the silence.*)

THE CHANTER. It is nothing—we shall meet near the ox-
hide. (*And after another pause*) Water is never tired
of flowing.

SAHDJI *gradually detaches herself from the couch. With
slow graceful bendings from the waist, she begins to dance.
Reverential gestures and oblivious abandon alternate as she
is torn between her loyalty to the vow of death and her desire
for life. The slow, stately steps of the funeral march give
way time and again to the sheer love of rhythm and dance.
She whirls, turns, writhes around the death couch, until suddenly her whirling brings her face to face with the death-
mask. She shrinks from it in superstitious horror,—then
gradually recovering herself, approaches and swiftly touches
it, hastening away before harm can befall her. Again she
comes forward and touches it, and cowers at her own daring.*

At the first touching of the mask, the CHANTER *has turned
away from the front face he has maintained throughout, and
cast his spear point to the ground. At the interval after the
second touch, he chants—*

THE CHANTER. When man is silent, God speaks.

SAHDJI, *becoming bold, snatches the mask from the pole,
places it on the ground and mockingly dances around it. She
then replaces it on the spear, and in wilder and wilder
gestures before it, hurls insult after insult upon it. Finally
completely fatigued, she has retreated backward to a position directly in front of the canopy couch, and throws herself
backward over the body. Reaching for the dagger, she
lifts it as* MRABO, *who has apparently been watching the
scene, appears suddenly in the doorway in arrested posture
of striding toward the couch. He recoils as he sees the up-*

lifted dagger, and covers his face with his shield, as SAHDJI
*plunges it into her bosom and turns in her death throes upon
the body of* KONOMBJU. *Quick curtain, just as the*
CHANTER *says—*

THE CHANTER. All clouds have lightning.   Darkness has
eaten her own child.

CURTAIN